NOT AN ORDINARY LIFE

Eileen my Younghusband

A unique, personal insight into wartime Europe. This is an important historic document of social, political and family history. A must read for anyone interested in world war two and women at war.

Perhaps the most fascinating part of Eileen's inspirational autobiography are the descriptions of her time in the WAAF. These chapters are hugely informative, and written with great clarity and honesty, as well as a lightness of touch. I would encourage anyone with an interest in the 'hidden' history of world war two to read *Not an Ordinary Life*.

Eileen Younghusband has lead a full and fascinating life as revealed in this remarkable autobiography. Her initiative and intelligence ensured that at the outbreak of war she played a crucial role in Fighter Command in underground Filter Rooms. Young wartime WAAF officers like Eileen Younghusband have not had the recognition they deserve for their work in defeating the enemy. They tracked invading aircraft while also tracking returning RAF planes accurately so that they could be rescued if they ditched into the sea. Eileen was posted to Antwerp and saved countless civilian lives by helping to intercept V1 and V2 rockets. She gives us a vivid insight into what it was like to be a woman in the front line of a devastating war and a witness to the grim aftermath of the German occupation. It reminds us and generations to come of the debt we owe to her and women like her.

Eileen Younghusband's autobiography? The title says it all. Very few lives will have seen such experiences. Now in her late eighties, she shows determination and heart, fighting for what she believes in as she did playing her part against Hitler's vengeance weapons 65 years ago.

It has been my privilege to have known Eileen for the last six years. I know her as an extraordinary woman with exceptional talent, commitment and wisdom; matched by a wonderful sense of fun! Her story is testament to it all.

This captivating read narrates the ups, downs and experiences in the life of an extraordinary woman. I previously knew of a few exciting snippets of her life; I now find that she has kept up that same blistering pace for nearly ninety years.

NOT AN ORDINARY LIFE

Eileen Younghusband

From London suburbs to French au pair, City clerk to secret War Room, V2 detection to V-Day, concentration camp guide to language teacher, pig breeder to busy hotelier and scrap metal queen – then a bachelor's degree in my eighty-seventh year!

How changing times brought historical events into my life

The right of Eileen Younghusband to be identified as the
Author of the Work has been asserted by her in accordance with the
Copyright, Designs and Patents Act 1988.

© the author 2009

ISBN 987-0-9561156-9-0

published by
Cardiff Centre for Lifelong Learning
Senghennydd Road
CARDIFF

cover and book design by Ian Spring
printed by Isis Printing, Ty-Rhiw,
Taff's Well CF15 7RZ
Second Imprint

set in Calisto MT 11/16.5

DEDICATION

I have written this book for all the young women who served in the Women's Auxiliary Air Force in the Filter Rooms of RAF Fighter Command in the dark days of world war two and whose work and dedication to duty have never been fully recognised.

War films have familiarised us with the Operations Room of coastal radar installations during world war two. However, little is known of the work done in the Filter Rooms of Fighter Command, the secret nerve centres for the defence of Britain. It was in these crowded and hectic underground rooms that radar information was collated, corrected and identified as friend or foe – all done at great speed. This vital information initiated air raid warnings and fighter interceptions, instigated Air Sea Rescue and advised artillery units for gunlaying. It was the secret link that defended Britain from invasion.

ACKNOWLEDGEMENTS

I would like to express my heartfelt thanks to Ian Spring for his immense help in editing this book and to those of my friends who encouraged me to write it. I would also like to thank John Greeves and Jacci Harries, my tutors at Cardiff Centre for Lifelong Learning who honed my writing skills and to the Centre who offered the facilities. I am grateful to Abbie Wightwick, David Richards, Catherine Bailey, Fred Mawer and Dorothy and Lino Scaglioli for their advice after reading the script. I must remember too the encouragement given me by my brother, Dr Dennis Le Croissette, who sadly died before he was able to see the finished volume.

My thanks also go to the Imperial War Museum where the archive film of the Filter Room, Fighter Command, was found and for their permission to reproduce still photos from it. I am extremely grateful to Lieutenant Colonel Simon West who unearthed the history of the work of the Filter Room, which has hitherto never been fully recognised.

Above all, my appreciation goes to the Women's Auxiliary Air Force, now the Women's Royal Air Force, which has had such a great influence in shaping my life.

CONTENTS

BEGINNINGS

I was born on the fourth of July, in the record hot summer of 1921. Both the date and the climate have affected my life. That summer sunshine produced the finest vintage of Chateau d'Yquem, the superb Sauterne, a dessert wine known as the Queen of Wines. The 1921 vintage became the Queen of Queens and wine became part of my future unexpected profession and a well-enjoyed hobby. The date I was born, revered as Independence Day in the United States of America, was the beginning of a bittersweet connection with that great nation, as I was to find out in later years.

But first things first. From the age of five I lived in a pleasant North London suburb, in an Edwardian semi-detached house with my mother's parents, my mother and father and my younger brother Dennis. My mother's parents, Tom and Emily Smith had come to live with us when we had moved from Finsbury Park to Winchmore Hill. My grandmother had trained as a cook and worked for a doctor's family in London before marrying Tom. She was petite but indomitable. They lived in an upstairs room and she prepared their meals over an open fire with a Dutch oven and a small gas ring. Whenever she went out, she would bring us back a penny bar of Nestle chocolate so we could collect the special picture stamps inside. Despite her no doubt hard life, she lived to a memorable ninety-three years, keeping most of her faculties to her final days.

Granddad was a wonderful typical Cockney with a great sense of humour. He had earned his living as a painter and decorator and had been an avid patron of Collin's Music Hall. He would amuse us for hours singing the famous old songs of his day – such as 'Away went Polly, her step so jolly, I knew she'd win, I knew she'd win'; obviously a race-goer's favourite! He liked his daily pint at the local and kept going until well into his eighties. Looking back, life could not have been easy for my grandparents but I never remember them complaining. I am sure their living with us helped us to move out to this pleasant suburb.

Our parents, Ethel and Harlow Le Croissette, were very special people and gave my brother and me a steady and happy start to our lives. They were never rich but they were never in debt. We were encouraged to learn and were instilled with a love of reading. From an early age, my mother would take us to the library and help us choose a book for the week. *Paddy the Next Best Thing* was my first favourite. This book by H E Hopkins was made into a much-loved film starring Janet Gaynor. My mother was a very clever and able person and had she had the advantage of a University education, would without doubt have achieved great success. She had a superb head for figures. When she was younger, before world war one, she had run the counting house for a couture shop, Maud Owen, in New Bond Street. She was there during the time of the Suffragette protests. She recalled how one day this band of militant women marched down New Bond Street, shattering the windows of the shops as they passed. The only place that survived was the establishment where she worked, owned by a female!

All her life my mother kept detailed household accounts, a habit that I have adopted to this day. I think it is from her my mathematical ability comes, which later led to my interesting wartime career with radar. My granddaughter Tiffany has also inherited this ability and this too has coloured her life.

My father came from an immigrant Huguenot family, the 'des

Croisettes' who had escaped from France after the Revocation of the Edict of Nantes at the end of the seventeenth century when a merciless persecution of Protestants took place. We have managed to trace the family back to the region of Picardy, in northern France, where they once owned a small manor. My father's near and distant relations seem to be the only family remaining with this name although some of them have taken it to both the USA and Australia.

My mother during those early days of the London bombing, during world war two when she was recovering from her first breast cancer operation, journeyed around London in her genealogical searches. She visited French schools, churches, museums and the Huguenot Society offices, tracing where our ancestors had come from and where they lived in London. Much of this took place during the London bombing raids in the Forties, when transportation was difficult. She found the original name 'des Croisettes' had been miswritten at various times in the eighteenth century, accounting for the name now being Le Croissette. She was resolute in her searches. She managed to unearth many birth certificates and other records. Eventually she traced an unknown part of the family who possessed an old family bible, dating back to the late seventeenth century, together with the coat of arms. This formed a base for our later searches. Subsequently at the National Library in Paris, I found a letter dated 1320 in which it is noted that Philippe des Croissettes loaned money to the then King of France.

French coat of arms

Father, a skilled cabinetmaker, worked hard and for long hours. Daily, he would catch the seven

3

o'clock tram, buying a workman's ticket and he would not return home until possibly seven in the evening. He could turn his hand to anything – mending our shoes, cutting our hair, teaching me the names of the stars in the sky, playing the piano by ear. He was always ready to help in any way. He never complained of being tired, despite the heavy workload of his daily tasks. He was also a superb gymnast, winning many medals in his early days. During my childhood, he volunteered as instructor to The Boys' Brigade. I remember being very impressed when he told me that he was able to do fifty grand circles on the upright bar, a feat I only really appreciated when I watched the gymnastic events during the Olympics. He had served during world war one as a despatch rider, experiencing the horrors of the Somme and Paschendale battles and then transferring to the Royal Flying Corps as soon as it was formed, still as a despatch rider. I treasure his Royal Flying Corps tie. Like so many of his generation, he barely ever spoke of his terrible experiences of the Great War. I learned a little of its horrors from a war magazine he subscribed to, where the character Old Bill, famous during that war, appeared once more as a cartoon.

As a family, we weathered the depression in the Thirties, we were always fed and clothed and I cannot remember ever feeling unhappy. When my father was on short time, he made furniture at home to sell, thus ensuring we could go to the grammar school and able to buy the necessary uniform. I remember helping him move the elegant furniture he had made in our spare bedroom, downstairs, to be transported to its new owner. After world war two, when eventually he could afford to buy a small car, this was his greatest delight.

Each day my mother, with her Ten Minutes Book, polished up our general knowledge and kept our interest going in current affairs. What is the longest river in the world? Who wrote *Lorna Doone*? Where is Guatemala? I still remember the questions and some of the answers. We had good friends, annual holidays in bed and breakfast guest houses in coastal resorts. One year it would be Leigh-on-Sea on the Thames estuary – another year Clacton. Sometime there would be special treats. I remember to this day being taken to the theatre for the first time, sitting on small stools outside the Old Vic for what seemed hours, queuing for seats in the gallery. We went to see *The Wandering Jew* with the then famous actor, Matheson Lang in the principal role. I can still recall vividly some scenes from it – especially the heavy cross, carried by Christ, as it passed the window of the upper chamber.

We were lucky with our other close relations. Although my mother was an only child, my father made up for it with two sisters and three brothers, all of whom lived in North London so we frequently met up with our many cousins. There seemed to be a strong work ethic running through the whole of the family as well as a love of education. Several of my elder cousins went to university, managing to complete their studies before the onset of war in 1939. I know their families saved and scrimped to pay their fees. I was not so lucky; the war put a stop to my going. It was something I regretted and vowed I would do sometime about in the future. I did not then realise that it would not be until I was eighty-six years old that I would finally graduate as a Bachelor of Arts.

My parents never showed overt emotion but always seemed happy together. There was not the constant hugging and kissing which seems essential today but we knew they cared. They showed it in so many other ways. There were always gifts for our birthdays and Christmas was very special. We would hang up a pillowcase at the end of the bed. By morning, it would be full of many small items. There was always an orange and always a lump of coal. The coal, Mother told us, was for the days when we had perhaps misbehaved and that it was taking the place of a present we would have had! They gave up their own pleasures to allow us to join in events, equally with friends whose parents were richer. They encouraged, praised our successes, and commiserated in our disasters. In return, they expected us to behave, to work hard at school and to get as much out of life as we could. There was a light wicker cane hanging up in the kitchen – it was never used but it was symbolic of the fact that discipline would be maintained if necessary. I loved and respected my parents.

Dennis and I from an early age went to the Baptist Sunday School. I joined in voluntarily and accepted all that I was told. Dennis never did. He questioned and needed to prove any statement at all times. These were the first signs of his scientific bent. Very soon, he would not accept the teaching. This eventually led to him becoming a confirmed atheist. I, on the other hand, entered for numerous Scripture exams, winning several book prizes. I must enjoy the torture of examinations since I have taken so many more in later years. I even became a Sunday School teacher. My closest school friend, Doreen Johnson, constantly reminds me that I signed the pledge, vowing to forgo the pleasures of alcohol. It took me many years before I broke this pledge but I can honestly say that when I did, I had no regrets.

It was not until years later when I announced my engagement to Peter, who was brought up as a Roman Catholic, his mother being a Newman, that I became cynical. When I announced the news to the Baptist Minister, the Reverend Clifford Wood, he became very angry and reviled me. He never spoke to me again. It was then I began to see the bigotry of religion. It took me rather longer to become sceptical of all religious teachings.

It was on my way to Sunday School when I was about seven years old that I first encountered a paedophile. I always used to go on my own; it was only ten minutes walk away. On this occasion, a man approached me and asked me if I liked babies. I would always talk

6

to anyone without thinking of anything bad happening. I answered eagerly. 'Yes', He replied, 'Look through that letterbox and you will see one,' and he pointed through the archway between two shops on the Broadway, which led to the doors of the flats above. Obediently, I did as I was told. I peered through the letterbox for some time but saw nothing. I turned back to him. 'I can't see anything', I said and then I saw he had exposed himself. I did not know what it was he was doing but I realised something was wrong. He then said to me 'Have you got something like this? Come and show me what you've got.' I pushed past him and ran on to Sunday School. I arrived crying but I would not tell anyone the reason for my distress. They sent me home and I ran back on my own. My father picked me and hugged me when I arrived home, still crying. He asked me what was wrong but I still said nothing but just went on crying. My parents never learnt the reason. I never told anyone and that was that. I can safely say I suffered no serious after effects although I remember the incident quite clearly. Nowadays it seems people think paedophiles are a new phenomenon. They are quite wrong. There were as many of them during my youth as there are now but they did not get the publicity.

Some years later, when I was about fourteen, Doreen, my best friend and I, whilst walking with our bikes in Grovelands Park, were accosted by the regular park-keeper there and asked to go into his shed with him. We were a little – but not much – wiser then so we turned on our heels and fled. We kept well away from him in the future but again we never told anyone. We just learned from the experience. I do not think I am any the worse for these events. I saw it as all part of growing up.

SCHOOLDAYS

After taking my scholarship exam from Winchmore elementary school in 1932, I went on to an excellent co-educated grammar school, Southgate County. Normally a fee of eight guineas a year was charged but many free places were offered when the income of parents was insufficient to fund this. I was fortunate to be granted a free place through winning the Latymer Foundation Scholarship on my exam results. Unbeknown to us, our house fell into the ancient parish of Edmonton and came within the range of this award. I had already decided to go to Southgate County, before I learned of the Latymer School in Edmonton. This school had a fine reputation but the journey would have been more difficult. Fortunately, the free place was transferred to my new school and in addition, I received a grant of £50 a year for three years. This seemed like a fortune in those days. It paid for my school uniform and any sports gear necessary and was a great help during those years of the 'Slump' following Black Thursday in October 1929. The effect of the heavy falls on the New York stock exchange reverberated throughout the developed world. It affected many British families in so many ways. With the downturn in the economy, many workers were laid off or put on short time. My father's company cut all the hours of their workforce so our family income was greatly reduced.

My brother, four years younger, was soon to follow me to Southgate. There we studied under the keen eye of a wise and learned Headmaster, Thomas B Everard, Cantab, MRCM, LRAM. In addition to normal subjects, he offered us opportunities to pursue music, drama, literature and art. There was a school orchestra, which played every Friday at the school assembly. We had yearly music and drama festivals and a Gilbert and Sullivan opera every autumn. Many of the masters and mistresses joined the musically gifted scholars in these productions. I remember playing St Joan in an extract from Bernard Shaw's classic at the Enfield Eisteddfod. My drama teacher chose me to play the part but she stipulated I use a North Country dialect since Joan of Arc was a country girl! 'Where be Dauphin?' I declaimed in my best Yorkshire accent!

The school had a wonderful collection of fine original paintings, loaned by Sir Philip Sassoon, which we were encouraged to search out, identify the name of the painter and title of the work. In addition, each morning at assembly, the headmaster would read out a quotation – either prose or poetry. For those interested, it was an opportunity to find the context. This was my special interest and together, my mother and I would search the libraries to find the answers. My bookcase today contains some fine leather bound books, which I won as quotation prizes. It is from this that my love of words has grown. All his students owed a lot to this wise headmaster and he is remembered to this day. Sports too were not forgotten. The boys played football and cricket, the girls, hockey and tennis. Athletics were encouraged and I specialised in both the 100-yard sprint event and the long jump, appearing in the team for the area's joint school games.

Because of the dedicated teaching by Mr Everard, other talented teachers were attracted to the school. They brought added skills, whether it was on the sports field, in the orchestra or an ability to relate to the problems of their students. In those days, most children left school at 14 years of age but if you went to a grammar school, you had to agree to stay on at least two extra years. Mr Everard arranged our schedules so that we took our General Schools and

Matriculation exams a year early, when we were fifteen or less. This allowed him, as he explained, an extra year in which to begin our real education. Thus it was that, before the age of 16, in the sixth form commerce, I learned to type, mastered shorthand, bookkeeping, basic economics and office routine as well as learning to speak reasonable French and German, in addition to studying normal school subjects. My brother early on decided he would be a scientist so he chose sixth form science This was to lead to his very successful future career as a space scientist with NASA. He worked for many years at Jet Propulsion Laboratory, Pasadena, California on the unmanned space programmes prior to the Apollo moon landings. I had a business career more in mind.

Life was not all study however; we had fun too. I went roller-skating at 'Alley Pally,' (the Alexandra Palace) nearby and played hockey for the school team. I regularly camped with my Girl Guide company. I even went to an International Camp in 1936 at Chamonix, on the slopes of Mont Blanc. That was a memorable occasion – twelve girls in a bell tent, each from a different country and speaking a different language. An unexpected August storm hit the camp one night, blowing down all the tents and carrying them yards away up the mountainside, resulting in a veritable tower of Babel! We all spent the night huddled together in a farmer's barn until we could rescue the tents, spread over the countryside, the following day. It was there that I first learnt the rudiments of meditation. After lunch each day, Chef Bricka, the French Guide captain in charge of the camp, told us to find a quiet spot alone and to meditate. She gave us a demonstration and off we went. It was a therapeutic practice I have found useful on so many occasions since.

That same year I saw my first television programme. The father of a friend had bought one of the first sets available. He was quite rich in comparison to my family, having made his money as a 'quack' pharmacist, selling 'Pink Pills for Pale People'. In 1936, the first ever television transmissions were being sent out from Alexander Palace. The area covered was very limited. Fortunately, at Winchmore Hill, only a few miles away, we were able to receive it successfully. I still remember the first programme I saw. It was the original production of *Me and My Girl* at the Lambeth Palace, featuring *The Lambeth Walk*. This song and dance had an interesting later connection with Hitler's Germany when it led me to a frightening encounter with Nazi Storm Troopers.

My parents were keen for me to learn to play the piano. I started at the age of six but although I spent hour after hour meticulously practising, even passing several of the Royal Academy of Music exams, I could never remember a tune or play a note without music. My brother was the real musician in the family. However, my music teacher entertained many foreign students during the summer holidays and it was there I acquired my interest in foreign languages and of course the chance of meeting French boys, including one, Rene Cadier, who many years later turned up in a most unexpected place.

The discipline and the teachings of my early years as a member of the local Baptist chapel had brainwashed me to remain a virgin until I married. This may seem very naïve these days and in retrospect, I wonder if it was worth it or the best thing to have done. Of course, we had boyfriends, exchanging them from time to time. Nor did it mean that from the age of fourteen, we would not permit intimate caressing but we never talked about what we did and with whom we did it. I recall fondly twilight trysts near the Leg of Mutton pond in Palmers Green with the favoured boy of the week. The modern generation imagine we behaved differently from them. Although we knew nothing about sex and our parents never discussed such things with us, we eventually found out about it in our own way.

IN THE SQUARE MILE

So far, my life seemed destined to follow the normal pattern of a typically unspectacular life. In those days, there was no financial help of either grants or loans for University studies. I celebrated my sixteenth birthday on July 4th, 1937 and two weeks later left school for good, armed with a matriculation certificate from the University of London with a distinction in mathematics as well as several certificates for commercial subjects from the City and Guilds Institute. Within the month, I was recruited for a post in the City of London with the Scottish Provident Institution, a life assurance company. I was to work in the cash department, sending out premium notices, checking on payments and becoming a dogsbody to the predominantly male staff. In 1937, women were barely accepted in the business world of the City but things were changing and I was the first female they had employed in the Front Office, permitting me to deal with the public, However, to show my more humble position, I had to wear the regulation overall, made from a hideous maroon scratchy material, designed for all female employees. Even the head cashier's secretary wore one of these ugly and uncomfortable garments. Meanwhile all the male employees wore smart city suits and ties. This was my first experience of sex discrimination. There were more to follow as the years went by.

One excellent by-product of my time in the cash department was to learn two important things from my boss, Mr Mitcham. The first one was how to tackle cryptic crosswords, which I have continued to enjoy as a favourite pastime ever since and the second one was to write the required date of posting on an envelope, in the space where the stamp was to go, for any correspondence prepared in advance! Very soon, I had decided that working in the cash department, sending out premium notices, following up unpaid dues, was extremely boring and unchallenging. I decided I would prefer to train as an actuary where my mathematical skills would better be employed. I realised it was a very elite career, needing a long training with few women accepted for it at that time but I set my sights in that direction and let the 'powers that be' know of my intentions. Sadly, future world events changed all that.

The journey into the centre of London took nearly an hour. First, I took a train from the station near my house to Finsbury Park and then changed to the Northern Line. This line was appalling. The trains were crowded and clanked slowly and noisily along the rails to Moorgate. Rarely did I find a seat. Nobody spoke. The men buried their heads in their newspaper. The women would bring out their knitting or just stare into space. Arriving at the final station, I would join the throng of office workers, hurrying along to the heart of the City. The Scottish Provident Office was at that heart, sited next door to the Mansion House, opposite the Royal Exchange and the Bank of England and only a short walk from the Stock Exchange.

I was mesmerised by the daily life in the City of London. Since we were adjoining The Mansion House, we witnessed many interesting sights – the annual Lord Mayor's Show, for example. Throughout the year, many international visitors would arrive there to pay their respects to the nominal head of London's business centre. I particularly remember the State Visit of Monsieur Georges Bonnet in 1937, obviously a controversial French politician since a group of Frenchmen lining the street alongside me were shouting vociferously *'L'assassin, l'assassin!'* as the procession of official cars went past I wondered what they meant. I later learned that this politician was associated with Serge Alexander Stavinsky, a French financier and embezzler whose actions created a political scandal known as the Stavinsky Affair. In the years leading up to world war two, the political mood in Paris was tense, aggravated by the economic depression. The 1937 Stavinsky Affair caused a corruption scandal in the radical socialist government, leading to bloody riots in the streets of Paris by right-wing extremists (primarily royalists).

Years later, during the war, I met a Canadian army sergeant whose father had been a colleague of Monsieur Bonnet. This association had caused his father to leave France hurriedly with his family and emigrate to Canada. This young soldier bitterly bemoaned the event as he had been studying to be a concert pianist at the Conservatoire in Paris, the move putting an end to his dreams. He confided in me that his father thought his son was getting homosexual tendencies through such an esoteric training so he stopped him studying music and insisted he train as an accountant. It had not had the desired affect, the young man assured me.

Lunchtime in the City of London was a magic time. I would cross the road to the Royal Exchange, eat my packed lunch as fast as I could and then continue past the Bank of England to Throgmorton Street and the Stock Exchange. I wandered amongst the milling brokers and jobbers, dealing shares in the street, whilst I soaked up the atmosphere. It was exciting and bred in me a love of share dealing, which has stayed with me throughout my life. I did not realise then how the war would later bring me in close working contact with many of those same brokers and jobbers I would see during my lunchtime wanderings.

I was to spend nine months travelling to the City. I carried an impressive hogskin briefcase, a present from my father, filled with my lunch of sandwiches and a piece of fruit together with a suitable book to read in the train. I usually chose a book that I thought would impress my fellow travellers. I recall lugging the heavy tome of *The Seven Pillars of Wisdom* for over a month with this intent. It never seemed to have the desired effect.

Early in 1938, out of the blue, my former German master, Victor Groves, telephoned my parents. He had just formed the School Travel Service and had remembered that I enjoyed learning French and German. He suggested that perhaps I would like to join his emerging company to help plan and co-ordinate school trips overseas. He made a proviso that I first should spend at least six months in France and then six months in Germany to perfect those languages. With my mother's encouragement, I had no hesitation in accepting. I was then almost seventeen.

My mother and I scanned *The Lady* magazine, a well-known source for advertisements for 'au pairs'. In those days, an 'au pair' was not the general dogsbody of today but someone who taught English to the children of the family and who lived as one of them. Our very first application brought success and by May 1938, I was on my way to Contrexeville in the Vosges Mountains, to the summer home of Monsieur Marcel Boucher. Not only was he the mayor of this well-known spa town but also a member of the Chambre des Deputés (a French Member of Parliament) and also the French champion fencer! My parents had no problem in letting me go. I think they considered I was levelheaded and could cope with most emergencies. They certainly did not put any objections in my way. I was eager to go and leave behind the boring work in the cash department.

Rail and boat tickets arrived from my future employers. Giving in my notice to Scottish Provident, I prepared for my journey to a new experience. I wondered whether I would manage to teach English to these children and whether they would like me but the thought did not unduly bother me. The main difficulty was to decide what to wear. I realised that there would be many formal occasions and I did not have much in the way of suitable clothes for special events. My mother, who was a wonderful seamstress, took it in her stride and quickly made me a couple of dresses and a new skirt and blouse for daytime use. I packed my bag and, in no time, I was making my way by train, via Paris to the eastern border of France. Germany was just across the River Rhine, a few kilometres away. Another adventure had begun. My life was about to change.

ON THE CONTINENT

Arriving at Contrexeville station on a late May evening, I was greeted by Madame Boucher, an elegant and at first rather intimidating lady. In those first moments, my mind went completely blank. I could not think of a single French word! But Madame was very understanding and before long, I found myself chatting freely with her as I realised she was able to understand me! That helped a lot. We drove through beautiful countryside in a large chauffeured Mercedes. As we entered the long drive to the house, I was overwhelmed by its size and the charming garden surrounding it. Le Val was a large and handsome villa, built in Georgian times, situated in extensive wooded grounds and furnished in a grand style. I was shown to my pleasant room overlooking the garden and then taken to meet my charges; Helene aged six, Jean nine and Francois eleven. It had been a long day; I was tired out by the journey and at seventeen, intimidated by the unaccustomed luxury of my surroundings. It needed a lot of courage to face the children. I need not have worried. They were delightful and they greeted me with well-rehearsed speeches of welcome in halting English. I took to them at once and felt I was going to enjoy this new post

Having regained my equanimity, I changed from my travel clothes to something more formal and went down to the sitting room to meet Monsieur Boucher. I am not normally shy but at this stage, I felt apprehensive as how to address this important man. I stuttered *'Bonjour Monsieur'*. He replied *'Bienvenue à nôtre maison'*. I began to feel more comfortable.

He was a tall elegant Frenchman who, although rather distant, greeted me graciously and escorted me into the dining room. There I was confronted with a long dining table, elaborately set with damask cloth, silver cutlery, elegant central silver candelabra and two large bowls of cut flowers from the garden. The three children joined their parents and we sat down for my first formal meal in my new home. We were to speak only French. This initial evening meal with my new family was a revelation. Every meal from then on was superb. Their Alsace cook was a star of her profession. Sometimes there were guests, perhaps politicians, friends and frequently foreign visitors. Always the finest French wines were served. Such a pity, corrected several years later, that I had signed the pledge not to drink alcohol! Sadly, I missed a great opportunity to sample some of the finest wines France could offer. However, I soon realised how excellent the food was and every meal became a gastronomic adventure.

Monsieur Marcel Boucher, as a member of the French government was often away but when home, he entertained frequently. I recall being present at a dinner with the then Rumanian Prime Minister, whose name I believe was Octavian Goga. He told me my French was far better than his! It was at that dinner that the cook prepared a Croquembouche dessert. This is a *pièce montée*, a spectacular mounted cake, consisting of many small profiteroles built into a tower around thick cream on a praline base and topped with a praline decoration of the Fleur de Lis.

Contrexeville is a well-known spa town in the Vosges Mountains. During my spare time, I often walked to the centre and mixed with the many visitors taking the waters. I only tasted it once and found the metallic taste quite unpleasant. However, its supposed beneficial effects attracted many foreigners, especially Germans from the nearby border towns. Of course, Alsace had been under German control in earlier years and there was still a strong affinity with this country on the part of many of the local residents.

I soon established a regular routine, teaching the children English for two hours every morning, having lunch with them in their study and playing games with them during the afternoon after they had finished their other lessons. At five o'clock, we were served English tea and a tartine, a jam sandwich made in a newly baked baguette. The children were beautifully behaved and keen to learn. They had two other live-in tutors, a German woman of about fifty for German studies and mathematics and a young French teacher for all other subjects. These two older women lived in a flat over the coach house and I had very little to do with them. Despite having private golf and swimming lessons several times a week, the children still preferred playing make-believe games in the woods with me. Their special favourite was Robin Hood when we made bows and arrows from the branches of trees using strong twine and we hid and played in the grounds surrounding the house. They enjoyed a life of wealth with every opportunity to succeed, an upbringing very alien to my own. Living this life of luxury, they could have had no idea of the turmoil that would take place in their lives in later years. I often wonder what became of them especially in view of what happened to their father after the war.

The days passed quickly. In late August, Monsieur Boucher, a major in the reservist army, went to annual camp near Strasbourg on the banks of the Rhine. The year was 1938 and unknown to most of us; we were heading for the Munich crisis. A few days after he left, Madame Boucher received an urgent call from her husband. He was very concerned. The German army was massing on the opposite bank. They had mined the river. He felt war was inevitable and it was too dangerous for me to remain. He gave orders that arrangements should be made for me to return home at once. I often wonder how much more he knew.

Both the children and I were most sad that I had to leave as we were getting on well. They treated me like an elder sister and their English was improving daily. We had all been looking forward to returning to their Paris home once summer was over. I had learned by then that Madame was very wealthy in her own right and owned three hotels, the famous Georges V, the Hotel Tremoille in Paris, and the Carlton Hotel at Cannes. I very much regret I never experienced the opportunity of living with the family in Paris and perhaps enjoying the delights of these famous hotels especially as I was to become an hotelier myself after the war.

I was given rail and boat tickets, and in no time I was in a crowded train, on my way to Paris. I was anxious, wondering if I would get home before war broke out. As I arrived in the late afternoon in Paris, already I could feel there was a sense of fear in the air. It was too late for my train to Calais. It had already left and there was not another until the next morning. I knew no one in the city but realised I

Invitation to return to Contrexeville

would have to find somewhere to stay. I walked the streets looking for accommodation for hours. Eventually I found a bed in the Centre d'Accueil in the Boulevard Haussman. This was a youth centre run by a religious organisation; the warden showed me to a curtained alcove where I was to sleep. The only other things in this space were a small chest of drawers and a French bible. I slept fitfully wondering whether I would get home safely. I still remember the breakfast next morning. In a huge bare refectory, I was served delicious hot chocolate in a large thick bowl accompanied by a warm baguette and a bowl of apricot preserve. I paid five old francs for my stay and then set off for the Gare du Nord and my train home. It came in from East France and was already crowded. Finding a seat was difficult. I eventually squeezed into a carriage, almost full. Everyone was speaking German.

I soon realised that these were refugees, mostly Jewish families escaping from Hitler's Germany. Their belongings were piled around them, bundles of goods tied up in old curtains and sheets as well as in suitcases and boxes. As the train left Paris for Calais and they were heading for eventual freedom in Britain, I could sense them gradually relaxing. Soon they were opening their luggage, extracting hidden jewellery. The tension left their faces. They put on their rings, brooches, and earrings and began to smile. I arrived in London to an unknown future.

AFTER MUNICH

T hat September of 1938, British Prime Minister Neville Chamberlain met Hitler in his mountain retreat and signed a useless piece of paper promising peace in our time. At least it gave us a year to build up our woefully inadequate forces and armaments.

I was home again and looking for a job. Before very long I was back working in central London as a secretary for Corke, Sons and Company, Paper Agents. Amongst their suppliers was a factory in Merken-bei-Duren in the Ruhr. Like the rest of the country, I had been lulled into a sense of false security by the hope of peace. I decided to holiday in Germany early in August 1939 and managed to get an invitation to visit the paper factory in the Ruhr before spending time in Bonn at the house of a professor who had taught my last German teacher, Jack Rolfe. It would give me an opportunity to practise my German as I still hoped I might get back in the travel business.

I set off on that sunny morning, feeling excited at visiting another new country. All seemed calm on the journey, except at the border the guards unceremoniously confiscated a copy of *Picture Post* I was carrying. I managed to understand their barked instructions. They said it was forbidden material. It seemed innocuous enough to me. I did notice there appeared to be many military uniforms on the streets.

A company chauffeur met me at Bonn and I completed the rest of the journey to the Ruhr in a large Mercedes Benz. We travelled at great speed through the new autobahns, built by the young men doing their *Arbeitsdienst*. Hitler had planned well. I had learned earlier from my German pen friend, Werner Eisner, how every young male had to do six months *Arbeitdienst* – work service. During this time, they built motorways and planted trees on the sides of the roads. The purpose of these trees, I discovered later, was to hide the movement of troops.

After the end of world war one, Germany had suffered from terrible inflation. Unemployment was rife. There were fears of the communists taking over control of the country. In 1933, Hitler had seemed then a saviour to the German people. The construction of roads and manufacturing supplies of arms offered work for those young unemployed people. It all seemed sensible at the time but no one realised that once Hitler tasted power, he would become a tyrant. His desire for *lebensraum* or living space had already manifested itself in the *Anschluss*, the takeover of Austria, when his troops moved in and occupied that country. This was only the beginning – but we all believed that the Munich agreement between Hitler and the other major European countries had put an end to that dream. How wrong we were!

Arriving at the paper factory, I was shown the manufacturing processes and given lunch in the canteen. The company specialised in producing unusual papers including luxury wrappings for chocolates and other fancy items. Everywhere was spotlessly clean and highly regimented but I could not detect a single smiling face amongst the workers who seemed under great pressure.

Returning to Bonn, I began my stay with the professor. He had a large roomy house and it was full of other students from several different countries. We had a lot of fun together despite the variety of languages spoken. When shopping in this attractive old town. I noticed that every shop window carried a photo of Hitler and each German as they entered, gave a salute before buying anything. I would hear them say *'Heil Hitler – ein kilo Karotten bitte'*, whilst raising their right arm! Even when they greeted their friends and anyone else including me, they always gave the Hitler salute. We would laugh and one day I went in the fruit shop and said in my form of German 'God Save the King and can I have some apples?' We thought it funny but the shopkeeper looked around anxiously to see if anyone else had heard us.

At first, we thought all that saluting was a joke but I changed my mind later that evening. A group of us went to the Stadtgarten and danced to a typical German oompapa band. They played *The Lambeth Walk*. My partner, a Welsh boy, and I started to dance the Lambeth Walk as we did in England. It was then a popular and innocent dance from the musical *Me and My Girl*, a current musical production performing in London. We had barely completed one circuit of the dance floor when two uniformed and armed storm troopers grabbed us and pushed us roughly off the floor. *'Swing ist verboten'* they shouted – 'Swing is forbidden'. It was only then I realised how dangerous the Nazi regime might be and I had fears for the future.

Returning home on August 15th, the news became worse. First Austria, then Czechoslovakia and the Sudeten land, country after country, was over-run by German troops. Hitler was still demanding *lebensraum* – living space. All the countries bordering Germany felt threatened, especially Poland. Finally, in late August 1939, Britain warned Hitler that a state of war would exist if Poland were invaded.

WARTIME

On September 1st 1939, German troops entered Poland, just after the signing of the Molotov-Ribbentrop Pact, with Russia agreeing to a non-intervention policy. The world was very surprised by this agreement, as Hitler's ultra right-wing party, the National Socialists, had come into being through the fear of Communism taking over Germany. Immediately on learning the news that German troops had crossed the border into Poland, Britain declared war on Germany. At 11.15am that day, we heard on the wireless, as we then called it, that we together with our then colonies were at war with Hitler's Germany.

Prime Minister Neville Chamberlain spoke to the nation:

I am speaking to you from the Cabinet Room at 10 Downing Street. This morning the British Ambassador in Berlin handed the German Government an official note stating that unless we heard from them by eleven o'clock, that they were prepared at once to withdraw their troops from Poland, a state of war would exist between us. I have to tell you now that no such undertaking has been received, and consequently this country is at war with Germany.

That same morning the postman brought the last letter I would receive from Berlin from my pen friend Werner. He wrote, 'I have been conscripted for military service and am being sent into the Infantry'. I found this most strange, as he was a fully qualified dentist. I had

25

been writing to him since 1933 together with another German girl, Hanneliese Nelb from Hamburg. She always wrote in English and, I now realise, must have been a member of the Hitler Jugend. She constantly mentioned hating the Jews and how wonderful Hitler was. At that time, I had never been conscious of any racial or religious differences between people and did not realise the significance of her words or realise such feelings would lead to the consequent Jewish persecution and inevitably the Holocaust. After the war, I never heard from her again and in a way, I was glad as I felt no affection for her. Werner on the other hand, writing in *Deutsche Schrift,* had never mentioned Hitler or politics in any of his letters, all of which I still possess. He wrote of his studies, of his love of music and of his family.

After the war, his mother wrote to my parents immediately postal communications were re-established with Germany. This letter was even more confusing. She asked if we were all safe, adding sadly 'Werner died at Arras in 1940, killed as cannon fodder.' It was not until 1980 when I visited his sister Gea in the American sector of Berlin that I learned the difference between these two German pen-friends. Whereas Hali, as Hanneliese was known, was obviously a full-blooded Nazi, Werner was officially considered a second-class citizen and thus expendable. He had great grandparents who were Jewish and although the bloodline was not close enough for him to wear the yellow star as a Jew, he was sent instead to the front line of the battle during the early days, to be slaughtered.

That first day of war is etched clearly in my memory. Barely had the announcement been made on the radio when London heard its first air raid warning, an ugly and ominous wailing sound. My brother turned to me and said 'We must put up the Anderson air raid shelter now.' We rushed into the garden and started to dig, a vain hope of protection if the enemy aircraft had arrived! We needed to excavate a deep trench and join heavy curved sheets of corrugated iron to ensure protection. Then we would have to cover them with earth for added protection. It would entail hours of work. Fortunately, it was a false alarm, caused, as I later learned, by a trainee radar operator making an elementary error and not sensing the echo on his cathode ray tube in order to check whether the aircraft response was in front or behind the radar installation! This would indicate whether it was one of ours – a friendly – or otherwise hostile. This error caused the air raid sirens to be sounded for the first time in Britain.

The rest of the year 1939 in Britain passed in an uneasy calm, which continued into the early months of the following year. We called it the 'Phoney War'. We had bombed Germany but only with propaganda leaflets, hoping that this would persuade the population to ask for peace. In Britain in the early months of war, many children were already evacuated from the big cities to more remote and less threatened areas. The 'Phoney War' caused many mothers to bring their children home again. London had expected to be bombed immediately. We were confused.

London was not the first target. From April 1940, Hitler's air force concentrated their attacks on our airfields and radar stations. We lost many aircraft during that time and we were already considerably short of the number needed to defend the country. Thanks to the radar warning system and the growing skill of our fighter pilots, we inflicted severe losses on Hitler's bomber fleet. This caused the Fuhrer to change his tactics.

What happened next can best be described in the words of Ernie Pile, a war correspondent in his article, *The London Blitz*:

The appearance of German bombers in the skies over London during the afternoon of September 7, 1940 heralded a tactical shift in Hitler's attempt to subdue Great Britain. During the previous two months, the Luftwaffe had targeted RAF airfields and radar stations for destruction in preparation for the German invasion of the island. With invasion plans put on hold and eventually scrapped, Hitler turned his attention to destroying London in an attempt to demoralise the population and force the British to come to terms. At around 4:00 PM on that September day, 348 German bombers escorted by 617 fighters blasted London until 6:00 PM.

Two hours later, guided by the fires set by the first assault, a second group of raiders commenced another attack that lasted until 4:30 the following morning.

The blitz in London

'They came after dark...' It was a night when London was ringed with fire and stabbed with fire.

They came just after dark, and somehow you could sense from the quick, bitter firing of the guns that there was to be no monkey business this night.

Shortly after the sirens wailed, you could hear the Germans grinding overhead. In my room, with its black curtains drawn across the windows, you could feel the shake from the guns. You could hear the boom, crump, crump, crump, of heavy bombs at their work of tearing buildings apart. They were not too far away.

Half an hour after the firing started, I gathered a couple of friends and went to a high, darkened balcony that gave us a view of a third of the entire circle of London. As we stepped out onto the balcony, a vast inner excitement came over all of us – an excitement that had neither fear nor horror in it, because it was too full of awe. You have all seen big fires, but I doubt if you have ever seen the whole horizon of a city lined with great fires – scores of them, perhaps hundreds.

There was something inspiring just in the awful savagery of it.

The closest fires were near enough for us to hear the crackling flames and the yells of firemen. Little fires grew into big ones even as we watched. Big ones died down under the firemen's valour, only to break out again later.

About every two minutes, a new wave of planes would be over. The motors seemed to grind rather than roar, and to have an angry pulsation, like a bee buzzing in blind fury.

The guns did not make a constant overwhelming din as in those terrible days of September. They were intermittent – sometimes a few seconds apart, sometimes a minute or more. Their sound was sharp, near by; and soft and muffled, far away. They were everywhere over London.

Into the dark shadowed spaces below us, while we watched whole batches of incendiary bombs fell. We saw two dozen go off in two seconds. They flashed terrifically, then quickly simmered down to pin points of dazzling white, burning ferociously. These white pin points would go out one by one, as the unseen heroes of the moment smothered them with sand. But also, while we watched, other pinpoints would burn on, and soon a yellow flame would leap up from the white centre. They had done their work – another building was on fire.

The greatest of all the fires was directly in front of us. Flames seemed to whip hundreds of feet into the air. Pinkish-white smoke ballooned upward in a great cloud, and out of this cloud, there gradually took shape – so faintly at first that we were not sure, we saw correctly – the gigantic dome of St Paul's Cathedral.

St Paul's was surrounded by fire, but it came through. It stood there in its enormous proportions – growing slowly clearer and clearer, the way objects take shape at dawn. It was like a picture of some miraculous figure that appears before peace-hungry soldiers on a battlefield.

The streets below us were semi-illuminated from the glow. Immediately above the fires, the sky was red and angry, and overhead, making a ceiling in the vast heavens, there was a cloud of smoke all in pink. Up in that pink shrouding there were tiny, brilliant specks of flashing light – anti-aircraft shells bursting. After the flash, you could hear the sound.

Up there, too, the barrage balloons were standing out as clearly, as if it were daytime, but now they were pink instead of silver.

Now and then through a hole in that pink shroud, there twinkled incongruously a permanent, genuine star – the old-fashioned kind that has always been there.

Below us, the Thames grew lighter and all around were the shadows – the dark shadows of buildings and bridges that formed the base of this dreadful masterpiece.

Later on, I borrowed a tin hat and went out among the fires. That was exciting too; but the thing I shall always remember above all the other things in my life is the monstrous loveliness of that one single view of London on a holiday night – London stabbed with great fires, shaken by explosions, its dark regions along the Thames sparkling with the pin points of white-hot bombs, all of it roofed over with a ceiling of pink that held bursting shells, balloons, flares and the grind of vicious engines. And in yourself the excitement and anticipation and wonder in your soul that this could be happening at all.

These things all went together to make the most hateful, most beautiful single scene I had ever seen.

These words of Ernie Pile awaken fearful memories. I recollect those days, those nights, so vividly. The capital city underwent constant bombing day and night. Those days and nights of terror and fear seemed endless. Night after night, it was impossible to sleep. The skies around London lit up with explosions. Every night we could see fires burning in the inner city. Every day we feared it might be our last.

This was the beginning of the Blitz – a period of intense bombing of London and other cities that continued until the following May. For the next 57 consecutive days, London was bombed either during the day or night. Fires consumed many portions of the city. Residents sought shelter wherever they could find it – many fleeing to the Underground stations that sheltered as many as 177,000 people during the night. In the worst single incident, 450 were killed when a bomb destroyed a school being used as an air raid shelter. Londoners and the world were introduced to a new weapon of terror and destruction in the arsenal of twentieth century warfare. The Blitz ended on May 11th, 1941 when Hitler called off the raids in order to move his bombers east in preparation for Germany's invasion of Russia.

We all grew up very quickly. My generation did not enjoy teenage years. We became adults before our time. Life in London daily became more difficult. Rationing was introduced. Food became scarce as merchant shipping brought in only essentials. It was a constant hunt to find enough to eat. We lived in darkened streets, darkened homes. Every window was reinforced with strips of paper tape against blasts, and blacked out with heavy dark curtains. The air raid warden would often knock at the door, warning any householder if the smallest chink of light could be seen. All cars and lorries had their lights shielded; only a small slit remained in the headlights.

Inner London and the docklands were the most severely damaged but the suburbs too were targeted. Yet people continued to work and live as normal a life as possible. Overhead, daily we would watch the dogfights between the Luftwaffe and our fighters. No one talked of defeat. The tenacity of our pilots aided by advance warning by radar finally caused Hitler to give up thoughts of invasion. Instead, he opened the second front against Russia.

My boyfriend, George Duncan, as a Territorial soldier, was called up on the first day of war. He was soon serving with the British Expeditionary Force on the continent – no letters and no news. Our forces in Europe were involved in heavy fighting. Things were going badly. The Maginot line was breached. Holland and Belgium were swiftly overrun by the Wehrmacht and the Allied Forces were in retreat. The army of the Reich was better armed and trained. German troops broke through the Maginot Line and moved swiftly through France, our troops were outnumbered and out-armed. In June 1940, the evacuation of our retreating army took place, followed by the miracle of Dunkirk when so many men were saved from the ravaged beaches. I wondered whether my boyfriend was one of them. Had he even survived the battles to get to Dunkirk? Everyday I learned of my friends' brothers or boyfriends being killed or wounded. I dreaded every letter, every phone call.

My boyfriend George
serving in Egypt

By then I was once more working for the Scottish Provident Assurance Company. Hearing I had returned safely from my au pair adventure, they contacted me and asked if I would return to work for them. Many of their young men had been conscripted and as they had already trained me, I could fill their place. Their City offices were evacuated to Woking in Surrey. Many City firms had either been bombed out or they had shut their offices and moved to safer premises away from London. I was happy to agree. This time I did not have to wear a maroon overall, I was needed. We lived in a large house at Woking during the week, returning home for the weekends to London. Nightly we heard the bombs falling on the Capital, many jettisoned close to us by the returning enemy bombers. The bark of the ack-ack guns kept us awake. I worried about my parents, living in the suburbs and still being bombed. After the office closed each day, there was very little to do. I decided to volunteer to help in the evenings at the YMCA canteen in the town, which offered food and companionship to the troops stationed in nearby barracks. When we heard the news in June of the Dunkirk evacuation, we were asked to stand by for daytime duties as well.

From the first day, as the battle-weary soldiers were arriving back from the Dunkirk beaches, they were dispersed by train to various centres. Woking station was the initial stop for many of the evacuated troops to receive any food or drink. The ports were too crowded and the men were moved out as soon as possible. We were asked to run the feeding stations on the platforms as train after train arrived, full of hungry and tired soldiers. My manager was only too happy to let me help. It was heart rending to see these men; some wounded, sometimes mortally, their uniforms filthy and torn. They could barely drag themselves out of the carriages for refreshments. Yet after a cup of tea and a 'wad', they still managed a smile and a thank you. One train would leave, only for another one to take its place. This seemed to go on for day after day. I wondered where my boyfriend was, whether he too had escaped. I had received no news from him for weeks. Every day I scanned the faces of the troops arriving at the station, every day I was disappointed.

On the third day, an amazing coincidence occurred. From one of the carriages, immediately opposite to where I was dispensing mugs of tea, there emerged a French pilot. He came straight up to me and hugged me. It was Rene Cadier, the French student I had met five years before when he had come to Britain for a holiday and stayed with my music teacher. He looked very different, tired, and grey-faced but he had recognised me. Of all the lucky chances to think he came to the very platform where I was working! I gave him a special welcome. We had little time for talk, just time enough to give him a large mug of hot tea and a packet of sandwiches for the journey. In less than half an hour, he was back on the train again and away. We said au revoir and hoped we would meet again some day. It would be more than thirty years before we did.

Meanwhile, for many weeks, the bombing of London had continued relentlessly; firebombs by day to show the way for the nighttime raiders. Hundreds of people were left homeless, many living permanently on the platforms of the tube stations, sleeping on the metal two-tier bunks provided, and leaving little room for the passengers. I will never forget the little 'old man' faces of children who never left the Underground for days on end. I will always remember my courageous London. As I travelled home at weekends, these were the scenes that stay in my memory to this day; everywhere devastation, shattered homes with personal belongings lying neglected in the streets, factories burned out, emergency services overstretched, London burning but Londoners who never gave up. As I looked through the carriage window on my occasional journey home, I could see land mines entangled on the telephone wires, ready to cause havoc if they fell.

From the summer of 1940, Fighter Command's young Spitfire and

Hurricane pilots began to turn the tide. With their skills and daring, they were causing unsustainable losses to the Luftwaffe. I, together with the rest of the population of the Home Counties, cheered every time we saw a German bomber in flames, crashing to earth. The success of the RAF and the then superiority of our Navy put a stop to Hitler's thoughts of invading Britain. Instead, he turned to Russia and began fighting on a second front, trying to extend his boundaries to the east. For Germany, this was a disastrous move. I did not realise then the significance of radar nor how this was what had helped the RAF to victory in the skies and enabled us to survive.

Fighter Command's special weapon
– the Spitfire

Little did I know how, in the near future, I would become part of that fantastic weapon of defence?

MY TIME IN THE WAAF

It was at this time that my cousin Eric, a graduate pilot from Cranwell College, was killed. He had won a Wakefield Scholarship to become a pilot. Now having qualified and received his wings, he was on a routine flight to Scotland. The weather was poor and his training minimal; he hit a mountain. His death affected me greatly. I was 19 years old, intensely patriotic and full of ideals. There and then, I decided to join the WAAF, the women's section of the RAF, in the hope of replacing him.

December 1940, I volunteered and was asked at the Recruiting Office, 'Do you want to be a cook or an MT driver?' I replied 'Neither, I want to be a Clerk Special Duties.' The Flight Officer appeared taken aback. 'How do you know about that?' she asked. I explained I had no idea what Clerk Special Duties entailed but I had asked a friend, already a WAAF, for which trade I should apply. She had been assigned to 'Special Duties' and suggested I should apply for this category. Unable to tell me more about it as she was covered by the Official Secrets Act, she added, 'Tell them you are good at Maths'. As soon as the enrolment officer heard this, she entered me immediately as Clerk Special Duties. It seemed there was a distinct shortage of women proficient in mathematics!

It took a few months before I received my calling-up papers but March 1941 saw me on my way to service life. Arriving at Innsworth Barracks, Gloucester for initial training, I entered a completely new regimented world. I learned how to salute officers, recognise the different ranks. I learned how to march, what ablutions were, how to pass a kit inspection and a myriad more Air Force requirements. This training lasted a few weeks.

I found myself amongst a mixed bunch of recruits, debutantes and prostitutes, vicars' daughters and academics. We all lived together in Nissan huts, heated by an antique boiler in the middle of the room, twenty odd girls, all equally as bemused as I was. I had lived a comparatively safe and sheltered life so imagine my surprise on the second day there to find a new recruit giving birth in the ablutions.

This was a month of hell but we got through, helped by a bit of humour and a lot of tolerance. By then, we had been kitted out with two uniforms, sensible black shoes, an overcoat and hat and of course 'blackouts'. These were the officially issued thick black knickers! After a passing-out parade we were separated into our different trades and sent off for special training.

My special duties category turned out to be Filter plotter; double Dutch to me at that time. The special duties category covered three different types of work; radar operators, Filter plotters and Operations plotters. A radar operator worked at the Chain Home radar stations linked around our coast, using information received by the radar equipment which was then passed on to the Filter Room. This special room was the hub of the whole radar system. Filter Plotters were responsible for displaying information on the gridded map table, received from the Group's radar stations. This was swiftly and mathematically analysed and corrected by the Filterer Officers. All personnel had to be fast and accurate. The tracks were identified as either friendly or hostile through information received from the Movements Control section. The filtered information was then past on to the Operations Room plotters who plotted it on their map table. It was this information, which was then used to give air raid warnings, scramble aircraft, organise air-sea rescue of ditched aircrews, and to give warning of any aircraft signalling Mayday or the SOS signal.

Anti-aircraft gun crews were informed of approaching aircraft for gun-laying. At the same time, it was passed to the Royal Observer Corps personnel who then carried on plotting the aircraft overland, using purely visual and sound information. Radar was in its initial stages and was at that time unable to be used successfully overland due to the interference to readings by metal objects, such as church spires and high buildings.

Now I was to learn the importance of radar, initially called Radio Direction Finding (RDF). This amazing invention (discovered by Watson Watt in 1936) gave our small air force the edge over the enemy. It prevented fighter aircraft having to patrol the skies constantly, allowing them to scramble only when the enemy was detected approaching our shores. It was invaluable as the RAF was

The laboratory at Bawdsey Manor where Watson Watts
produced Radio Detection Finding – later radar

lacking in aircraft and trained aircrew in those initial years. I was proud to think I was to become part of this special organisation, just one small cog in this amazing machine.

Contacts with home and friends were sparse. I would receive an occasional airgraph letter from George who, I finally learned, had been one of the last people to leave the Dunkirk beaches. He had acted as Beach Master, getting the troops on to boats and organising the evacuation of the injured. It is only in recent years that I have learned that he and a fellow military policeman, being keen rowers, had found a boat and had rowed boatloads of soldiers out to a waiting rescue ship, making ten journeys. Finally, the ship's captain had said 'No more, lads. We're full to the gunwales. You jump aboard and we are off.' George was immediately sent overseas again with the Seventh Armoured Division; to the Middle East, I guessed. From there the occasional air letter he was able to send usually took weeks to arrive. I had no idea where he was stationed.

There was no time for worrying in my first month of training, as there was so much to learn and absorb. As trainee Filter Room plotters,

Information on the Filter Room table showing details of enemy raids

courtesy of the Trustees of the Imperial War Museum

we went to Leighton Buzzard to learn the necessary techniques before taking up our positions at one of the seven Fighter Group Filter Rooms, as part of the radar defence system. We learned that throughout Great Britain, Filter plotters were connected by telephone to the radar stations forming a defence chain around our shores. The information from the radar stations was calculated from the responses on their cathode ray tube screens. In the Filter Room, for each new filtered track, a numbered magnetic plaque was placed on the map table, together with counters showing position, height, estimated number of aircraft and whether they were showing Identification Friend or Foe (IFF). Speed was essential as the aircraft were moving all the time.

After we passed the final test, proving we were both fast and accurate, once again we were separated and sent off to different Fighter Group Headquarters, where the Filter Rooms were located.

A busy watch in 11 Group Filter Room, Fighter Command HQ

courtesy of the Trustees of the Imperial War Museum

There were seven of them, spread around Britain and Northern Ireland. These were the vital nerve centres which co-ordinated the information received from the chain of radiolocation stations covering the entire coastline of Britain and Northern Ireland. After the plotting of aircraft, the Filter Room Controller, already notified of all friendly aircraft movements by the Movements Liaison team, could then identify them as friend or foe. This was passed on to the Operations Rooms which controlled fighter interception operations, monitored our bomber raids, initiated air raid warnings and other land and air defences against the Luftwaffe attacks and most important, instigated air sea rescue operations. At all times, speed and accuracy were of paramount importance.

I was posted to 10 Group Filter Room at Rudloe Manor, Box, a few miles from Bath. We worked underground in cramped and uncomfortable conditions. Air conditioning and heating were very primitive. There was a lot of air activity in this region as it covered the coast from the Isle of Wight to North Wales and there was considerable bombing of the ports and the factories as well as regular Coastal Command patrols looking for U-boats. We usually worked a three-watch basis, eight hours on duty, plus a half hour handover period, each end of the watch, to liaise with the incoming or outgoing watch, and then fifteen hours off. After eating, sleeping, doing one's laundry, having parades and inspections, there was not much time left for other activities. We were billeted with civilian families in surrounding villages. I was sent to Corsham to the house of the local coal merchant. I had an aunt living in Bath and I managed occasional rare visits to her but there were very few chances of much time off. Life consisted of work, sleep, eat and then back on duty.

During my time at Rudloe, I was given the task of designing a map table with a distorted grid, as it would appear on a globe. This was a complicated process and needed some special calculations. On the strength of what I achieved, in the late summer of 1941, Wing Commander Rudd recommended me for a commission. He was a great er and organiser who ran 10 Group Filter Room superbly. I had previously applied for an Intelligence commission but he insisted he would block it. He explained Filterer Officers were needed desperately and he intended to prevent me from leaving this work. A few weeks later, I was called up to Air Ministry for the Intelligence commission interview. I was put in a room and left there for over two hours. People looked at me from windows high up in the room but nobody came. Realising the Wingco's warning that he would prevent me being considered for any other commission other than Filterer, had succeeded, I left without being interviewed and returned to Rudloe Manor. I was destined to be a Filterer Officer.

In September 1941, I was posted for the necessary technical

training. This took place at the famous Bawdsey Manor, the place where Watson Watt had first worked on RDF. The idea had come to him after investigating sonar responses from icebergs, as used by the Navy. He wondered whether radio waves would give similar responses from the metal of aircraft. It was from Bawdsey where he planned the Chain Home stations, to be eventually linked around the coast of Britain and Northern Ireland, as well as establishing the first Filter Room.

The training was intense. We had to learn how radar worked, know the siting of all the stations to evaluate their accuracy and learn about the ever-increasing new types of detection being designed. The scientists were constantly bringing out new inventions. Each one increased our ability to give advance warning of raids or aided our bomber and fighter crews to perform more accurately. Our job was to use the information displayed by the plotters, assimilate and collate it and estimate the correct position, number and height of all aircraft from the information displayed from the overlapping radar stations. Speed and accuracy in assessing and estimating the position, direction of flight, height and numbers of aircraft, as well as recognising friend or foe, were essential. This information had to be instant as the aircraft were constantly moving. We were all young women, many under twenty-one years of age. We were not to have reached the 'age of caution', as instinctive action was needed for the work. There could be no hesitation. We had previously taken an initial psychological test, based on the one given to fighter pilots, to gauge our response time. This training was probably one of the most difficult of any I have ever received. Those of us on the course worked hard to pass the final test, as the need for trained Filterers was vital for Britain's defence network.

I was then sent on an officer training course, as a cadet at Loughborough College. Here I learned how to give commands, take parades, and behave as an officer! I was immensely proud of the white cadet band I wore around my hat. After graduation, we received the sum of £50 with which to buy our uniform, topcoat and hat. We were appointed to the rank of Assistant Section Officers, equivalent to Pilot Officer. After that, we had to pay for all uniform replacements and cover our Mess bills, out of the small monthly salary we received. Many officers received extra from their parents but I had to make do on my monthly RAF pay. I have since learned that male officers of the same rank received a much larger sum and flying crew nearly four times as much as we did. At the time, the pay did not seem important. I was proud to serve my country and thrilled to accept the responsibilities thrust upon me. I was just twenty years old.

Having passed the course, we all wondered where we would be sent. My posting was announced as 9 Group HQ, RAF Barton Hall, near Preston, Lancashire; a part of Britain I had never visited and whilst there, never liked. The winter of 1941 in the north was bitterly cold. It snowed for days on end. Coming off duty at midnight, we had to wait outside the entrance to the Filter Room, in the biting wind and snow, for the RAF bus to take us back to the Mess. This did not help to make for an easy life. We arrived back at our billets, hungry, cold and unable to sleep. After six months there, I was promoted to Section Officer, equivalent to a Flying Officer in the RAF. I would receive £12 a month pay. There was little chance of further promotion, unless someone died, since by then all the Filter Rooms were fully manned with the essential personnel.

Preston as a town had nothing to offer and we never felt welcome. Having always understood that Lancashire people were friendly, I had expected this to be so. I never found any signs of it. They ignored us in the streets. We were pushed out of the way in queues. The civilian women looked at us with suspicion. There was nothing to do and little to see. Air activities in that region were sporadic with occasional heavy raids on Liverpool and other manufacturing centres, all very different from the continuous bombing in the south. The Filter Controller I usually worked with, Squadron Leader Meinerzhagen, was arrogant and haughty. I remember him complaining bitterly that his father had not been informed when Radio Luxembourg, which he owned, was raided by our Special Operations forces. Our forces had successfully destroyed the unit and captured a German radar scientist! I looked forward to my next posting. Anywhere must be better than this place.

To add to my misery, I developed chickenpox and spent my twenty-first birthday in hospital, with 86 spots on my face and goodness knows how many elsewhere! The only thing my stay at 9 Group was memorable for was that I drank my first glass of alcohol there. For many years, I had abstained for reasons I cannot now remember, possibly some influence of the Baptist chapel I attended in my youth. This breakthrough came about on a bitterly cold winter's evening. I was invited out to dinner by the Royal Observer Corps Officer, who said he would take me to the Moorcock Inn at Clitheroe, on the side of Waddington Fell in the heart of the Forest of Bowland at the head of the Ribble Valley. I was told this was the best dining to be had anywhere in the area. Never before had I been to a high-class restaurant. I have forgotten my escort's name and what he looked like. I do remember he was much older than I was and he must have been quite rich as money was no object. Arriving there, I decided it was time to sample alcohol for the first time.

We started with a pre-dinner Rye Highball. During the excellent meal of roast venison, shot in the locality, we consumed a bottle of Burgundy and then after the dessert and with our coffee, we finished with a Van der Hum liqueur. It was then I found I had a strong head for liquor because on returning to base, due to report for duty at midnight, I managed to work the night watch, carrying out my duties successfully. I must admit however that I had no difficulty in sleeping when I came off duty at 8am. My escort got nothing out of the evening except my company throughout dinner. I am not sure what else he had expected.

There was one particularly memorable occasion whilst on duty there. A new invention had been added to our defence repertoire. It was code-named Aspirin. It was to be the antidote to Germany's Knickebein. This was a radio beam guidance system using two beams designed to help the Luftwaffe bombers find their target. When flying towards this target, as soon as they detected the second beam intersecting the first, they would drop their bombs without having to rely on visual sighting.

The Allies countered this system by using Hallicrafters S-27, the only device capable of detecting the Knickebein beam. They soon developed jammers to interfere with the system. Since the Knickebein was called 'Headache' by the British, it was only logical to name the jammers 'Aspirin.' This was to be the first occasion when Aspirin would be used. A Luftwaffe raid was scheduled to attack the shipping at Liverpool. We understood that Aspirin was to be tried out with the intention of jamming the German beam and sending the enemy on a wrong track. It was highly successful in this instance. The beam was redirected towards Southern Ireland. Dublin received a heavy bombardment, to their great surprise. We were delighted because it was well known Ireland's capital

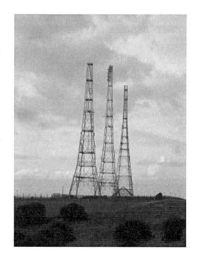

Chain Home radar towers, RAF Swingate

city was a haven for German spies, aiming to infiltrate Britain. The whole Filter Room applauded.

How ecstatic I was to learn that, after eight months at Preston, I was being posted back to 10 Group at Rudloe Manor. This time I would live in the mixed Mess in the Manor House. I had never before been in a mixed Mess and I gained a completely new view of life in the RAF. Many air crew, after operational duties, were posted here for a rest period but this did not stop their high spirits. There was always some crazy activity involving them going on when we were off duty. What I found interesting was the different way the female officers reacted to being in a mixed Mess. Many of them had come from girls-only public schools, several from Roedean. They were always very self-conscious, primping and preening themselves as they entered the dining hall. I had been co-educated from my early days and had no such problems. As far as I was concerned, we were all part of the same team. The permanent personnel too were interesting. The senior officer was Air Vice Marshall Augustus Orlebar, a pilot in the Great War with many 'kills' to his name, he had also won the famous Schneider Trophy Race. He was a hero to us all. It was here too that I breakfasted with Rex Harrison. He was an Army Liaison Officer, responsible for the Air Raid Warnings section. I am afraid I never took to him. He often sat opposite me during breakfast and barely deigned to speak to us lesser mortals. He was a very messy eater, his toast and marmalade oozing from his mouth whilst he was eating. He was not the glamorous film idol I had imagined! Although still married but separated from his wife Connie, he was in the middle of a turbulent affair with Lilli Palmer, the beautiful and well-known actress. Each evening he would carry on a long and amorous conversation with her from the public phone in the Mess. We were all able to hear every word as he spoke to her in his well-honed modulated tones. Peter Hoare, a famous theatrical producer, also served at Rudloe. He was a sergeant and spent most of his time providing entertainment for the troops. On one occasion, he produced the famous *French without Tears* in which Harrison had himself once appeared. I took the minor part of the French maid in this production!

Hamilton Kennedy, still a civilian, was a frequent visitor. He wrote *You are my Sunshine, my only Sunshine,* a great favourite with the other ranks. I fell for him and managed a few dates on his expense account. It was here too that I first met Wing Commander Kenneth Horne, before he linked up with Dickie Murdoch. His then wife was a Filterer on my watch so we often all went out together. She later left him for a Polish pilot and broke his heart. I adored Kenneth; he was a lovely person. As well as being a radio favourite, he was also chairman of The Triplex Glass Company but was doing his service with the RAF.

The Filter Room was operating from the caves below Box village, just a few miles from Bath. It was during this period that Hitler launched the 'Baedeker' raids, bombing our most beautiful cities, chosen from this famous German guidebook. They included Exeter, Bath, Norwich and York, then later Canterbury. Bath was bombed constantly for three day and three nights, killing many civilians and destroying vast numbers of beautiful buildings. Several WAAF who were spending their off-duty periods in Bath during this time were killed and we had the sad job of notifying the parents. This was a heart-rending task. Then came the calm and another city was targeted and their turn came for devastation. I remember these raids with anger when people complain and condemn the Air Force and Air Marshall 'Bomber' Harris for bombing Dresden!

Despite the tragedy of the raids on Bath, my time there was a very happy one. I was able to see my aunt and my cousin Daphne, sister to the Eric Padfield, whose death had inspired me to join the RAF.

By contrast, her brother's death had persuaded Daphne to become a pacifist We did not argue, we just agreed to differ.

Living near the site of the Filter Room obviated the daily coach journeys to the Mess that I had endured at Preston. The conviviality of the mixed Officers' Mess provided some great social occasions. On the other side of the valley was RAF Colerne, occupied at that time by a squadron of Polish and Czechoslovak pilots. These men, who had escaped from their country, had also lost contact with their families. They were intrepid, sometimes reckless, pilots but brave and interesting men. They added a lot of spice to our off-duty activities.

After almost six months, I was posted once again. 11 Group Filter Room, based at the headquarters of Fighter Command at Stanmore, Middlesex. This was a great boost to my morale as only the fastest and most accurate Filterers were sent there. It was the busiest and most important Filter Room in the country, controlling the coast from the Fens to the Isle of Wight, including all activity over London. More aerial activity took place in this region than the rest of Britain put together.

A tense moment filtering enemy aircraft

courtesy of the Trustees of the Imperial War Museum

Installed in No. 2 WAAF Officers' Mess, Stanmore was the highlight to date of my RAF life. It was a thatched house, opposite Stanmore Common. My fellow officers were all interesting intelligent women. I met the extraordinary and talented Zoë Hicks, an offspring of Augustus John, Mary Hogg, a niece of Quentin Hogg (afterwards Lord Hailsham), Peggy Strickland, designer of the famous trade mark the Yardley Bee, two dancers from the Palladium, my very special friend Kay Tanner – my watch leader, who eventually became PA to the Chief of the Air Force in the Far East, Air Vice-Marshall Goddard, and many more. No. 2 WAAF Officers Mess, Bentley Manor, was reserved for those of us working on secret projects. We were unable to talk about our work other than amongst our colleagues. We would occasionally accommodate WAAF Officers on similar secret projects. I recall 'Bomber' Harris's PA spending a few nights with us whilst he was visiting Fighter Command. Since she was likely to know future bomber movements, she slept in our Mess in case she talked in her sleep!

We also had eight WRNS Officers billeted with us who were working at Canons Park, a few miles from Stanmore. We never discussed our work with them nor did we know what they did. In fact, I only found out what this was by a strange coincidence nearly forty years later. I was visiting friends in Houston. One afternoon I noticed, on a shelf in my host's den, an unusual wheel.

'What is that, Skeet'? I asked.

He replied 'What do you think it is'?

'Is it an Enigma wheel'?

'You're right'.

It turned out that my host was the first American sent to work at Bletchley Heath, after the USA learned of our ability to decipher the German Enigma code. He then told me that he had later moved to Canons Park where he worked with some WRNS Officers. It was then I realised he was referring to our colleagues. I learned for the first time they were code and cipher officers, engaged in deciphering Bletchley Enigma information. He told me he had a book they gave him. Without revealing that I knew them, I asked him to find it and added 'Don't tell me their names, I think I may be able to tell you at least some of them!' I was able to his great surprise to tell him the names of at least four of the signatures on the front page. This was one more of life's strange coincidences. It had taken me all those years to break down our code of silence.

Work in the Filter Room, deep underground, was hard and intense. We spent long night watches filtering the tracks of a thousand bomber raids – both German and later British – monitoring the dog fights over the sea and checking on shipping in the Channel. If it was a busy night, there was little chance of respite. We might perhaps have fifteen minutes during an eight-hour watch when we would make our way to the canteen for a drink and a sandwich, invariably consisting of chopped raw cabbage and marmite.

We did our best when off duty to have some social life. We would arrange a Mess party or join the male officers at their Mess just up the road. We frequently received free tickets for the ballet or a theatre. We would sometimes make our way up to the West End for a visit to a nightclub. Zoë Hicks would take several of us up to the Café de Paris to meet her father, Augustus John. He would be holding court with his friend Dylan Thomas and other luminaries of the art world. All the girls were propositioned in turn! We relaxed when we could and made the best of a demanding life, taking our pleasures where we were able to find them.

Many advances in radar techniques; the use of Window to deceive the Luftwaffe, GCI, (Ground Controlled Interception), AI (Air Interception) whose use was pioneered by Cat's Eyes Cunningham, OBOE, and Happidromes – all took place during my time there. Of course, due to weather conditions, sometimes there were quiet days and quiet nights. The hours then spent underground in uncomfortable conditions could get very boring. Many plotters would occupy themselves 'binding'. This was the name given to the chatting, which took place between a plotter and the radar operator at the other end of the line. They would probably never meet but many friendships were formed over the air on such occasions, especially if they had been on duty together when there had been heavy air activity. This relationship between radar operator and plotter was of great importance since it was vital to have complete co-operation in order to pass on the relayed information as correctly and swiftly as possible.

It is important to emphasise that many of both the WAAF plotters and the Filterers had husbands, boyfriends or brothers who were flying in the bombers or fighters they were plotting. We always knew which squadrons were operating. Imagine the strain when five hundred bombers were plotted out on a mission and initially only four hundred and fifty returned. The others might gradually find their way back, having been shot up. Many never returned. Everyone in the Filter Room continued doing their work despite their anxiety over the fate of their loved ones. Their discipline and devotion to duty could not be faulted.

As officers, we were given other duties during the periods when bad weather prevented many air operations. Even then, there were occasionally hours of doing nothing. Two of us managed to get a contract with William Ritchie of Edinburgh, greeting card manufacturers. Section Officer Williams, known to all as Willi, and I would use these quiet nights to compose verses for both birthday and Christmas cards. I might start off with 'The Yule time log is burning bright' and hope I could make a suitable rhyme. We were paid the princely sum of one shilling and ninepence per line, less than 10p, for our efforts. This meant a lot as it was a great supplement to the twelve pounds a month we earned. This sum had to cover our Mess bills for food, drinks and replenish our uniforms and underwear.

In order for us to understand how our work in the Filter Room was used and to emphasise its importance, we were sent on occasional short visits to other units who relied on the information we supplied. For this reason, I visited the Air Sea Rescue unit at Dover. They relied on our correct calculation of the position of ditching aircraft from the Broad IF signals we received, for their forays to rescue crews from the Channel. We always gave first priority to any Broad IF response reported by a radar station. I can recall one occasion when I tracked a returning bomber, which had suffered extensive damage. I received the Broad IF signal long before the aircraft response itself came in. The bomber was constantly losing height. I tracked it for several hundred miles and finally lost the signal. It was later I learned that the Air Sea Rescue boat had picked the crew up from a position within half a mile from my last calculation. It was this sort of event that made all the hard and stressful work worthwhile.

I was delighted to have the opportunity of visiting the Dover boat station and go out in the motor torpedo boat for one of their Channel rescue trips. Despite my normal ability to feel seasick at the slightest motion of the waves, on this occasion I was so interested that I completely overcame any problem in that direction. On a subsequent occasion, I spent three days with two other WAAF Filterers at a bomber station in the Lancashire area so that we could emphasize to them the importance of turning on their Identification Friend or Foe switch (IFF) and reassure them that the German radar was not able to pick up this signal.

We often found returning fighter and bomber crews were difficult to identify for this very reason, as the pilots were frightened to turn on this aid. It was essential to reassure them of its safety. Many bomber crews had no idea how radar was constantly tracking them and monitoring them for

Air-sea rescue motor torpedo boat in action

the first two hundred miles or more of their missions.

It was at this time that I learned that my now fiancé George had been wounded at El Alamein and that, during his convalescence, he had met an ATS signals girl in Cairo, got her pregnant and married her. Letters had been infrequent and many were lost in transit. I had to hear this from his sister and it was many years later that he told me how ashamed he was for the way he had treated me. These things happened in wartime. He had had a bad time in the desert fighting. His Dunkirk experience had been horrific. How could I blame him? I suppose I was upset, I cannot really remember. Life at Fighter Command was incessantly demanding with no time for remorse, only time to get on with the job. Things happened that way during wartime. It is in the latter years I have felt more affected by it.

I was to meet up with Kenneth Horne again, now the Wing Commander in charge of the Balloon Barrage station at Stanmore. His wife had by then left him for the Polish pilot. He was very cut up about this and poured out his troubles to me. I was a good listener. We became friends and, when he was posted to Equipment in Whitehall, I visited his office on one occasion and met his colleagues. They were Wing Commander Armitage and Squadron Leader Richard Murdoch. This was where the great partnership between Kenneth and Dickie Murdoch began. On my first visit there, they were doing *The Times* cryptic crossword together, in itself as good as any comedy performance! He went on to do many radio programmes, *Monday Night at Eight* and the RAF comedy *Much Binding in the Marsh*. As he did not know much about the WAAF side of the RAF, he asked me to write some of the dialogue.

I had by then briefly met Sergeant Quentin Baillie of the Royal Service Corps. He was an interesting man, a scholar, world traveller and a writer. We got on so well that we decided we would work our way around the world after the war had ended. I had met him just before

Sketch from a book found on
a dead German soldier

I received my commission and on my subsequent first leave, he sent to my house three hundred daffodils by means of congratulation. My mother who had met him just once thought him charming. During an operation in Europe, he had found a sketchbook on the body of a dead German soldier. He sent it to me; I still have it, wrapped in the tarred paper used in those days, in which it arrived. I was never to see him again.

I later learned he had been transferred to a Special Services unit. I do not know what really happened but he was wounded during a later raid on the French coast. He subsequently wrote to my mother saying he could never see me again as he had been so badly injured. He would only be a burden to me if we got together. He asked her to break the news and that was all. I have tried on many occasions to find out whether he had died from his injuries or if he had returned to his home to Dundee. I could find out nothing. It is one of the tragedies of my life. I feel I abandoned him

A SWIFT ENGAGEMENT

It was some months later, in May 1944 that I met my future husband. His father, Captain Jimmy Younghusband, owned the Stanmore Riding School, one of the most famous in Britain. At that time, each Filter watch was encouraged to organise a 'Wings for Victory' event. The idea was to encourage the public to invest in National Savings Stamps for loan certificates to pay for the war effort. My 'B' Watch decided to run a garden party in the grounds of Hill House, a property taken over by the RAF. The Filter Room was built at the far end of the large garden. The grounds seemed ideal for the event, having a lake surrounding a small island.

I was appointed organiser and the public were to be invited. No activity offered would cost them a penny, as they would receive a National Savings stamp for every entry fee paid. This, we hoped, would encourage them to save and would provide government funds for supplies to the Forces. We secured prizes from local businesses, all of whom were most generous and, on the day, we received great support from the local community. One of the activities suggested was pony rides so I approached Captain Younghusband whose stables were opposite the site of the event and asked if he would provide a couple of reliable ponies and two stable girls to help. As an ex-cavalry officer, he was more than willing to co-operate. The event was a great success and 'B' Watch raised the greatest sum and won the prize of a £500 Savings Certificate. We decided to donate it to the children of a member of a Fighter Command aircrew. We heard of a sergeant fighter pilot who had recently been killed and whose children were being educated at The Blue Coat School in Kent. We made contact with these two children and 'B' Watch adopted them for the period of the war. These are two more people whose lives were briefly intermingled with mine. I often wonder what their future was.

After our successful garden party, I returned one afternoon to thank Captain Younghusband for his cooperation and to tell him of our success. It was that day I met his son Peter who also was serving in the RAF. He had volunteered in the early days of the war for aircrew. He had grown up with the two de Havilland boys and he had often flown pre-war in one of their aircraft in return for them having riding lessons. Unfortunately, during initial training he failed his morse code test As there were many volunteers at that time and few vacancies for aircrew, the RAF transferred him to other duties. He was bitterly disappointed, as he always had wanted to learn to fly. This desire had been born when he was very young. Amy Johnson, the pioneer woman aviator, had become a client of his father. She had taken up equitation prior to her solo flight to Australia in 1930, as she believed it would help her manipulate the aircraft's controls more easily. She had landed in her small Gypsy Moth on the Riding School's training field and he had been photographed standing beside her. This was one of his most treasured memories. He became a physical training instructor and was seconded to the entertainment section, since he had played in a semi-pro dance band before the war. He eventually ran the station dance orchestra at RAF Northolt as well as his other duties.

On our first meeting, Peter persuaded me to book his RAF band for one of our Mess parties. This I did and we became friendly. I was invited to swim in the lakes in his father's grounds and before long our friendship turned into something more. We became engaged within two months and we married barely five months after meeting. Did we rush into it? I often wonder. We did not really know each other at all. I knew he liked motor bikes. This is what got him from his home to RAF Northolt on his days off. I also knew he played the drums in a semi-pro band before the war as a hobby. He had worked in the Denham film studios as a trainee film editor until he became sick due to the fumes of carbon tetrachloride used for washing film and had then spent several months at sea. I had no idea how we would earn a living after the war or whether we were sexually compatible. The time we spent together was so short. I was seldom off duty and even then, the times rarely coincided with his one day off a week. This is how it was; no one knew what tomorrow would bring. I had already lost two people I loved. You learned to grab happiness when you found it.

It was during the early summer of this year that Hitler launched the first of his secret weapons, the V1, known to many as the doodlebug. These pilotless aircraft were launched from underground ramps in the Pas de Calais area. Many thousands of them flew over the Kent coast heading for London. These weapons had an unforgettably threatening sound. When the sound of the engine cut out, you knew it would fall to earth and explode, often killing many and causing untold damage. London once more was the butt of these fearsome weapons but their reliability was often suspect and many landed in outlying districts. No one was safe. The coastal artillery shot down many as they crossed into Kent on their pre-destined course and the fighter crews shot down many more.

The terrifying V1 flying bomb
en route for London

Some pilots would tip the wing of the V1, causing it to crash in open countryside or over the Channel but many reached London, causing panic and death in their wake. Our Filter Room was increasingly busy tracking these devilish craft. We would come off duty totally exhausted but hyped-up with the strain. After hours of concentration and stress, we were in a state of tension and found it impossible to sleep but we had to keep going. No one gave in. It is difficult for people of today's generation to understand our discipline and dedication to duty. We believed we were fighting for survival. We lived by the exigencies of the Service.

In late August of that year, we received warning that Hitler was preparing to use a second secret weapon. We were given no details but told to listen out for the code word BIG BEN. Our plotters would receive this signal from one of the radar stations. On 8th September 1944, I was on a daytime duty when my Bawdsey plotter called out the code word for the first time. Orders were that the first Filterer Officer

to receive the code word must stand on a chair and shout out 'BIG BEN' three times. This I did. The whole room sprang to life. We were apprehensive, having no idea what to expect. That was the day the first V2 rocket was launched against Britain, landing in Chiswick, killing several people and causing immense damage. Londoners had yet another danger to face. I had taken part in a historic event.

From that day onwards,

A V2 rocket is launched

58

many more were launched, totalling over 1,000 in all. One later landed opposite our home in Winchmore Hill. My mother received considerable blast injuries. My brother and I often wondered whether this was the cause of her later illness. Houses all around were seriously damaged and many people killed or injured. The V2 was terrifying, it was impossible to hear it. Its speed was supersonic and it travelled on a high trajectory. Radar could not detect it. The fear this weapon instilled in Londoners was immense. Meanwhile the Allied troops had landed in Normandy and were pushing forward, liberating France and moving into Belgium. Peter and I were engaged in July and we planned to marry on 30th September of that year. Plans were made hurriedly.

I had met a Belgian family on one of my days off when visiting my parents in Winchmore Hill. They spoke no English and had, only two days previously, been evacuated from Antwerp on the last boat to leave Belgium. There were five in the family, two adults and three teenage children. Told to report to a police station after being billeted in a house near my home, they were at a loss to find it. I noticed they looked worried so I had asked if I could assist Delighted that I spoke French, they then begged me to help them. It ended up with us becoming friends and I asked their daughter to be my bridesmaid. Her presence at the wedding would add a little spice to the proceedings! Organising the reception offered more headaches. Providing the food proved quite a challenge. Peter's family fortunately kept some chickens and a cow. Other friends and family members gave up their precious ration coupons to provide dried fruit and other ingredients for the wedding cake. The head chef from the No.1 RAF Officers' Mess offered to make this for me and produced a spectacular three-tier offering.

Due to clothes rationing, I had to beg coupons for the material for my dress. Elaine Garrard, one of my fellow officers, made it for me.

She eventually made her name in the fashion industry and ended up as a director of Courtaulds. Many of the presents we received were antiques and other personal treasures belonging to the guests. There was little to be found in the stores. We were specially honoured when Sir Frederick Handley Page, the aircraft tycoon, gave up his coupons and provided us with two handsome woollen blankets, which I have to this day. Even the venue for the reception was a present from one of the Riding School clientele. Somehow a tasty buffet appeared, with contributions from both friends and family from their limited supplies of rations. On the day of the wedding, I was on duty until

Our wedding present from 'Raff' – Bill Hooper
of 'Pilot Officer Prune' fame

midday, and then had lunch in the Mess before arriving at the church at 3.30pm. I remember clearly what the menu was that day; brown stew followed by apples and custard made with dried egg!

The ceremony took place in a Catholic church as Peter's mother and both her sons were brought up in that faith. When I first met Canon Goggin prior to the ceremony, he asked me my name. When I replied 'Eileen Le Croissette', he smiled and remarked 'Ah, one of us!' 'No', I hastily replied, 'My family were Huguenots. We were persecuted after the Revocation of the Edict of Nantes. That's when my forefathers came to Britain!' He never tried converting me after that. Peter and I managed a brief three-day honeymoon at the Old Place Hotel in Rottingdean, Sussex and then it was back on duty for both of us. Peter and I saw little of each other. Our times off duty rarely coincided.

POSTING OVERSEAS

M any more V2s continued to fall on London. By November, Belgium was liberated and Antwerp, a vital port, was free. This was the first port suitable for landing Allied soldiers, arms and supplies and of vital importance. Immediately Hitler launched a series of attacks. Both V1s and V2s bombarded the port by day and night, threatening the essential supplies to the advancing Allied troops, by then pushing their way on to Germany. Few people realise that over 1,600 V2s were aimed at Antwerp, 500 more than those launched against London, causing vast devastation in that port. Many missed their target and landed in surrounding areas. These supersonic weapons were responsible for killing both allied troops and local inhabitants whilst also destroying much needed vital supplies.

Due to the lower flight path of these V2s to a nearer target than London, the RAF were able to employ mobile radar units, capable of tracking part of the flight of these rockets. This had not been possible for those directed at Britain due to the greater distance and higher trajectory. Since their speed was supersonic, however, it was impossible to intercept them in flight. Another method of prevention had to be found. Because of our specialised training, eight Filter Room WAAF Officers and eight other ranks were ordered to go to Belgium together with Flight Officer Ann Richmond, one of our Scientific Observers. We were to join a special unit at Malines (Mechelen). It was essential the officers going were able to understand logarithms. This unit later became 33 Wing, 2nd Tactical Air Force and came under the supervision of SHAEF headquarters in Paris. I was to be one of the eight officers chosen. This unit was destined to provide a means of defeating the assault on Antwerp.

Now I had to telephone Peter at RAF Northolt to tell him the news that I was being posted overseas. Normally married women were never posted abroad but we had already signed an agreement that due to our specialised training, we could be sent anywhere at a moment's notice. I was not able to explain what I did, where I was going or the importance of the work we were going to do. I recently found a note Peter wrote, trying to understand why. He wrote 'I love her so much. Why has she gone away? Did she have to go? Does she love me?' He must have been so very unhappy.

Those of us due to go on this operation were then told the purpose of this newly formed unit. Its work was to calculate the position of the launch vehicles of the V2s and to destroy them. The launchers consisted of a lorry and trailer carrying the V2 rocket. These vehicles would leave their base and find a suitable terrain in which to hide, prior to the launch. This could be in the woods, by the coast or near high buildings; anywhere they could find cover. The rocket would be winched to an upright position for firing. After the launch of the V2, the vehicles would then return to base for re-loading with another missile.

Our unit, 33 Wing, was linked to No. 9 mobile radar units, which would move freely around Belgium. They were capable of making fixes on a small section of the launch trajectory. This information was fed to our unit at Malines. As soon as our team learned the position of the fall of shot, we would make the necessary calculations, extrapolating the flight curve back to the launch area. Five minutes was the maximum time allowed for this. These calculations would be sent to Intelligence for instant checking and the information obtained would be coupled with readings from sound equipment from the Survey Regiment. The final information was then passed to patrolling RAF fighter aircraft, enabling them to destroy the launch vehicles before the launchers moved back to their base. The RAF used fast moving Mosquitoes equipped with torpedo bombs for this task. They patrolled in sections over the anticipated areas of launch. It was essential our calculations were made at top speed, as the launchers would move off in fewer than twenty minutes after the rockets were fired to return to base. You have to remember there were at that time no calculators or computers. All our calculations were made solely with slide rules, pencil, and paper!

I, together with the seven other Filterers chosen, received orders to go to Malines, 10 km from Antwerp, to set up and man this unit to carry out these calculations. Thus five weeks after getting married, together with my future colleagues, I flew in a Dakota to Ghent and then travelled by Jeep to Malines. I was to spend almost nine months overseas, apart from my husband. However, this was the exigency of war and it never occurred to me to complain or consider it unusual. Peter found it very hard to comprehend, as once again, I was unable to tell him what I was going to do and why I was being sent to Belgium.

Life in Malines, a Flemish-speaking town, was very busy and intense for us. We had to master the calculating techniques swiftly. I was billeted with Ignace Kennis, a tall thin lugubrious man in his mid-fifties. He was a well-known artist and lived with his wife in a very old house, full of heavy furniture, dark velvet curtains and walls covered in religious paintings and metal crosses. I rarely saw him and throughout my time there, had little conversation with either of them. Perhaps they resented my presence. At that time, the Belgians were desperately short of food. They were collecting acorns and grinding them to use in place of coffee. It was a common sight to see people of all ages ransacking dustbins in search of something to eat.

The Officers' Mess, shared with members of the Survey Regiment, was previously a Soldatenheim for German troops. Initially we feared the water might have been poisoned after their retreat so we were only permitted to drink beer, wine or bottled water. Furthermore, we were not allowed to buy or eat locally grown fruit or vegetables since the fields had been fertilised with human excreta. It was feared we might become infected with typhoid or cholera. Canned cabbage, beans and potatoes were our standard staples at mealtimes. Life was not easy but soon we became a very close and dedicated group, Army and Air Force working closely together.

The Operations Room was in the bank building opposite. It was here on a four-watch basis we carried out the work of estimating the position of the launch sites from which over 1,600 rockets would eventually be launched. The number of launches increased as the weeks went by. Many missed their target causing hundreds of civilian casualties in addition to the Allied troops who were landing at Antwerp. Others damaged the ships and destroyed their cargo or demolished the warehouses. The V2 was not a precision weapon and many landed in our vicinity. We were only ten kilometres from Antwerp. One that failed to detonate sat outside our bank premises during all our time in Malines. However, as our calculations of the position of the launch lorries became more accurate and our fighter crews more adept at destroying many of these vital launchers, we felt we were getting the better of the enemy

Coming off duty at midnight to get to my billet entailed walking across the empty Butter Market. My heavy shoes echoed across the cobbled surface. During the first days there, we suspected that a few German snipers were still hidden in the town so the late night walk on my own was somewhat daunting. There was a nightly curfew in the town, only recently liberated. I would see no one.

There was little to do during our free time. Our only relaxation was playing hockey. As I had been playing for Fighter Command, I was soon enrolled in the team. The games were extremely tough. Our team was mixed, some Army, some RAF and some WAAF. The teams we played against were all male. The local Malines team included several members of the Belgian national ice hockey team, most of whom were over six feet tall. They were very hospitable and it gave us a chance to meet some of the local people, as we would go back to their clubhouse after the match. I made great friends with the Conrad family, two of whose sons, Pierre and Theo, played in the home team. They lived close to our Mess and owned a large timber business. They felled trees in the Ardennes forest and processed them into usable timber. This then provided wood for the still flourishing furniture manufacturing businesses for which Malines was famous.

Christmas that year was an uneasy time. The Rundstedt offensive in the Ardennes, later known as the Battle of the Bulge, had started. The weather was appalling and our aircrews were unable to fly to support our troops. The news we were getting was bad. General Rundstedt's aim for this new offensive was to split the Allied forces, allowing his Panzer divisions to move north and re-take Antwerp. Malines and our unit were on that route. Fighting was intense. The US Army lost many men and tanks in the operation. Our own tank regiment suffered severe losses. For a time, we feared the worst, realising that, if the Germans made a breakthrough, there was the risk of their forces reaching Malines en route for Antwerp. In the meantime, we had to continue our vital work. During the period when our air activity was at its lowest due to weather conditions, the intensity of rocket launches was at its height. The fighters, which targeted the launch vehicles, were unable to operate. The enemy took advantage of the situation. Increased numbers of V1s and V2s were falling daily on our troop landings. Christmas came and went and as soon as the weather improved, our air activities were able to recommence. Fortunately, by the end of January, Rundstedt's Ardennes offensive was defeated and we breathed a sigh of relief.

On a rare day-off early in January, I went with Pierre Conrad in one of the company trucks to visit their saw mills near Bouillon in the south of the country. As we passed through the Ardennes region, the snow was beginning to melt. All around us on the route, revealed by the melting snow, were the frozen bodies of the troops who had taken part in the battle against Rundstedt and his Panzer divisions, together with the shattered remains of many tanks, German, American and British. I still get shivers down my spine when I remember the scene.

NOT SO GAY PAREE!

By now, our unit had been transferred from Fighter Command's control to that of Supreme Headquarters Allied Expeditionary Force (SHAEF), based at the Palais of Versailles in the French Capital. In late January 1945, I was sent to Paris for special training for two weeks and I was billeted in Les Petits Ecuries, the stables, of that famous palace. Fortunately, they had removed the horses! Paris was a sad city. Food was short. Daily, collaborators were being exposed and punished. The women who had consorted with German soldiers had their heads shaved. The men who collaborated received harsher punishment from the Resistance fighters. As I entered the Palace of Versailles, I was shocked to see the sorry state in which the retreating Germans had left it. A year before the war I had visited there and seen the beautiful furniture and priceless paintings. These were all gone, stolen by the invaders. Yet in the spring of 1945, the cafes were still full of customers and the flower sellers were offering their blooms at the street corners.

During my visit, I contacted my brother's French pen friend, Roger Sirdey, initiating a long and still-continuing friendship with his family. At sixteen, he had joined the Resistance movement. He was working in a hardware shop whose owner was the leader of the local Resistance cell. Roger acted as the delivery boy and made deliveries on his bike to the German barracks opposite. He had learned some German whilst at school so his orders were to make friends with the soldiers and listen to the conversations around him. Any useful information that he overheard, such as details of troop movements,

Paris liberated

was then passed on to the Resistance., some local people, having seen him chatting with the soldiers, believed he had collaborated with the enemy. They seized him and started to beat him up. Just in time, his boss intervened to save him and explained the useful work he had been doing. It was a strange time. People were suspicious of each other and only too willing to accuse others of collaboration.

Paris at once brought to mind the Boucher family with whom I had worked and stayed just before the war in their summer home of Contrexeville. I had often wondered how they had fared. On one of my free days, I set off to find them. I located one of Madame's hotels, Hotel Tremoille and anxiously entered the foyer. It was immediately obvious that the American forces had taken it over. A major, seated in reception, greeted me warmly. I introduced myself and explained I had come looking for the Boucher family. Immediately his attitude changed. He demanded to see my papers, asked what I knew of them and why I was making these enquiries. I showed him my credentials and explained I had once worked for the family as an au pair before the war. He seemed very suspicious of me. He said 'I cannot disclose anything to you, it is better you forget about them'. He would not tell me more. I left perplexed, trying to imagine what had happened during the occupation.

It was many years later before I learned the truth. Marcel Boucher, the Deputé, was a collaborator. Alsace Lorraine had once been in German hands and there was always some support remaining for the Herrenvolk. The organisation in the Vosges that he headed, Les Compagnons de Jeanne d'Arc, was pro-German. In Paris, he had offered his wife's hotel to the German invaders. It had then become a Gestapo Headquarters and a scene of torture. After the war, Marcel Boucher was named as a collaborator and he fled the country. I learned later that Giscard d'Estaing finally gave him a pardon but not before his wife had divorced him. I still wonder what happened to those three children I taught so long ago.

On my return to Malines, the Battle of the Bulge was over, Rundstedt was defeated and his bid to split the Allied Forces had failed. Our own position was now safe. Meanwhile the combined efforts of 33 Wing and Mark 9 radar units, together with the fighter pilots' success resulted in the gradual destruction of all the V2 launch vehicles, despite Germany still having vast supplies of missiles. This meant that by early March 1945, the port of Antwerp was secured and free of bombardment. Our activities became less frequent and finally on the morning of 8th May we would learn that peace had been declared; the war in Europe was at last over.

I crossed the road early that morning after night duty, just prior to that momentous announcement. I was returning to the Mess for breakfast. A small black open car stopped alongside me, in it were two RAF officers, both wearing pilot's wings. On the side of the car was written in chalk the words 'Ex-POWs'. They hailed me with great excitement and said, 'Great, you are the first British girl we have seen since 1940!' You can imagine my surprise and their joy. They were from a Wellington crew shot down in '40 and ever since, they had been in a prisoner-of-war camp near Hanover. A few days previously they had taken their opportunity to escape, stealing an SS car as their guards, sensing defeat, had quietly faded away! The two airmen had travelled through Germany at night and finally reached Malines. I immediately took them into the Mess for a substantial celebratory breakfast. I tried to imagine their feelings, freedom after almost six years incarceration. They were able to drive a car once more, talk to an English woman and eat whatever they chose, rather than prison rations. The transformation in their lives must have been enormous. I realised how relieved they must have felt.

It was about 11 o'clock that morning that we learned peace had finally been declared. Germany had surrendered; the war in Europe was over. The two pilots insisted they wanted to return to Rotterdam right away and take some food to the nurses who had cared for them after their aircraft had crashed. My commanding officer decided a couple of us should remain with them, as they would be 'bomb happy' with the excitement of their freedom. After collecting tins of corned beef, packets of biscuits, jars of jam and anything else we could find from the Mess kitchen, we set off. Travelling through Holland was a delight. Everywhere there were celebrations. In village after village, we met parades of farm wagons, filled with branches of the golden flowers of the gorse bush, a tribute to their Royal family, the House of Orange. In the towns, the street and bars were full of people celebrating, delirious with happiness at the news of peace at last.

When we eventually reached the banks of the River Scheldt, we were devastated to find all the bridges destroyed. After all our efforts, it seemed we were to be unlucky. Rotterdam was on the far bank and we were unable to cross. We drove up and down the river bank looking for help. Eventually we found a ferryman unloading his small boat, which he used to bring supplies to the nearby villages. We asked him to take us across the river but sadly, he told us it was forbidden, as it was too dangerous. There were still small pockets of snipers in the city and the river was mined. With four extra people in his small craft, it would be too low in the water and might hit one of the mines. The two pilots were so disappointed that they could not express their thanks to these Dutch women who had saved their lives five years earlier. The ferryman then offered to deliver the food. Reluctantly, we decided to give him the box of supplies together with the names of the nurses and the hospital, since he promised he would get it to them. At the time, he seemed sincere enough but of course, food was short everywhere and could be bartered for other necessities. I often wonder whether they ever did receive it.

Retracing our steps through happy celebrating Holland, we arrived back at the Mess by 6pm. By then I was exhausted although elated, having not slept for 30 hours. My mind was working frantically. This would be the end of the V2s, the end of the killing – at least in Europe. Maybe we would all be going home. It had been quite a day. The air of excitement was palpable. We all had ideas of being home in a few days. We had no idea what the RAF intended to do with us now that the V2 threat was over.

On our return, the medical officer decided I needed to unwind and gave me a tablet to help me sleep. Immediately after taking it, as I got into bed, I realised everyone was going to Brussels to celebrate. After all, it was VE Day! How could I possibly sleep through that? So up I got, had a quick wash and back into my uniform. When the MO saw me getting in the once-SS car with the pilots, he said 'You'd better have one of these!' and thrust a Benzedrine tablet in my hand! Three of us crammed into the car with the pilots and off we went. I cannot remember much about that night except that we were feted and kissed by the people in the streets of Brussels. They handed us flowers and bottles of wine. I was just about coming alive again, when the rest of the party were worn out and ready to go home! That was my first and last time taking a 'downer' and then an 'upper'!

PEACE

Sample peace as if it were
A rich rare wine, sipping gently,
Fearful, lest by lust, the glass will slip
From your testing hands,
The precious liquid spilled and lost
And having sipped, compare
Its fineness with the taste of blood
Or bitter parting tears and fear, fear
That chokes. Then pause and taste again
The rich intoxicating wine of peace.

Meanwhile back in Britain, Peter was hoping I would return home at once now the war in Europe was over. I was not so sure. He was therefore very upset and surprised when I wrote to say that I would have to stay in Belgium until early July. The war-torn regions needed help, we would all be found new posts. Town mayors were being set up to work with the local councillors. I waited to see what they had in store for me. I suppose I had become accustomed to the discipline of the Services and was prepared to accept whatever was my next order. I had only been married a few weeks before I went to Belgium. It was now almost a year later. I barely knew Peter. We had met only four months before our marriage and much of that time we had spent apart. It did not seem real to me. Then I received my orders.

THE CAMP OF SILENCE AND DEATH

I t came as a great shock. The orders I received led to an experience that has had a lasting effect on me. Because I was fluent in French, I was detailed to work as a guide and interpreter at a little known but infamous holding camp, which had eventually became a concentration camp. It was called Breendonk and known as *Le Camp de Silence et de Mort* – The Camp of Silence and of Death. The senior Air Force Officer commanding the area had given instructions that

The entry over the moat
to Breendonk
concentration camp

all personnel should visit the prison. My duty would be to escort them around and remind them of the atrocities perpetrated there. Thus as many service personnel as possible would learn of the sufferings of the Belgian people and the barbarism of the invader. I was there for about three weeks. Each day I would show around a group of airmen and explain what had taken place within those walls.

Every morning, as I arrived, the outer courtyard would be filled with Belgian prisoners, mostly young men between eighteen and thirty years of age. They were known as 'the black ones', collaborators, many of whom had joined the SS. They resented my daily appearance and showed it by swearing at me and even urinating in my direction. I would ignore them and march past with my head held high. I will never forget that

74

time I spent at Breendonk.

Only half an hour's journey from the sophisticated city of Brussels, in the Flemish-speaking countryside of Belgium is the old fortress, known as Breendonk. It has never been a beauty spot nor a site visited by foreign tourists. Yet there are many people who will never forget it or its wartime name. Some of the survivors returned to tell me of their experiences and their suffering there.

Built prior to world war one, many battles have been fought around its walls. The deep moat offered protection to its occupants over the decades and its dungeons hold untold secrets of the past. However, the years of the German occupation of Belgium saw the most infamous chapter in its history. Soon after the German forces swept through Northern Europe and overran Belgium, they turned

The compound used prior to the bath torture

this fort into a prison and eventually a concentration camp. They filled it with Jews, gypsies, homosexuals, members of the Belgian Resistance and political prisoners. In it, the conquerors fabricated their own brands of horror.

The walls, built of huge blocks of stone and surrounded by a deep moat appeared impregnable. The latest occupiers added barbed wire fences and armed guards. Inside, the cells, each a bare eight-foot square and about seven feet high, were cold, dank, and comfortless. Incarcerated within these cells, the prisoners had left reminders of their sufferings on the chalk walls. Many had marked off the days of their imprisonment. Others had scratched messages with their fingernails. I remember especially one, which said *'trahi par ma maitresse, Leonardine Boissons de Courtrai,'* (betrayed by my mistress, Leonardine Boissons of Courtrai). Another cell wall bore the face of Christ. I could only imagine the time it had taken to etch this figure on that wall. I wonder whether that prisoner lived to take his revenge.

During many of the daylight hours, the prisoners were pinioned upright against the far wall by their ankles, their hands stretched above their heads and manacled. There they remained until the guards decided to release them. Their only relief came at mealtimes, just twice a day, when their hands were released. Then to reach the scant food offered, pushed through a cat-hole in the door, they were forced to crouch on the ground, to eat as best they could. At night, they lay on the uneven stone floor, covered only with a thin blanket.

Among the many chambers of the prison, one was especially infamous. Here the Gestapo conducted their daily sessions of torture. Prisoners lay naked on a solid wooden table, resembling a butcher's block whilst an electric current was applied to the bare moist parts of their body as they were interrogated. They suffered indescribable agonies, burns, convulsions, and even death. When they became unconscious, their torturers threw them upon a low wooden slatted bed. Jack-booted guards stamped on their legs, invariably breaking bones, to bring them back to consciousness. The shattered slats bore witness to the force used. This was not all. With a horrible sense of calculated cruelty, their captors forced the next candidate for torture to stand behind a screen in the chamber, listen to those screams of anguish, and anticipate their own fate.

In the courtyard, daily shootings took place; the victims tied to wooden stakes already brown with the blood of those who had died before. In a nearby area, the guards buried Jewish prisoners up to their necks and left them to suffocate and perish. The more fortunate prisoners, not destined for immediate death, were harnessed to an enormous wheel from dusk to dawn and forced to push it around for hours on end until their arms were raw. They were drawing water up from a well, the only source for the whole site.

The policy of the camp commander was aimed at eliminating the weak by any conceivable method and he pursued this policy with sadistic vigour. One of his many ways of doing this occurred during the weekly bath time. The prisoners, made to strip, waited naked in a compound in the open air, winter or summer, rain or shine and then were forced into baths filled with scalding water. Afterwards, once again they were subjected to a further wait outside before being permitted to dress and return to their cells. Without doubt, many already sick succumbed to the harsh measures and died. Yet despite all odds, some prisoners survived and when the Allies liberated the region in the autumn of 1944, these broken men and women were able to tell the liberating forces of their ordeals and of the many atrocities they had witnessed. I had the privilege of meeting some of those who had been released in the final days and heard their personal stories of the tortures they suffered.

My tour of duty lasted only three weeks; the memories of those three weeks remain forever etched on my mind. The world will never forget Belsen, Auschwitz, Treblinka; I will never forget Breendonk.

HOME AGAIN

By mid-June 1946, 33 Wing 2nd Tactical Air Force was disbanded and all personnel flown back to the UK. By then, Peter and my in-laws had converted the bothy over the stables into a cosy flat for us. Below the horses could be heard, snorting and stamping their feet. Peter, when off duty, had installed a bath in the kitchen, with a wooden cover. This now doubled as a worktable.

Peter had no idea when I would return but had been able to use the flat on his days off from RAF Northolt, where he was to stay for a further nine months before his turn arrived to return to Civvie Street. He was delighted to know I would be coming back to Stanmore. My feelings were slightly different. I had experienced so much since I had left. I was apprehensive of meeting my husband again. On arriving back at Fighter Command, I got a message through to him and we met the following day. We were to be together for three weeks and then only when we were both off duty. It felt strange to be so close to someone I hardly knew.

By now with no further need for radar, the Ops and Filter Rooms were dismantled. We all had to remuster; the RAF word for a change of direction. I was informed I was being sent on an EVT course, (education and vocational training), for a period of two months. This course was designed to teach those sent on it how to instruct others on a variety of subjects, which could be of use to RAF and WAAF personnel after demobilisation. We would learn some elements of psychology and be shown how to pass on whatever particular knowledge we possessed which might be of use in civilian life. We all had different skills. On my return to Stanmore, the RAF decided that my task would be to give English lessons to a group of Polish Fighter pilots and help them improve their accent. These men, all aircrew and mostly senior officers, planned to stay in Britain since Poland was now in the Soviet controlled zone. Poor men, after all their sacrifices, they were unable to return to their homeland and their families.

I left for the course and Peter was on his own again. There were about 30 of us, both sexes and all ranks, in a large mansion 'somewhere in Lancashire'. Whilst there I realised I was pregnant. Morning sickness before attempting my first test lesson was no fun. However, I weathered the course and in fact enjoyed it. Returning home, Peter and I decided I should stay in the WAAF as long as I could as it meant extra income, since he would not be demobilised for some months. Although I could have been demobbed in September, I soldiered on until Christmas. I thoroughly enjoyed teaching 'real' English to these eighteen Poles, in place of their current RAF slang, whilst trying to improve their accent. I based my teaching on the sounds used in Pitman's shorthand; I had known

Inscription in *Poland's Progress*
– presented to Eileen by
her Polish pilot pupils

it would come in useful one day! My charges were all senior officers, pilots with vast operational experiences and a wealth of medals to prove their gallantry. They included a veteran pilot, Group Captain Bayan, who, although he had lost a hand during world war one, was a highly successful pilot in world war two

They all had so many exciting and sometimes sad stories to tell. One I remembered particularly. Squadron Leader Sponarovich told me how, during his service in Germany, he had met a young German Jewish civilian. This man had managed to hide his race and remained in Germany throughout the war. When he learned of the death camps and how the bodies of prisoners were burned, he put in a tender to purchase the ashes. Knowing how his fellow Jews would try to hide their jewellery by secreting them in the various orifices of their body, he realised he might find some of their valuables still amongst the ashes. I was horrified to learn how anyone could profit from the sufferings of his own kin.

Finally, almost six months pregnant, I received my discharge from the WAAF in early January 1946, leaving many of the friends with whom I had worked so closely for so long. To my surprise, however the RAF asked me to continue teaching the Poles from home as a civilian. They offered me the princely salary of twenty-eight shillings an hour, far more than I received as a WAAF Officer. Peter meanwhile whilst still in the Air Force was getting outside gigs for his band, Peter Younghusband and His Music, plus a growing reputation. I wondered what my future held. I could not visualize myself just sitting at home, baby watching.

FACING CIVILIAN LIFE

On March 27th, 1946 our son Clive was born. My mother-in-law insisted I went to a private nursing home in Stanmore. This turned out to be the recently vacated home of the last Prime Minister, Clement Attlee. It had been taken over by one of the riding school's clients, Dr Eleanor Bergmann, a Austrian Jewish doctor who had managed to escape just before war started. I admit I did not enjoy the ordeal of giving birth. It was five days hard labour. I was not helped by any of the aids mothers are given these days. In fact, one of the nurses managed to start a fire in my bedroom. She repeated a dose of a drug I had already taken. This caused me to vomit over an electric cable, which immediately burst into flames. I had to stop her throwing water on to it and perhaps electrocuting herself!

The baby was fine, a healthy boy of 7lbs, 6 ounces and very active, a quality that remained with him throughout his life. We had decided to call him Clive Francis, after Sir Francis Younghusband, the soldier and mystic, a distant relative of Peter's father. After it was all over, my local GP, Dr Byworth, finally arrived. Ignoring me, he took out his diary and consulted the astrological details of my new son. 'Ah,' he said 'Aries under the influence of Jupiter, this young man will have an interesting life'. And so he did, but sadly, a life cut short at the age of 50 years. Of course, I was proud of my new son and never thought about what sadness there might be in the far-off future.

The following day Peter was demobbed. He received a new three-piece utility suit and a £32 gratuity. I had received £100 but no clothes. This was the sum total of our capital except for a small amount in my Post Office savings account. Then, on his first day as a civilian, Peter conducted an 18-piece dance orchestra for the Hunt Ball of the Old Berkeley Hunt. This was the most important booking he had ever undertaken. It was quite a week for all of us. The next question was where would we find a regular income? There was no chance of me getting a university education, much as I wished for one, since only the male officers returning from war were offered this chance. This was my second experience of sex discrimination. I could not go back to train as an actuary with a small baby. Peter's pre-war job as an assistant to the film editor in the Denham Studios no longer existed as no films where being made. Although the dance orchestra provided some income, it was not something we could rely on regularly.

We would have to take any opportunity offered. Thus, I became a part-time secretary to my father-in-law at the Stanmore Riding School and Peter a sales representative with Jamal, a hairdressing product company. As he was a great raconteur and an excellent driver, he enjoyed the freedom of travelling around the country making new contacts despite the fact that the prospects were not enormous. At least the company provided us with our first car. Previously we only had motorbikes. Peter had worked his way through a variety of makes from a Norton to a Velocette. The current one, however, was his pride and joy. It was an Aerial Square Four.

His semi-pro dance band activities continued to prosper. Everybody was celebrating a return to a more normal life. He played on many interesting occasions as well as at private parties in enormous mansions whilst I acted as his business manager. He did a lot of work for Nuthalls Caterers at the Victoria Halls in Southampton Row and soon became very good friends with the general manager, Vernon Herbert. Through him, we were introduced to good food and fine wines. Even though, by law, it was forbidden at that time to charge more than five shillings for any meal, Vernon, through his contacts, took us out to incredible meals in amazing restaurants. I recall Vernon inviting us to dine at the Trocadero in central London, where he was a friend of both the general manager and the maitre chef. The head waiter placed a large menu in front of us. This remained throughout the meal to hide the dishes we were being served. We had a fantastic choice. No way would it have cost only five shillings although that was the total of the food bill. I guess the copious bottles of wine we consumed made up for it.

Living as we did over the stables at Stanmore, horses were very much part of our lives. We could hear them below us at night, when they became restive. Clive from an early age would sit in his pram in the yard, alongside the manure heap, as the horses were being groomed. His proud grandfather had him sitting on a pony at the age of two. He was known by all the clients and greeted as they arrived for their riding lesson. Peter and his brother Derek had both ridden from the age of three. Even I learnt to ride, taught by Mary Handley-Page.

Captain Younghusband provided horses and riders for many of the film studios in the vicinity as well as doubling for some of the stars. He replaced George Arliss in the riding scenes in *The House of Rothschild*. He taught Elizabeth Taylor to ride for *National Velvet* and Janette Scott for *The Thirty Nine Steps*. Many of the stars became friends and joined the elite riders on the famous Sunday ride. Ann Ziegler and Webster Booth pushed Clive's pram down to the nearby pub for a Sunday morning drink and Ronnie Shiner always came up and chatted to him. Clive had no idea who all these famous actors were but he gurgled and smiled at them nevertheless.

In September 1947, we had a surprise invitation to spend a week's holiday with a cousin of Peter's mother who owned the West Country

Inn, four miles outside the village of Hartland in North Devon. This small hotel, on the borders of Devon and Cornwall, sited on high land one mile inland from the sea, was a delightful spot. Petrol was rationed until 1953 so the hotel was not very busy except for the bars, filled each night with local farmers and their workers. Tourism was non-existent. We managed to save enough petrol for the journey and drove down to this part of Devon, new territory to both of us.

We enjoyed our stay, the first holiday either of us had since our three-day honeymoon, three years previously. Mr and Mrs Lowe were then in their early sixties. She was a rather large and formidable lady and had married late in life. Her husband, Victor, was a White Russian and, as he informed us, a relative of Nikolai Rimsky-Korsakov. We only had his word for that. Victor was a small man and obviously well controlled by his wife who held the purse strings. Mrs Lowe was the one with the money. She did all the work; he spent his time listening to music.

The hotel was on the border of North Devon and Cornwall. It was situated on Bursdon Moor and from the windows, we could look out to the Atlantic. This was the rocky coast of Devon, where in the past the wreckers had operated, tempting passing ships on to those rocks and stealing their cargoes. Returning home, we settled back in the usual routine. Some months after our visit to Devon, the owners, Mr and Mrs Lowe, decided to buy a second property in Wincanton and to our great surprise, in March 1948, they wrote asking us if we would like to take over the running of the Hartland property at a joint salary of £320 per annum plus food and accommodation.

Peter was always a countryman at heart. His favourite hobbies were fishing, shooting, and growing things. Life at Stanmore was becoming a little difficult. Peter's mother was killing us with kindness. We felt we were not in control of our lives. Tommy, as she was known throughout the riding world, was a character but a little hard to live with. Furthermore, she had not taken kindly when Captain Younghusband asked me to take over the riding school accounts. In fact, each night, she copied my entries in her own writing and tore out the sheets I had entered. However, Tommy was a very generous person and if we mentioned there was anything we needed, she would produce it for us. It became overwhelming. We thought it time we stood on our own feet so we made the decision and said yes to the offer! That is how we became hoteliers. On May 2nd 1948, we took over management of the West Country Inn.

PETER BECOMES MINE HOST

The first night, the two bars were filled with the locals, farmers, their workers and nearby tradesmen, all wanting to see what the new landlord was like. They took to Peter immediately. He talked their language and had a great repertoire of jokes and of course, he enjoyed his glass of beer. We inherited a part-time barman, Bill, and a cleaner named Flossy. Everything else we had to do ourselves as well as looking after several acres of land, very soon under cultivation by Peter. There he grew fresh vegetables for our restaurant and reared turkeys for Christmas and even kept a pig. We were able to feed it on waste food from the restaurant as well as Russian Comfrey from the garden. The government was encouraging people to keep a pig to supplement the available supply of meat. Every six months you sent it to the nominated factories where it became ham and bacon, half was then returned and the Government paid you for the other half.

Clive was now nearly three years old and took to the country life at once, loving all the animals there. He became used to meeting new people all the time and his gregarious nature became obvious even then. He loved helping in the garden, especially weeding, sometimes too enthusiastically. Peter was not too pleased when his son pulled up a row of newly sprouted beetroot seedlings, whilst chanting 'dirty old docks!'

This old inn, known as the last in Devon as it was just over the border from Cornwall, had ten bedrooms, two bars, a restaurant and a long narrow tearoom. A Devon travel guide described it as 'a lonely house in a lonely parish'. We realised we had a tough job ahead of us attracting people to stay when petrol was still restricted and we were very much 'off the beaten track'. I had to learn to cook but that was no hardship as I had always been interested in food preparation. As a child, I had watched my mother who was a master of the art. The hotel kitchen was large and I cooked, with the aid of numerous cookery books, on a large coal-fired Aga. At first, there were only occasional meals required and a few bar snacks. Food rationing was still in force and anyone staying had to give up ration coupons if they stayed more than two days. Fortunately, in the country, with farmers nearby, things were not quite as difficult as in the towns. Eggs, milk and cream were easily accessible and the rabbit catcher would call once a week. Peter's hobbies of shooting and fishing added to the menu with snipe and plover, salmon and trout and the occasional woodcock or pheasant. I became adept at making Devonshire clotted cream. Initially resident guests were sparse, mostly passing sales reps and a few landowners who visited weekly to oversee their farms. Occasionally we welcomed families for a Devon holiday, enjoying that beautiful unspoiled corner of Britain but travel was difficult because of the fuel shortage. Petrol was still severely rationed until the early fifties.

Then one day the following headline appeared in the *Daily Express*:

THE YOUNGHUSBANDS BEAT THE PETROL BAN!

We had hit on the idea of flying guests from Elstree aerodrome in a small plane to the hotel for the same cost as a first class rail fare. A pilot friend would ferry guests in his Auster to a nearby farmer's field. There we erected a drogue to indicate the wind direction. A friendly RAF pilot, from a local air base, dropped this to us when flying past. We would meet the guests in our station wagon using our legal red petrol. Our guest list multiplied and we soon built up a reputation for good food despite rationing, with home-grown fruit and vegetables, our own chickens and cream from a friendly farmer, the game Peter shot and even our own pig, fed on the remains from the kitchen!

Fortunately, one day the officers from the nearby Territorial Army camp at Cleeve, near Bude, found us. The camp was in use from April until October each year. From then on, we regularly provided regimental dinners for visiting TA Artillery Regiments. Many well-known people signed our visitors' book, all serving as TA officers. These included Colonel Edward Heath of the Honourable Artillery Company, Sir Colin Cole who later became Garter King of Arms and Robert Henriques, the writer and broadcaster. Their support boosted our takings and the profit considerably.

Things were going well. Clive, five-years-old in 1951, started at Hartland School, five miles away. He went there with several farm

The West Country Inn, near Hartland, North Devon

children in a small bus and thoroughly enjoyed it. His London accent acquired some Devonian overtones. During that summer, we engaged three newly graduated students from Oxford University to help us, John Russell a budding poet, Peter Gammell and Bobbie Furnival. Two had served as soldiers and Bobbie Furnival had been conscripted as a Bevin Boy, to work in the mines during the war. As you can imagine, they were a great asset and stimulating company.

This was the summer of the polio epidemic in the Isle of Wight. Several families switched their holiday from the island to this remote part of Devon, to escape the epidemic. Then fate struck. Bobbie Furnival came down with what the doctor thought was 'flu. He was so ill that we moved him from the damp cottage they had rented at the coast, into the hotel. Two days later the doctor diagnosed polio. We were all quarantined, including the holiday families who had come to us to escape just such a chance. Fortunately, Bobbie recovered and no one else caught it but it was a very bad moment.

The next help we took on, a couple whose references we checked assiduously, produced a very different problem. The man, under the assumed name of Jimmie Barraclough saw our advertisement in the *Morning Advertiser.* He made his plans carefully. Having answered our advertisement and sent us excellent references, which he had stolen from a fellow employee in a Yorkshire hotel, he picked up a prostitute at the White City dog-racing track. We thought his application sounded suitable but before employing him, we phoned the Mayor of Keighley who had given one of the references. He gave the so-called Jimmie Barraclough a glowing report. Unfortunately, it was for the wrong man. We did not think to describe him – ginger hair, balding slightly, with a stoop and who always walked with his hands clasped behind his back! It transpires the pseudo-Barraclough had stolen these papers from an innocent night porter from a local hotel where he had taken a temporary job as a kitchen porter. Both the Mayor and ourselves were obviously completely unaware of this. Never again did we employ anyone without checking both references and a full description.

We picked up the couple from Barnstaple station. Jimmie was a hard worker. He got on with the customers, made friends with Clive and offered to exercise our water spaniel, Fuss. His 'wife' helped in the kitchen and was a cheerful and friendly woman. All seemed to be going smoothly. Two weeks after their arrival, we were due to drive to Torquay for a meeting with the lawyers of the owners of the Inn. Immediately after we drove off, Jimmy ordered a taxi and left the hotel. His wife asked him where he was going but he fobbed her off with some excuse of getting some necessary supplies. We returned in time to open the bars at 6 o'clock to find the woman in tears. 'Jimmie's gone and I think he has taken all your money too.' she sobbed. How right she was! He had made off with the hotel cash and all our jewellery but had left the so-called wife behind. He even took the small amount of money I was looking after for the Women's Institute, which I subsequently had to refund to them. There was no safe in the hotel and normally we left the cash in the locked wine cupboard. We could only bank once a week in Bideford, ten miles away, due to the petrol shortage. Thinking the wine cellar with its glass door was unsafe, I had carefully removed the money before we left and hidden it in our locked bedroom. Apparently, Jimmie was a jewel thief and was really looking for gold and other items of jewellery. After breaking into our bedroom, he unfortunately also found the week's takings.

We had thought it strange whilst driving through Dartmoor on that day, when a gang of prisoners working out on the moor gave us a friendly wave. We wondered why. Peter turned to me and asked with a chuckle, 'Who are your friends?' In fact, it seems these prisoners recognised our car, a station wagon with a rather unusual wooden body. On his arrival, Jimmie had told us their suitcases had been stolen at Paddington. His unfortunate partner, Linda, did not realise that this was yet another lie He had instead taken them to be stored at left luggage whilst she was absent, planning to pick them up later. On their day off the previous week, we had loaned Jimmie and his partner our car to visit Barnstaple to buy replacement clothes. His partner in crime admitted they had gone to Dartmoor instead. He had stolen some of our cigarette and tobacco stock to give to his former fellow prisoners. No wonder the prisoners had waved at us, when they recognised the car.

We later found he had only recently been released from a long-term imprisonment there, just a few weeks before his con trick on us. He had a long criminal record as a confidence trickster. Apparently, it is customary for prisoners during their exercise period to walk with their hands clasped behind them. He had acquired the habit during his previous confinement in Dartmoor prison. I now check everyone carefully who walks like that.

He had picked up his so-called wife, a London prostitute, at the White City dog track after seeing our advertisement for a living-in couple. He had planned it well. Before taking the train from Paddington to Devon, he had secreted their luggage in a left luggage slot, telling the poor unfortunate woman it had been stolen. He was intending to dump her too. All this was in preparation for stealing from us and making a getaway. Oh, the joys of finding staff for hotels! He was arrested six months later, having committed four more similar crimes. Any money or belongings found on criminals are returned to the owners but I am afraid there was nothing left of his haul from us. What finally happened to the jettisoned Linda, I do not know but she was as shocked as we were; only to find he had left her to face the police, whilst stealing her few treasured possessions. They suspected her of being in on the scam and temporarily took her into custody. I almost felt sorry for her.

The following year, 1952, saw another change in our lives. To our surprise, Mrs Lowe, Peter's second cousin and owner of the West Country Inn, decided to buy a hotel in South Africa and sell one of her two properties in Britain. She offered us the chance of managing the Wincanton hotel but we decided against it. It was a much larger hotel and I was then not certain we had enough experience to manage such a large hotel. I still cannot believe I turned the offer down! This meant we had to sell the West Country Inn on her behalf and thus put ourselves out of a job. We managed a successful sale of the property for a sum five times the amount the Lowes had paid for it seven years previously but that did not help us much. Our future was in the balance.

A CHANGE OF TACK

A friendly customer, Major Malins, about to rejoin the Army oversees, heard of our dilemma. He offered us a cottage and fifteen acres of land at Higher Huish near Barnstaple, if we would keep an eye on his large mansion and estate there. It suited him to have someone he could trust on the scene. We would have a home, a chance to live off the land and no rent to pay. Peter, always a countryman, was tempted by the thought. I, being a Londoner, was more apprehensive but we had no alternative. We accepted the offer and planned to raise pedigree pigs. It was very different from the comfortable, though busy, life of innkeepers. Daily living was tough; the cottage was without mains water and we had to use an outside pump. There was no electricity, just Tilley lamps. Our only neighbours would be the farm manager and his family and Clive would have a long trek to his new school. It was half a mile from the cottage to the main road. However, we decided to try it. It was a great change for me, brought up in a London suburb with all facilities to hand.

We had saved a little capital. With this, we built up a herd of pedigree and cross breed pigs with the help of Sammie, our pedigree boar, a Red Lynch Field Marshall. Every month we went to market and sold the piglets. It was a hard and not very financially rewarding life. Peter loved the open air and the countryside. I was not so keen but did my best to adapt. I became quite good at selling the piglets at market. However, after almost a year, we realised we could not make much of an income doing this and the primitive conditions were getting us down. We looked for another option.

Peter's father told us one of his cottages near the riding school was empty. A firm selling an animal feed called Ful'O'Pep, a subsidiary of Quaker Oats, offered Peter a sales rep's job covering Hertfordshire and Essex. It was a cold and miserable winter's day when their letter arrived. We had run out of paraffin for the Tilley lamps and the logs for the fire were running low. We had spent a very wet day lifting fodder beet from a muddy field and our backs ached. The thought of getting back to a more hospitable life was most appealing, we said yes to both offers, without any hesitation. We had to write to our army friend, explaining we had found life impossible at Higher Huish and hoped he would understand our reason for leaving. We sold our pedigree herd of pigs to a rich widowed lady nearby who had acquired a young strong Polish lover who was anxious to farm. We packed what possessions we had in our station wagon and returned to Stanmore.

Unfortunately, our piggy life had not yet ended. Three months later, we received a writ from the new owner of our pigs, suing us under the Warranty of Goods Act. One of the pedigree pigs had given birth to thirty-two piglets, none of which had survived and she was claiming the mother pig was faulty! In the meanwhile, she still owed us for all the dead stock, weighing scales and the like. The judge in the Barnstaple Court was reported in the local paper as saying 'I know nothing about pigs. What is a poor judge to do?' What he did was to make them pay us for the dead stock and we had to reimburse her for one in-pig sow! This was blatantly unfair since the pig, a pedigree Dartmouth Baroness, had already had one very successful litter whilst in our ownership so we could not see that she was 'faulty goods'. However, we accepted the ruling and settled back into a more civilised life on the outskirts of London. Peter travelled the two counties, visiting farmers and selling his animal feed. Clive went to school in Stanmore and I helped my father-in-law with his office work. Deep down, we both missed the hotel scene; we had enjoyed our taste of hotel life

However, fortune was on our side. Vernon Herbert, our old friend, who had stayed with us at the West Country Inn on several occasions, contacted us. He thought we had the right abilities for the hotel and catering industry and asked if we would come and run the Winter Gardens at Ventnor on the Isle of Wight for his company, Nuthalls Caterers Ltd.. It was a tempting offer. I had missed the friendly life of the catering trade whilst Peter was not making a fortune selling chicken and cattle feed. Once more, we committed ourselves and jumped into the unknown.

SERVING OVERSEAS!

It was January 23rd 1953, midwinter and the day we were to view the business that we were to manage. Throughout Britain, the weather had been foul. This was the year when many areas suffered from flooding. The winds were at gale force. We drove to Portsmouth and took the ferry to Ryde on the Isle of Wight. The crossing was very rough, the waves flooded the decks and being no sailor, I disgraced myself immediately by being seasick. Peter and Clive had no such problems; both loved the sea. I just prayed for dry land. Vernon Herbert met us at Ryde and drove us to Ventnor, then a smart resort on the south coast of the island. The Winter Gardens had become bankrupt in the hands of the previous tenants. Nuthalls Caterers Ltd had taken it over and intended to make it pay. It was in our hands to make that happen. This time our salary would be £650 a year but no accommodation.

We realised there would be a lot to do but we decided to accept the challenge. We moved over to the island in March. By then a smart new bar had been built. There had been extensive re-equipping and re-decoration of the ballroom, stage, kitchen and restaurant. It was up to us to plan a profitable summer programme. The season lasted with luck from late June until early September. The previous management had facilities for a small bar and a cafeteria. They offered a season of concert-party type entertainment in the ballroom-cum-theatre. The reason for their failure, we realised, was that visitors would only attend one concert during their stay as the programme never changed. The box-office takings failed to cover the expenses. We had to come up with a new look.

We lived on site for the first few months, sleeping in the artistes' dressing rooms and storing our furniture and belongings where we could. We began looking for a house and decided to apply for permission to build on an attractive plot we found in upper Ventnor, a site with wonderful sea views. Clive enrolled in the Catholic junior school, where on hearing he had been christened by the Church of England, the priest in charge baptised him as a Catholic, given that his father had been educated at the Oratory and his grandmother was a relative of Cardinal Newman. We were never asked for approval. Clive however seemed to settle in there fairly well.

The first thing we did was to christen the updated bar 'The New Elizabethan' in honour of our newly crowned Queen. After a lot of thought, we proposed to run the Winter Gardens on the lines of a continental cabaret for four nights each week, offering a talent competition, a music night and visiting speciality artistes, coupled with a dance on Tuesday and Saturday and a Palm Court Concert on the Sunday. This programme would give visitors a wide choice of entertainment during their stay. On cabaret nights, the ballroom would be laid out with individual tables and chairs. There would be no entry fee but they would have to order drinks. We trained the waitresses to ask positive questions. 'What will you have to drink'? This was more likely to get a sale than 'Would you like a drink?' In the event, the Talent Night became so popular that we eventually had to charge a small entry fee. Peter emceed these evenings with great skill and aplomb and managed to persuade at least a dozen acts to 'have a go' each week. It was a real hit.

Our resident quartet, the Doug Carver Trio, rose to every occasion, accompanying the singers or providing background music for other acts. The trio was one of the first to play electric guitars. The rest of the week's activities were also usually well patronised, especially the dance nights. This was the beginning of the Rock and Roll era. The Sunday Palm Court concerts were popular with both Island residents and visitors. We augmented the in-house musicians with several talented local amateurs. I became 'the disembodied voice' and read a poetry prologue and epilogue as well as announcing the programme. This mean I would spend Sunday afternoons searching for appropriate poems to read. These would range from Masefield's *Sea Fever* to extracts from Tennyson's works as well as verses from some of the more modern poets. I thoroughly enjoyed those Sunday evenings.

Very soon, we had an additional task. Ventnor pier had been split in two during the war, as were all the piers around the British coast. This was to prevent possible landings of enemy forces. Making it usable again was quite a mammoth task of rebuilding. A new bar was constructed at the end and named The Caribbean Bar, echoing Princess Margaret's recent trip to the island of Mustique. A well-

The ballroom at the Winter Gardens, Ventnor

known local architect, Basil Phelps, went to town on the project and decorated it with palm trees, coconuts, and even the odd stuffed monkey sitting amongst the foliage. Our work now entailed management of the entertainment here, in addition to providing luncheons in the Winter Gardens café, an ice cream parlour, full time bar service as well as the evening events.

The weekly programmes were a great success and the Winter Gardens prospered. It seemed the residents of Ventnor and the trades' people were pleased with our efforts since I was elected to the District Council as an Independent Councillor. My slogan was 'Vote Younghusband for a progressive Ventnor' and I canvassed in our very old Morris with its dickey seat and outside brake handle. I had always been interested in politics. At one stage during the war when stationed at Stanmore, we would discuss what we would like to do when peace came. I had said I would like to go into Parliament but at that time had no definite leanings towards any political party. It was just an idealistic dream. However, settling for local government, I looked forward to the experience. Once more, I encountered the old enemy of sexism. The male members would use Rotary or Masonic reunions to discuss council projects and come to the meetings with a *fait accompli*. Once more, I had to put on my fighting boots as the only female councillor and press for my views to be considered.

Peter and I knew that on the Isle of Wight, as in many resorts just after the war, trade would be limited to the summer months. We considered how we could extend it. We went on to propose a Spring Time Festival. The Winter Gardens would offer free entertainment from early May until June and this would continue from the end of the tourist season until the end of October. The town would benefit from early and late groups of visitors, taking advantage of cheaper prices. The hotels and boarding houses were pleased with the suggestion and planned their own publicity to support the scheme.

We contacted volunteer organisations to arrange quizzes, concerts and competitions and had a great response. The first year's efforts were highly successful and Ventnor continued this programme for several years in the future even after we had left.

Head Office must have been pleased with us because after two years, they offered us a promotion – to run the two banqueting halls in London at their Southampton Row headquarters. This would be a big challenge for both of us, neither having received any formal catering training but we agreed to take it on. We had at the time no idea of the differences we would encounter, employing London staff as compared to our local helpers from the Isle of Wight. It would also mean giving up the house we had built in Ventnor. This had been very special to us as we had purchased the plot, designed the house and watched it being constructed. Our builder, Jim, had a great sense of humour and when the roof was ceremoniously tiled, coinciding with the very day that the infamous murderer Christie was hanged, he placed a note in a milk bottle and incorporated it in the top of the gable at the front of the house. It read 'Christie had it today!' I am sure it is there to this day and any new owners probably have no idea about it! We were sad to leave our first real home but realised our future necessitated the move.

We did not realise that this would coincide with a downturn in the economy and it would take us almost two years before we were able to sell Clinton House. Fortunately, one of Captain Younghusband's cottages at Stanmore was again vacant so we moved in there. I was now living once more within sight of where I had served during so many of my years as a WAAF officer. I wondered what had happened to the many able young women I had worked with there. Had their boyfriends, their fiancés, their husbands returned safely? Had they found a niche in post-war Britain?

LONDON CALLING

Our new post entailed commuting to The Victoria Halls in the centre of London daily, returning home well after midnight six days a week. There were two banqueting halls, both operating nearly every night of the month, each with a large bar. Once more, it was very hard work, operating with no kitchen facilities on the site. The Liverpool Friendly Society, owners of the building, did not permit any cooking on the premises so all meals were prepared at Camden Town in another branch of Nuthalls. The food was then transferred to us at Southampton Row, to be kept in hot cupboards. This meant a lot of organisation to ensure the food remained hot and attractive for service. There were two banqueting halls, both operating nearly every night of the month, each with a large bar.

Most the staff, both waiters and bar staff, were employed on a casual basis, many of them foreign. Each event had different staffing requirements. West End casual workers, we very soon found, were both difficult to control and up to every trick to make an extra pound. They sought any opportunity to steal food or drink or make money out of the customers. Many spoke poor English. It was a nightmare. Finally, we paid a restaurant manager a permanent retainer fee of an extra £10 a night to be on our side. This was a fortune in those days. He would frisk the tails of the waiters' dinner suits and extract sides of smoked salmon, bottles of wine or spirits from the hidden poacher pockets. The message soon went out that the new management was on the warpath.

The bar staff offered a further challenge. They always made certain the manager's liquor stock results were OK since there were regular spot checks on these by company stock takers but they still managed to fleece the customers. They were completely different from Isle of Wight staff, which had consisted mainly of locals and generally could be trusted. In London, we had to have eyes in the back of our heads and other places too! A favourite trick of one particular barmaid was to count a customer's change into her hand so they could see it, then hand it over, whilst palming a coin, usually a half crown. She would adjust her dress, whilst dropping the coin down her cleavage. These coins were secured in place by a string tied round her waist, over a petticoat! We only uncovered this trick when Peter noticed how frequently she went to the cloakroom. I followed her one day and then heard the coins clinking as she retrieved them into her handbag. We had to call the police after this discovery. It certainly acted as a salutary lesson to the others.

We never knew until the last minute how many waiters would be arriving, as they were booked through an agency and every night was a different type of function. It could be a formal dinner dance, or a knees-up, a Masonic function or a school reunion. There were works' Christmas dances or pensioners' get-togethers. Each needed a different staffing arrangement and we were completely in the hands of whoever turned up on the night. Around midnight or even later, we drove home to Stanmore, completely exhausted.

During the second winter season, we learned the company had been taken over by an unknown finance group. They moved our friend, Vernon Herbert, sideways and one of the company's men was put in as joint general manager. It was obvious Vernon would eventually be forced out. Backed by John Christie of Glyndebourne Opera, whose contract he had gained for Nuthalls, and supported also by the previous company Chairman, Vernon decided to leave.

He then bought the Norfolk Arms at Arundel. In addition, the Glyndebourne catering contract, which Nuthalls had for many years, was transferred to him. He continued to run this until 1984. We realised that we could no longer work happily or successfully under the new regime, especially as we were friends of Vernon Herbert. We decided to resign and seek new horizons.

Once again, we had to take stock and decide the direction we would take. We thought perhaps we might take over a small Inn tenancy with a brewery and at last have our own business. However, after contacting several breweries and having initial interviews, it became apparent our meagre capital was far too small for any viable or pleasant business. Then out of the blue, we were approached by Simonds, the Reading brewers, following an interview we had with their Tenancy Manager. Their Hotels Department had been told of our previous experience and there and then, they offered us a joint hotel management post at their Reading branch.

It was a run-down city centre pub/hotel with a few rooms, minimal food capabilities and a bad reputation. We took it on and once more had to re-build a business. The customers in the centre of Reading consisted mostly of Irish workmen building the Aldermaston underground atomic research site, some locals and an occasional prostitute – hardly a welcome clientele. We noticed there was a shalalee hanging behind the bar, obviously used to keep order! We had to change the whole atmosphere of the place. We put up the prices, eliminated the drunks and 'ladies of the night' and started to offer a limited food menu. Fortunately, we came under the jurisdiction of a great mentor who was our general manager and who supported us whole-heartedly. H C Davies had started life in a Lyons Corner House when he was 14 years old and had learned the hotel and catering business from A to Z, finally working his way to General Manager of the Hotels Department of Simonds Brewery.

He had a great influence on us and I personally owe him a great debt.

We managed to turn around the Reading pub and change the clientele. One of the small snug bars we converted into a lunchtime buffet. Contacting a nearby Polish grocery store, we borrowed interesting items from his stock to fill the shelves. We had a selection of his salami sausages, all sizes and shapes. Some were long and thin, some tied with string, some short and fat, some red, some brown, some ochre. The lunchtime snack bar became a popular venue for nearby office personnel. One day H C Davis called in to see what we were doing. He looked at the display of sausages and turned me and said 'And what, Mrs Younghusband, are those?' Cheekily I replied 'Men I have known, Sir.' From that moment onwards, he and I became great friends. Obviously, he had the same sense of humour as I did.

After a while, Peter and I decided to redecorate the rather tatty hotel rooms and lounge during our spare afternoons. As we were doing this one day, there was a knock at the front door. Coming downstairs in our paint-smeared clothes, we found it was the Brewery managing director, Duncan Simonds. He was as much surprised to see us in our painting gear, as we were to see him. He had come to see how we liked the job! We must have made a good impression because a month later, in November 1956, the company offered us a promotion to the management of the Goddard Arms, one of their top hotels, in Swindon. It seems the Reading pub was our testing ground.

Meanwhile, Clive had been attending Presentation College as a dayboy. This was a private Catholic preparatory school in the town. If we moved, this would mean another change for him. Deciding to accept the promotion, we enrolled Clive as a boarder at the school. He had had so many changes of schools, we felt it unfair to move him yet again. I still ask myself, were we right? He was only eight years old.

GOING WEST

In the Fifties, the Goddard Arms was the prime hotel, restaurant and banqueting venue in Swindon, a town that was expanding rapidly with many London companies moving there. The Plessey Company, Garrards Engineering and Pressed Steel all relocated to this Wiltshire town. British Rail had their long established engine workshops there.

We realised this would be yet another challenge especially as the previous manager had been fired. He was very popular with the existing staff and our arrival was look upon with scant approval. However, it was a much more congenial atmosphere to work in. Swindon was a rapidly growing town with plenty of opportunities for new business. The hotel clientele consisted mostly of visiting businessmen. The Goddard Arms was the preferred venue for banquets and dinners for most local organisations like Rotary and Round Table. Many of the large companies in the town entertained their guests there. Five masonic lodges used the hotel facilities for their monthly meetings and annual Installation and Ladies Nights. The rooms in the hotel were fully booked from Monday to Thursday with good weekend occupancy as well. It was one of Simonds' prime hotels producing excellent profits for the company so once again we had to maintain high standards and profitable returns.

We lived in the hotel although we had no sitting room, only two bedrooms, one for Peter and me, and one for Clive. We quickly organised for the corridor to be shut off, giving us a long narrow area where at least we could be alone and perhaps relax. We had to put memories of our lovely house in Ventnor out of our mind. We very soon found we were working a 120-hour week. We were unable to leave the hotel together for more than three hours, without prior permission from Reading and there were no such things as days off together. There was a large and very busy restaurant and two popular bars. The hotel rooms were generally fully booked and we had functions in the ballroom at least twenty-three nights a month. Our joint salary, living-in, was initially £650 per annum, rising to £750 after the first year, with an occasional end of year bonus. We were allowed two weeks vacation but we had first to have a stocktake of liquor and food before leaving and also on returning to duty. However, we certainly learned a lot there. I managed to take my City and Guilds 151 cookery exam and a National Trade Development Diploma in wines and spirits, which helped me to carry out a very demanding position. The restaurant gained accolades from both the AA and Egon Ronay.

Peter took over responsibility for the bars and wine service and I did most of the office controls and worked closely with the chef and restaurant manager. We had a variety of assistant managers to help us, and a full team of kitchen, reception and restaurant personnel, supplemented by a special team of part-timers for the banqueting programme. Initially we had a difficult time with the staff, as the previous manager had been dismissed for unspecified irregularities. He had been very popular with his staff but did not have very much control. They had run things their own way for some time. It took us a few months to gain their loyalty but when they saw we were fair and that all tips received went into the pocket of the staff and not the management, we won them over. In fact, I am still in touch with several of them from those far-back days.

With such a busy working life and living in the hotel, we were glad at that time that we had decided it would better for Clive to be educated at a boarding school. We were not able to attend many of the school functions and I realise now that was unfair on him. Whether we were right not to have moved him nearer to where we worked, it is difficult to say. He had moved schools so frequently that we felt he needed stability in his education especially as we could not be sure that we too might be moved again without much notice. We realised that Simonds owned a large number of hotels spread around southern England. It was a hard decision to take and one Clive did not easily understand. Later, in 1959 when he became 13, it was time to move from his preparatory school, so we transferred him to Ryde School on the Isle of Wight, on the recommendation of Vernon Herbert who had once been a pupil there.

That same year, the hotel industry decided to form a professional body, entitled the Hotel and Catering Institute (HCI). During the initial year, those who had been in management for at least eight years, were offered direct entry in order to form a core membership. Otherwise, entry would be by examination, usually after several years at college. By then I had ten years experience in the industry so I applied for direct entry to the Institute in March 1958. To my disgust, I was turned down, because the powers that be imagined that being a woman, I only did the flowers! Once more encountering sex discrimination, I decided to challenge them. I said I would take the exam that June. Initially they demurred, informing me that students needed to undertake a four-year college course to pass. I told them that if I thought I was fit for direct entry, then I should be able to pass the necessary examination. I had to be persistent and finally they agreed to send me the curriculum. It consisted of the following six subjects, Hotel Law, Food and Drink, Nutrition and Hygiene, Bookkeeping and Accountancy, Maintenance and Stock Control and the Economic Structure of the Industry.

I considered I could manage most of the subjects but I asked the company lawyer to give me details of all laws relating to the industry, such as the Licensing Law, the Shop Act, Tax Laws and up-to-date Health and Hygiene regulations. I knew I needed to know more about nutrition so all my spare moments were spent in revising and filling in the gaps in my knowledge. Furthermore, the organising committee of the HCI insisted it was up to me to find a venue for the examination and to arrange for an invigilating officer. I contacted the local education committee in Swindon and they suggested I joined the schoolchildren at a local grammar school as they were taken their GCE exams the following June. I had three months to prepare for the six subjects on the syllabus. The first day of the examination arrived. It would last for three consecutive days, two subjects daily, each of three hours duration, totalling 18 hours in all; quite a marathon. Then I had to wait until September for the results.

The summer passed slowly, I had almost forgotten about the exam. On 6th September, just as we were leaving for our annual two-week vacation, my receptionist rushed out with our mail, including a letter from the Hotel and Catering Institute. As we drove out of the car park of the hotel, I opened the letter. To the chagrin of the organisers of the Hotel and Catering Institute, and to my immense pleasure, I read that not only had I passed but also I had gained the highest marks in Great Britain that year and had been award the Sir Francis Towle Gold Medal! That was my one great effort for sex equality. As we started our vacation, I shouted with elation.

WHAT ABOUT THE REST OF THE FAMILY?

The lives of my close family by this time had changed considerably. My beloved mother, who had given my brother and me such a love of learning, sadly died of a recurrence of breast cancer three years after the end of the war. It was thanks to her efforts that the link with the French side of the Le Croissette family was uncovered. She had walked around London during the war years, despite the bombs, visiting old churches and French schools where the Huguenots had taken refuge in the years after the Revocation of the Edict of Nantes in the late seventeenth century. She managed to trace an unknown branch of the family, owners of an old bible, The Benfleet Bible, giving details of the early settlers in London. From this, the web site on the family has grown, thanks latterly to Gwyneth Cheeseman. We had now found that our forefathers lived near Senlis in Picardy. We even found a coat of arms.

My mother had suffered greatly but bravely fought the terrible disease of cancer to the end, even maintaining her beloved household budget records to the final weeks. I still consider her one of the greatest influences in my life. My father later re-married, unable to face living alone. Dennis and I were happy for him when he set up home with May Martin, a widowed friend of my mother's. They moved away from London to Wokingham, having given up his job as a cabinetmaker, to go pig farming with May's brother. This venture however was never a great success. He was kept busy, as always, making and mending everything possible for the farm and being taken advantage of, for very little recompense. His new companion

110

died after only a few years. He was alone again.

Dennis, my brother, after his two years National Service in the RAF (happily post-war) had continued his studies in electronics, gaining an external degree from Imperial College at the University of London. This led to a teaching post at the then Regent Street Polytechnic. There he obtained his Master of Science degree and wrote many scientific papers together with his much respected mentor, Dr John Yarwood. On the strength of his growing reputation, he was offered a post as reader at the newly chartered University of Southampton. Whilst there he undertook special research in gas discharges related to geiger counters. This formed the subject of his thesis for his doctorate. In those early post-war years, there was no money available for research and he had to find assistance in the private sector. 20th Century Electronics came to his rescue and provided the equipment for his research. Finally, as a result of his efforts, he gained his PhD degree in 1953. Several years later, he felt he was being held back by the lack of investment in science and the constantly delayed decisions by academic committees. This was a common complaint in post-war academic circles.

The sight of the liners departing for the USA stirred his desire to visit that vast country. He remarked to me that he wanted to reach the other end of the 'bus route'. By 1957, he had secured a teaching post at the University of Kansas at Lawrence. I always remember him coming to Swindon to say goodbye before his departure. I asked him if he would like a photograph of me and his answer was 'Why? I am going to see you all again'. Little did he know then how ultrasound photography would figure largely in his life in later years. Although we had been working and living apart for some years, I knew I would miss him tremendously and it would be some long years before we would meet up again. However, I knew he was ambitious and I wished him well.

Meanwhile, Clive, our only son, had been at a boarding school from the age of eight. Hotel life, when one is likely to move around from place to place, is not congenial for a young child's education. Changing schools so frequently in his early years did Clive no favours. So reluctantly, we decided, if his home kept moving, at least his school must remain the same. Thus, from 1954 to 1958, he attended Presentation College in Reading and at the age of thirteen, moved on to Ryde School on the Isle of Wight. It took him some time to settle there, regarding school as a prison, as shown by a comment in one of his letters in which he wrote 'two boys escaped today'.

In later years, he complained to me that we did not visit him as frequently as did other parents. I felt sad about this but we had acted in what we thought was his best interest since we were so tied by our work. The alternative would have been a constant stream of changing schools. The hours we worked in the hotel profession in those days were penal. As managers, we had no fixed days off and little chance of ever being off together. Working conditions in the hotel industry have vastly improved today.

Peter's family meantime were having great success at the Stanmore Riding School. Their horses were used in many of the films of the day at Pinewood, Elstree and Denham studios. Derek, Peter's brother was working for J Arthur Rank Screen Services and by now had married a glamorous showgirl called Rusty. They had just had a son named Quentin. Unfortunately, neither Peter nor I saw much of our families in those days. I regret that but so many lives were disturbed as returning service personnel tried to re-establish their lives. Priorities were different from those of today!

LEARNING TO BE AN ENTREPRENEUR

In 1959, after my success in the Hotel and Catering Institute Examination, we felt ready to start our own business and have a permanent home again. We had finally sold the house in Ventnor and now had a small capital sum to invest. The publicity I received had had an immediate effect. We received offers from several breweries offering us a tenancy of one or other of their licensed houses, thus enabling us at last to run our own business. This was exactly what we were looking for and we welcomed the challenge. Our search for a suitable opportunity took us around many areas of the West Country. From the various country inns we saw, we decided to apply for the tenancy of The Duke at Bratton, belonging to Ushers Brewery of Trowbridge. This was an attractive building in a lovely village in the heart of Wiltshire,

Captain Younghusband provided horses and riders for many films

A tenancy agreement gives one the right to run one's own business but with the proviso that all alcohol and tobacco supplies must be purchased from the brewery granting the tenancy, whilst paying them a yearly rent. Ushers, an old-established family brewery, based in nearby Trowbridge, was a delightful and helpful

113

company and we subsequently had a happy ten-year relationship with them. In November 1959, we tendered our notice to Simonds' hotel department, leaving Swindon at the end of the year.

However, prior to our taking over our new business, we had a delay of a few months whilst the existing tenants were moving out. We spent this time in Norfolk at Snettisham, helping Mr and Mrs Lowe run their hotel, The Ingoldisthorpe Manor. Mrs Lowe, Peter's second cousin, had recently returned from South Africa. She was the person who had originally offered us our first entry into the hotel business by suggesting we took over the management of the West Country Inn in Devon, so we were delighted to help her. Since her latest hotel was very near to Sandringham, there were many royal connections using its facilities. However, we never enjoyed life in Norfolk; it was much colder as far as the weather was concerned but also the local residents too were a little chilly! They all seemed to have delusions of grandeur, living within the aura of royalty! We were relieved to learn we could finally take over our own business in the spring of 1960.

On 6th May 1960, we moved to the Duke at Bratton, near Westbury, Wiltshire. The Duke was an old established hostelry, named after the Iron Duke, The Duke of Wellington. It lay under the northern slopes of the Salisbury Plain and near the famous Westbury White Horse, carved into the chalk hills. The village of Bratton and nearby Edington were the scene of a famous battle in the twelve century, between Guthrum the Dane and King Alfred. Alfred won and this changed the history of England. After his defeat, Guthrum converted to Christianity and the separate regions of Wessex and Mercia were formed. The Battle of Edington took place on and around Picquets Hill, the name we later gave to our future home in Wales. I would see this hill daily for the next nine years, from my bedroom window.

Prior to our arrival, as well as two licensed bars, the Duke had provided bed and breakfast accommodation, a little bar food trade and ice cream sold to the locals from the back door! We had rather more ambitious plans. It was an attractive building dating back to the seventeenth century and had originally been a coffee house providing sustenance for the passengers of the stagecoaches en route to Bath from Reading, whilst the change of horses took place.

There were eight bedrooms, several bathrooms, two bars, a visitor's lounge and an attractive dining room, surrounded by a large and pleasant garden. The bars and other rooms all had attractive carved oak beams. A wooden pavilion in the back had been for many years the venue for Sunday School outings; no alcohol served there! Now it would serve as additional storage and an outside kennel for our black Labrador bitch, Negra. Negra was Peter's responsibility and he soon trained her to the gun. There were plenty of opportunities for a day's shooting around us. I was not a doggy person as I had been pushed off a breakwater in Folkestone by a large black dog when only two years old. The water was deep on the other side, already filled by the incoming tide. I nearly drowned. I have never feared water but ever since that day, I have had a built-in fear of dogs and they seem to recognise it. I must admit I eventually managed to accept Negra who was placidity itself.

On that sunny day in May, the laburnum tree overlooking the bedrooms shone golden with cascades of blossom. The sun was high in a blue sky. The formalities of stocktaking and valuation of all furniture and equipment took several hours. Finally, we handed over the cheque in settlement and bade farewell to the outgoing tenants. At last, we were in business for ourselves. Six o'clock promptly we opened the doors to the two bars, having stocked up and polished all the glasses and bottles afresh. There were fresh flowers on the counters and the one member of the bar staff we had retained took up his position in the public bar. Peter took over the lounge bar and I

The Duke at Bratton

stood by in the background. It seemed the whole village poured in that evening to take a look at the new innkeepers. This was the beginning of another adventure, long hours, some risks, new friendships and a great learning process, leading, we hoped, to ultimate success.

We had enough experience in management to watch all the staff carefully, as the trade was renowned for fiddles. After the first night, it was evident that the barman we had inherited thought we were new to the trade and had evolved his own form of private enterprise. We soon realised he and his wife who came in each night for a drink had a very clever trick going. He would give his wife the drink she asked for, together with change from a pound note, without her ever proffering any money! Our London experience had made us wise to these sorts of tricks so he lasted less than a week and was soon sent on his way. We decided not to get the police involved at this early stage in a new area. Our hunt for reliable staff began.

We decided in the future only to use bar staff from the village, as there was less likelihood of dishonesty. It was then we found Mattie

116

Parker, the Welsh wife of Fred from Tonypandy who looked after the extensive gardens of a rich and eccentric widow in the area. Mattie knew everyone, was a wonderful worker and a veritable treasure. She ran the public bar for us from then onwards until the day we left, nearly ten years later and as an added bonus, always kept us provided with delicious Welsh cakes!

Very soon, we decided to open the restaurant for lunch and dinner and to provide all meals for the residents. This coincided with the building of the cement works at Westbury by the Associated Portland Cement Company (APCM). Before long, all our rooms were occupied throughout the week by their organising team. This consisted of the site's new resident manager, the chemist, several engineers and technicians and the architects. It was a lifeline for us and gave us a great start. These cement 'bods' stayed with us for over two years and became almost like family. At first I did the cooking and we gradually built up a reputation for good food and reasonable prices, but I knew I would soon need additional help. I enrolled several young people from the village as chambermaids and to help in the kitchen. I must have taught at least a dozen young Bratton girls to cook. We then found John, who had trained as a chef in the Navy and had cooked for the Prince of Wales. He was young but enthusiastic and we soon had a great team.

Before long it became obvious we needed a well-trained waiter to take over the restaurant as our menu went up market. We were attracting a lot of custom from many Army units in the area as well as local businesses. Press advertisements failed to produce any possible candidate locally. It was then we had the idea of contacting our friend Antonio Franco. Since 1958 we had been visiting his hotel, Las Mercedes, in the then unknown small Andalucian village of Torremolinos – long before it gained its future notoriety. With a growing British clientele, he quickly agreed when we suggested he should send his waiters over to us, in turn, for a period of around six months. They would help us and we would teach them English. At the same time, they would get to know what British visitors were looking for on holiday. This arrangement continued throughout the whole of our time at the Duke and we trained over twenty of his 'boys' both as waiters and chefs. They in turn added a 'cachet' to our growing reputation for good food and service and at the same time, were a great catch for the local girls! I meanwhile began to learn Spanish – from a book.

Antonio Barranco, the first arrival, came in November 1960. His English was good enough to be understood and very soon, he became fluent. He was a great help and a wonderful personality. He had left school aged 13, when his father, who had fought against Franco and his army when they arrived in Malaga, had been imprisoned as a Communist and then executed. Antonio had to start earning a living to help provide food for his younger brothers and sisters. After training as a carpenter, he realised the growing tourist industry in Southern Spain was offering great opportunities and before long he had risen to assistant head waiter at the Mercedes hotel. He was a fast learner, could cook, had a smattering of several languages. In addition, he was an expert at the Japanese art of origami. At our first Christmas at the Duke, he decorated our bars with many of these creations and he became a great popular figure with the locals. They called him Norman Wisdom because he looked like the actor and had almost the same sense of humour! We owed him a great deal. Our trade was growing rapidly. Once more, this meant long hours for Peter and me but at least we were working for ourselves. We engaged local staff for additional help in the kitchen and the bars. Antonio worked six days a week. With his ability and charm, he received many tips, which later helped him on his return to Spain to put a deposit down on his first home for his wife Magdalena and little daughter Loli.

After the School of Infantry, based in nearby Warminster, found us, we provided facilities for much of their entertaining. At that time, they were using Salisbury Plain for their programme of training officers from many foreign countries of the Western Union. During their orienteering exercises, they would use our bars for their lunchtime break. They would arrive with their hay boxes, set them up outside the Duke and provide a hot curry lunch. The officers would consume this in the bars and of course top it up with a pint of ale. We met many interesting and sometimes notorious people from countries far and wide on these occasions. Idi Amin, then a major, was one of these. He was an enormous and very sullen man. On entering the bar, he had to duck his head down as he passed under the low beams. Like him, many of the African majors and colonels who attended were later involved in military coups in their respective countries. They either succeeded and became president or they were executed. We learned that a colonel's rank was a particularly dangerous one!

I often wondered why the Army trained so many foreign officers. Finally, a lieutenant colonel from the School of Infantry gave me the answer – an excellent one it was indeed. He said, 'If we train them, and there is any trouble later on in that part of the world, we will know how they will react. It doesn't mean to say that our troops will be doing the same thing!' An interesting strategy.

After our first Spanish waiter, we went on to employ Emilio who after the warmth of Andalusia, had to experience the coldest winter for years in 1962/3. I bought him long johns and sweaters but he still was cold. It started to snow on Boxing Day and our residents, all employees of the cement works, had to walk to work. They found walking along the railway tracks the easiest way by far. We always left satisfying casseroles in the Aga for the night workers so they

Manolo and John offering a stirrup cup at the Telcott Hunt
meet at the Duke at Bratton

could eat when they returned at whatever hour. The snow turned to ice and did not disappear until March of the new year.

Each year we became better known and the trade increased. We gained both a mention in the *Good Food Guide* and a flattering write-up in the *Egon Ronay Guide*. Emilio was followed by Leonardo, a couple of Manolos and several Pepés. Peter and I continued to work long hours with few days off. I managed to get to London occasionally to judge the Junior Salon Culinaire entries for Hotelympia and Peter managed a couple of days fishing on the Wye but there were few holidays. Our increasing reputation meant longer hours and greater stress. In 1961, I had an abdominal operation coupled with a termination but soon had to get back to work. I shared the cooking duties with the chef and we found our business increasing after favourable entries in the food guides. People would enter the bar, clutching their book and if we were not there, they would be disappointed and ready to complain.

We would try to take an occasional holiday, usually driving to either France or Spain but this needed a lot of organising. We would have to find and pay suitable relief managers – not always easy to do. Otherwise, we rarely had a day off together. Peter looked after the bar and liquor ordering and since our residents were able to stay in the bar as long as they wished, he had many late nights. Coupled with overwork and the sudden death of his mother in 1967, Peter suffered a serious breakdown the following year. This necessitated a spell in hospital and a recuperation period away from the hotel. I was worried.

His absence coincided with the August Bank holiday and a full

Some of the entries for the Pram Derby outside
the Duke at Bratton

house of residents attending the Edington Priory Church Musical Festival. This was a prestige occasion when many famous choirs appeared and people worldwide attended the services. On the bank holiday Monday, the village was also holding their annual Pram Derby, beginning and ending at the Duke, the busiest day in our year. I awakened early that morning to prepare the early morning teas, served to the residents in their rooms. On entering the kitchen and going to the storeroom, I found the door blocked by a soft-feeling object. My initial thought was 'It's a body!' On pushing open the door, I found a large bag of detergent, normally kept in the laundry. This was the cause of the blockage. Immediately I realised something was seriously wrong. Then I noticed the laundry window had been smashed. I went to the back storeroom where all the spirits and cigarettes were kept in a locked cupboard. The door had been forced and the shelves were empty. I realised we had been robbed. All the bottles of wine and spirits had gone, together with the stock of cigarettes and tobacco. They had even taken several kegs of beer. What a disaster, no stock left and the busiest day of the year to cater for! But the show had to go on.

The current Manolo took up the morning tea to the residents and prepared their breakfasts whilst I contacted the police for help, the brewery for urgent supplies and notified the insurance company. The response was immediate. The police arrived and we found the thieves had doped Negra, our Labrador. They had entered through a back window, blocking the kitchen door with the sack of detergent and they made their getaway through the lane at the back of the garden. Apparently, this same gang had been operating throughout Wiltshire for some time, always targeting licensed premises, with the same modus operandum. They were never caught.

The brewery sent immediate replacement of wines, spirits, beer and cigarettes. The police took fingerprints. By eleven o'clock

122

when all the decorated prams arrived on the forecourt for the Pram Derby and the bars were filling up, things were operating as normal. Everybody seemed oblivious of what had happened in the early hours – except for Manolo and me. By then I was a quivering wreck but just managing to carry on. Then Major General Christopher Man appeared. He was the current Head of the Army Commissions Board at Westbury and an ex-Japanese prisoner of war. He was a special friend of mine and on seeing the police; he asked them what had happened. Learning of the burglary, he came up to me, put his arm round my shoulders and said 'And what about you?' This was the first kind word I had received and much to my surprise, I burst into tears; not anything I do easily. Then I collapsed.

My doctor was summoned. He took one look and gave me a morphine injection. He allowed me to stay to the end of the Pram Derby and then he whisked me home to his house in the nearby village of Steeple Ashton, where I fell into a deep sleep. My wonderful team rallied round, fed the residents, looked after the bars and despite the calamitous beginning, the day was a resounding success. I awakened later that evening to the sound of a heavenly choir! It was a group of King's College choirboys, also staying at my doctor's house. They were practising their contribution to the evening service at the church festival. By then, feeling calmer, I returned to the Duke.

Life was never boring. There were always new experiences, new people to meet. One day it was Robert Morton, the actor, who arrived. He admired the truckle of Cheddar cheese we were serving, and insisted I order one for him! Another day, the one-time members of the crew of the Dambusters walked through the door, Mickie Martin amongst them. After a session in the bar, we ended up playing one of the games that was popular in the wartime RAF Officers' Mess! We were all blindfolded, crawling around the floor, armed with rolled up newspapers, trying to target each other! On a further occasion,

Lord Reith arrived unannounced. He was very distant and had a distinctly regal air. Peter Cook and Dudley Moore used us as the base for one of their comic routines in *That Was the Week That Was*. They dressed as cave men and climbed on to the Westbury White Horse. We never knew who would be next to walk through the door. However, almost ten years of hard work and long hours with little time to relax, coupled with Peter's illness had taken its toll. I was running out of steam and Peter was losing his art as a raconteur. We had to think seriously of changing direction.

We had recently bought the Court Farm House in the village – a beautiful fifteenth century building, built two years before Columbus arrived in America. It was thatched, full of oak beams and with a lovely garden. We thought carefully and made our decision. We gave the brewery notice of our wish to leave. The terms of our tenancy meant we might have to wait up to a year before new tenants could be found. In the meantime, we were making plans. We realised we would get nothing for goodwill despite having built up a substantial and profitable business. That was how it was with a tenancy. On handover, you receive the value of the ingoings – furniture, fittings and stock. Sometimes an understanding stocktaker, knowing the business was a very good deal for the incoming tenant, would place a higher value than normal on some of these items but this was not a guarantee.

We were now in our late forties and for many years had each been working for up to one hundred hours a week. Thinking about our future, we decided we would set up a private catering service for weddings and other special events in the area. Our new house was large enough and offered adequate kitchen facilities for preparations. We knew there was enough trained local staff to call on for these occasions and we could then choose how much to take on.

This meant we could have some holidays abroad and even visit my brother, now in California. During so many years, there had been little opportunity for holidays. Whenever we managed to go away, it had meant finding management cover during our absence. This had on several occasions led to problems with our staff. So the thought of being able to travel without any worries was a pleasant sensation to muse upon whilst we were working through the last months of our tenancy.

SCRAP METAL QUEEN!

During our time at the Duke, we had bought a couple of cottages in the village, which we often used as additional bedrooms for the Duke's guests. Now we would be able to let them to officers from the Warminster School of Infantry so this would provide a small rental income to help with expenses. We were coming to the end of our tenancy and planning our future.

Then the strange hand of fate entered the scene. In the past, I had usually tried to give our visiting Spanish waiters an opportunity to visit other hotels in the vicinity. Pepé Cubero was the current Torremolinos incumbent in our final months at the Duke. One day I took him back to my old hotel, The Goddard Arms at Swindon to lunch there. The staff still remembered me and when they heard me talking in Spanish, they told me there was a visiting Spanish couple staying in the hotel. They were having great difficulty in making themselves understood. Apparently, they spoke very little English and had been asking for assistance. It was suggested that I find them and see whether there was anything we could do to help.

We finished our lunch, drank the last drops of our Rioja wine and went searching for them. We eventually tracked them down in Room 24, their bedroom. By then it was about two o'clock. Stupidly I had forgotten about the Spanish habit of taking a siesta so I knocked on the door. A rather gruff and heavily accented Spanish voice called out *'Quién está?'* Who is it? 'A friend of Spain,' I replied in my best Castilian accent. Back came the order 'Enter, friend of Spain!' So together with my young Andalucian waiter, we went in. We found a couple in their early sixties in bed!

Overcoming my confusion, I explained haltingly that I had been told they were looking for some help and I wondered if there was anything we could do. I introduced Pepé and explained who we were. Then we heard their story. Señor Orbegozo, who came from the Basque region of Spain, was the owner of a large steel mill. He bought scrap metal, added additional metals such as molybdenum, melted it into ingots and then extruded it in order to make car springs and also steel for high grade knives. At that time, Britain was issuing permits to some foreign manufacturers to purchase scrap steel from our surplus stocks. These permits were much sought-after, as vast amounts of steel were needed for rebuilding in the post-war period. He had been the lucky recipient of one of these permits and had been purchasing a special category, No. 4 bales, as well as steel turnings, from a scrap dealer in Swindon. However, after several successful deliveries, his supplier became greedy and had inserted lumps of concrete within the bales, increasing the weight and robbing his client of the scrap equivalent.

Señor Orbegozo was looking for a lawyer to sue this man but he also needed a translator. To my great surprise, during our conversation, he suggested I should act on his behalf. I realised that my Spanish was not up to such an onerous task but I suggested I would put him in touch with someone who had been giving me some private lesson. He was delighted. I made the necessary phone call to Brian Steel, a teacher at the nearby Public School, Dauncey's at West Lavington. Subsequently he acted on Señor Orbegozo's behalf arranging, I believe, a satisfactory compensation, and he received an appropriate remuneration.

Pepé and I left the couple, still in bed, when we had concluded our discussion and we returned home. I imagined I had now left the matter safely in the hands of others. However, three weeks later, one morning as I went into the lounge bar, to my surprise I found both Señor and Señora Orbegozo sitting at a table by the window, enjoying a glass of wine. I went up to them, greeting them warmly and asked what they were doing. Imagine my surprise when this opulent steel magnate told me he thought I was a good businesswoman and he had come to offer me a job as his purchasing officer for scrap steel in Great Britain. He said he would pay me fourteen shillings per ton and he wanted four thousand tons a month of No. 4 bales and turnings. Getting over my astonishment and jumping in with both feet, I agreed I would take on the challenge! He said he would send me my air ticket and I was to fly to San Sebastian where he would meet me. We would then go to the British Consulate and sign an agreement and how soon could I come? That is how three weeks later; I was sitting in the Consul's office in San Sebastian and signing on as a scrap metal dealer.

On my return, I realised that my knowledge was sadly lacking on the subject of scrap and that I would have to do something about learning more. I decided I would find out what exactly a No. 4 bale was. By phoning around, I learnt it was a bale of pressed clean steel, i.e. without any treatment of paint or solvents, usually consisting of the trimmings from sheet steel used for car bodies and white goods. I also learnt turnings were the clean bits of steel scrap when metal was ground or turned into shapes. Then I needed to know both the buying and selling prices. This required a little more careful planning. First, I rang up several metal producing firms such as Pressed Steel, in the guise of a secretary, asking how much they charged for bales of their scrap metal. I followed this with calls to several scrap metal merchants asking them for their purchase price for No. 4 bales. Before long, I had the upper and lower figures from which to work.

I had once done a favour to a well-known steel fabricating company in Swindon, who made car bodies, when they had a strike on their hands. They needed to meet with the Communist leaders of the striking union but did not want the press to find out. They had approached me and I had offered them our personal sitting room at the Goddard Arms for the meeting. So contacting the managing director, I reminded him he owed me a favour and had he any No. 4 bales to sell! After he heard the story, he immediately offered me a guaranteed thousand tons every month towards my purchasing target. This was a start. I realised I would need help to get the next 3,000 tons of the quota. I decided to approach the then chairman of the Chamber of Shipping. He happened to be the son of Clive's godmother. I asked if he could recommend a good and reliable scrap dealer, who could assist me in purchasing and shipping. He was most helpful and put me in touch with John Lowenstein who had a very large business in this field, shipping regularly from Dagenham. We made contact by phone and it was agreed we should meet for lunch in London. John suggested the Baron of Beef, a restaurant in the City used for many business deals. I imagine he was wondering who this woman from Wiltshire was, who wanted to ship 4,000 tons a month to Spain!

The day came. I arrived on time outside the restaurant and there was this elegant young man in his late twenties waiting for me. In a rather condescending fashion, he informed me, the supposed country cousin, that he was very well known here and we would get an exceptionally fine lunch and very special service. I recall how we entered the foyer and then descended a wide impressive staircase to the restaurant. Below, awaiting our arrival, was the restaurant manager, in his morning coat and sporting a red carnation in his buttonhole. He was smiling broadly. My escort turned to me and said, 'I am a regular here, I come very frequently'. As we reached the foot of the stairs, the restaurant manager ran up to me, threw his arms round my neck and said in heavily accented English 'Allo,

Mrs Young'usband, how nice to see you again', and gave me a hug! Amazingly, it was Jean Braconnier, a young potential manager we had trained at the Goddard Arms. My escort was more than surprised and I think I went up considerably in his estimation from then on! I thoroughly enjoyed my lunch and we certainly did have the best attention possible.

Obviously, this scrap metal project would be ongoing and demanding. I decided to form a company that would cover all future activities when we finally left the Duke. This was the birth of Younghusband Sales and Development Agency Ltd, with a schedule of operations covering many areas. We could have run businesses ranging from boating pools to holiday camps, deal in all kinds of metal, cater for weddings, offer hotel and catering consultancy and pack herbs! This would cover any of our business ventures from then onwards.

The scrap metal project fared well during the next three years and was very profitable to us all. There were several occasions when I needed to return with John Lowenstein to the Hernani steelworks. These were only minor problems and we all managed to work well together. Then General Franco decided to put his finger in the pie. His regime had always had bad relations with the Basque region where Hernani was situated. They had offered the strongest resistance against him, during the Spanish Civil War. Therefore, when his industrial friends told him they wanted to buy scrap steel from Great Britain, he insisted on a change in the method of issuing of permits. Instead of Britain allocating permits to export scrap steel, he would issue the permits to import these goods. The consequence was all his friends got the permits and the Basque companies lost out. Sadly, that was the end of a very interesting sortie into the manufacturing world for Younghusband Sales and Development Agency. We had to look to other sources of income.

STARTING AGAIN

This all happened after we finally left the Duke on 6th November 1968. It was a sad day in many ways as we had many happy memories of our time there and had made many friends. However, we would be staying in the village and would have more time to enjoy the beautiful area around Bratton. We loved The Court Farm House and Peter was delighted with the garden, which he soon made his own.

Three years earlier, my father, on the death of his second wife, had become very lonely. One day he phoned me and asked if he could come and join us at the Duke. Of course, we had said yes. Within a short time, he fitted in with the routine, becoming a great help with his carpentry and joinery skills. The staff loved him and he seemed settled and happy. Some weeks before our move, he was invited to join his cousin and visit the elder son of his favourite brother, then living in South Africa. He went by boat, enjoying a luxurious trip on the Windsor Castle. After visiting his nephew Frank Le Croissette and Dorothy his wife in Cape Town, they all went on a trip along the Garden Route and saw the beautiful southern coastline of South Africa.

Sadly, after the trip, he returned home looking very ill. Within days, it was confirmed that he was suffering from lung cancer. He had always smoked, rolling his own cigarettes filled with a strong tobacco called Digger Shag. Even as a child, I would go into the local tobacconist to buy his weekly two-ounce quota. I am sure it was the constant smell of tobacco in the house that had convinced both Dennis and I never to smoke. This habit coupled with his work as a cabinetmaker and shop fitter, where he was constantly exposed to wood dust, was the cause of this terrible disease. I could not chide him for smoking. He had endured four years as a soldier in The Great War, experiencing the horrors of the Battle of the Somme and of Paschendale. Later he worked long hours under very tough conditions to ensure his family had the best possible start he could offer us. Smoking was one of his few pleasures.

Just prior to us leaving The Duke, he had a major operation to remove one lung and rebuild his chest wall. The surgery left him considerably weaker. He joined us in our new home some weeks later, after a period of convalescence. He had always been a strong person and seemed to be recovering well. After several weeks convalescence, he was able to use his beloved car again and visit his stepson in Manchester and other distant friends. However, he couldn't get used to living in the old fifteenth-century house. It bothered him that the beams were not regular and aligned. He found it difficult to adjust. He was missing the company of the staff at the Duke. We gave him his own bed-sitting room and bathroom but he never settled in the Court Farm House. His illness had changed him and made him bitter. Sadly, within four years, the cancer re-occurred and he died in 1972. He was a fine man, who had lived a good life but one filled with hard work and very little relaxation. I think his greatest pleasure was to know how well his son, my brother Dennis, had done. Before my father died, he had the satisfaction of learning that Dennis as manager of the space instruments department at Jet Propulsion Laboratories, Pasadena, (JPL), was responsible for all the instrumentation on the successful Surveyor unmanned probe landings, sent to the Moon in preparation for the manned Apollo spacecraft. In addition, Dennis's department provided instruments on the Mariner probe to Mars and on Voyager, which travelled out past our solar system and is still journeying in space today.

After my father's first operation, he regained enough strength to undertake his first transatlantic flight to visit Dennis in Pasadena. There he was able to meet Jill, his so far unknown daughter-in-law who Dennis had married in Philadelphia. Jill was born in Cambelltown, Australia. Her mother was a schoolteacher from Kent who had emigrated there whilst her father was a fifth generation Australian of Scottish descent. Jill had a brilliant academic career, specialising in library science. She was a great partner to Dennis. He as a scientist and she as a librarian were both meticulous in everything they did. They had the same sense of humour and the same taste in wine!

My brother showed my father the California that he had come to love. They visited San Francisco and Santa Barbara. They did a little gambling in Las Vegas and enjoyed the beauty of the desert surrounding Palm Springs. Dennis, by then, had lived in the USA for more than fifteen years and was now an American citizen. This was an essential requirement for anyone working for NASA. He had progressed from being a lecturer at Kansas University at Lawrence, to Assistant Professor at Drexel College of Technology in Philadelphia where he published his much-used textbook *Transistors*. There he became a pioneer of biomedical engineering and launched the initial training programme for both doctors and scientists in this sphere. Because of this and since he was a specialist in instrumentation, he had been headhunted to join NASA at JPL. He took over as manager of the then troubled Surveyor programme. This unmanned probe was designed to land on the Moon. Its complex instruments were to act as probes of the moon's surface and atmosphere. Dennis rescued the programme and seven Surveyors were launched, sending back vital information. These instruments included a television camera, an alpha scatterer, the probe for soil content and the computer. The successful landings sent back reports from these instruments, giving details of the atmosphere, the soil and pictures of the environment on the moon. All this was essential knowledge for the astronauts in the forthcoming Apollo landings. On a later mission, one of the astronauts managed to walk to the Surveyor module nearby, retrieving both the camera and computer and returning it to Dennis.

When NASA curtailed any further unmanned space probes due to increasing costs, Dennis became manager of the Biomedical Engineering Department and, together with Richard Heyser, conducted many pioneering experiments with ultrasound equipment. Simultaneously he also took on responsibility for the Department of Extra-Terrestrial Life where experiments were undertaken involving sending out mathematical messages into space. He told me it might be generations before any responses might be received but one day there would be a response, of that he was certain. My father, the cabinet maker, was rightly proud of his son.

THE CABINET MAKER

Not for him, precision tools that come pre-packed
and only need a plug be fixed, no, not for him.
His skilful hands used rasp and gouge and moulding planes.
Their graded blades stacked carefully in their case.
His tools all sharpened, cleaned – his saws and drills,
His vice, the metal rule, French polish pad made neat,
Chisels, brace and bit meticulous in that chest.
A five-year stint to learn his trade for next-to-nothing pay,
A mere five bob a week he earned and at the end, that piece
That special piece that those apprenticed make,
A box of walnut, all inlaid . 'It's parquetry,' he said,
'Cross-banded too and lined as well with finest yew'.
His proudest moment when he held the scroll,

His hard-earned indentures none could take away.
What would he say of present craft,
all stapled, stuck and tacked?
No joints or dovetails, no tongue and groove, no craftsman's art,
Not proper wood but chipboard, laminates, Formica topped,
and thrown together, nothing screwed, no skill, epoxy glued
Buy the pack and take away, read the hints and self-assemble.
His life was hard but bravely lived
But cancer struck him long before his time.
No masks, you see, to stop the dust. Not then.
Just lungs that clogged. That's how my father died.

CATCHING UP WITH CLIVE

Our son Clive had remained at Ryde School until he was 16 in 1962. He was never a keen scholar, much preferring to find out things on his own, rather than being told. He was anxious to get out into the world at the first opportunity and was trying to decide whether to be a farmer or an hotelier! There was no capital available to set him up in a farm so hotel keeping it had to be. He decided he wanted to train properly and not just pick it up as he went along as we had done. A previous assistant manager at the Goddard Arms, Bryan Evans, a Welshman, had now assumed the lofty position of banqueting manager at the Savoy Hotel, London. There he had been re-christened Evangeloni Brioni! We contacted him for advice. He arranged for Clive to be interviewed by Silvino Trompetto the maitre chef, together with the general manager, Michael Shepherd. They agreed to accept him for a place in the five-year management training scheme when he became seventeen. They insisted however that he spent the intervening year getting some experience elsewhere.

Once again, our contact with Antonio Franco of Las Mercedes Hotel in Torremolinos came in useful. He agreed for Clive to spend a year there with the opportunity of gaining experience in the kitchen, restaurant, bars and reception. Within a very short time at the age of just over sixteen, Clive arrived in the Costa de Sol, not knowing a single word of Spanish. His French teacher at school had stopped him learning French after the first year, saying he would never become a linguist. By learning through necessity, within three months, Clive was speaking Spanish fluently. Once again, it proved he was better at finding things out in his own way. He had a great year in Spain, finally becoming Antonio's assistant in opening a second hotel, El Delfin.

On his return to England, armed with new confidence, he returned to the Savoy and began five years of hard but valuable training. His first two years were spent in the kitchens under Silvini Trompetto, affectionately known as 'Tromps'. Clive began in the garde manger (larder) and moved through all the 'parties.' The kitchen was run on the brigade system with the different parties or departments, as designated by Auguste Escoffier in the late nineteenth century.

Kitchen training covered experience in the hors d'oeuvre section, fish, roasts, entremetier (vegetables) and the patisserie departments. The hours were long and split into two halves, 9am to 2.30pm, and 5pm to 10pm. The kitchen was hot and steamy, the pressures to produce top quality food at all times enormous. The two and half-hour afternoon break was spent in the nearby AM Club open to off duty catering staff where they spent the time perfecting their snooker technique.

Training at the Savoy Hotel entailed a six-day working week with minimal pay. It costs us more to keep him in London for those five years than it would have done to send him to a top university. However, the knowledge he gained was invaluable in his future career. Many were the times when returning to his flat in Belsize Park late at night, the police would stop him. They would insist on searching him, especially looking in the heavy box he carried. This contained his full set of kitchen knives, something every potential chef owned and guarded with his life. He had to show his Savoy pass to persuade them he was just returning home from work and had no ulterior motive!

His third year saw him working as a commis waiter in the main restaurant. The commis did all the carrying of the dishes for the station waiters to serve the clients. This entailed walking miles during every service; from the kitchen to the restaurant, clad in a long white apron and with aching feet, along extensive corridors, up and down huge flights of stairs, over acres of thick wool carpet. When he came home on occasional breaks, his feet would be bleeding. It was not an easy life by any means. There were, however, compensations. His great moment came when the Queen Mother dined there and requested that only English waiters serve her. Since so many of the staff were foreign, the trainee management students were recruited for this occasion. They were issued with white gloves and told to do their best! This was an honour indeed. Another great memory was the day of the funeral of Winston Churchill. The staff was able to see his coffin, carried in the Royal barge on the Thames, as it passed the windows of the River Room. Winston was a regular client of the Savoy. On this solemn day, the waiters who usually served him arranged to keep his special table unoccupied. Together they contributed to pay for his favourite dish. With reverence, they carried in and placed on the table an ice carving of a swan, bearing amongst its wings his favourite Beluga caviar; a touching gesture by a usually tough and cynical group of waiters.

Clive's main complaint about working in the restaurant was, if he received a good tip, on occasions as much as £25, he had to put it in the tronc. This is the customary method of dealing with tips. Every level of staff receives a proportion of the monthly total, dependent upon rank, the maitre d'hotel getting the most and the unfortunate commis the least

The next six months were spent in the Audit and Control Office. Amongst other activities, this entailed learning how to check on any illicit staff activities and ensuring the profit margins were reached. Six months bar training followed and this was succeeded by a most interesting year spent on the front office reception desk. Here he was to meet many notables of the time; Elizabeth Taylor, Bing Crosby, who practised his golf shots along the corridors of the Savoy bedrooms, Lord Thomson of the *Times* newspaper and of course the Beatles. On several occasions, he helped John Lennon and his fellow musicians escape the waiting press hordes, by escorting them out of the rear entrance of the hotel. Finally, in 1968 he finished this arduous but incomparable training. The Savoy management students received no certificate at the end of their course. They were told that anyone needing to know whether they had completed the training successfully should write for a reference! These five years were to hold Clive in great stead in the future.

Almost immediately, he was offered a post as assistant manager at the much-respected North British Hotel in Edinburgh, part of the British Transport Hotel chain. He spent a happy year in Scotland where we were able to visit him and were accommodated in a most sumptuous suite in this Victorian hotel. He also spent some time at their Turnbury and Gleneagles Hotels to widen his experience and later was promoted to senior assistant manager at the Station Hotel in Hull; not quite so pleasant a posting. He was ready to spread his wings. He answered an advertisement in the trade magazine, *The Caterer*, for general manager of a large outside catering concern in Wales. On being invited to an interview, he found it was with Hamard Caterers of Barry, a company owned by our friends Chris and Vivien Pollard. His London training was just what they wanted for their expanding business and he was immediately offered the position. This led to him managing many diverse events, ranging from Royal occasions for both the Queen and the Prince of Wales, several Welsh Eisteddfods, Cardiff City banquets and most of the Jewish celebrations of bar mitzvahs and weddings in the area.

By this time, we had left the Duke and he came home from time to time to his own room in the Court Farm House. We had met many of his girlfriends from London, Wiltshire, Scotland and now Wales but he showed no signs of settling down. After two years in Wales, he felt that he had proved himself and was ready for a change in order to broaden his horizons. It was in early 1970 that my brother, by then in Pasadena, California, wrote to Clive suggesting he might like to get some American experience and Dennis would guarantee his expenses if Clive could get a visitor's permit. The demands of outside catering were getting frustrating and he felt he would like to get back into hotels again. This opportunity of visiting America was tempting so he gave in his notice, obtained the necessary visitor's visa and armed with friends' connections and addresses, set off on this new adventure. Little did we know what it would to in later years.

Arriving in New York, he telephoned one of the contacts he had been given and was invited to spend a few nights as their guest. They were most hospitable and showed him their New York lifestyle. Then he set off, hitchhiking down the Atlantic coast to Florida where he spent a week with the cousin of one of my WAAF friends. He found American hospitality generous and welcoming. Bussing and hitching his way through the Southern states, he arrived in Houston to a welcome from yet another Good Samaritan. He spent two weeks with Skeet and Mary Kent Stewart and was treated like their own son. He visited the Houston Space Center, ate oysters in Galveston, saw the Presidential Library in Austin and tasted the temptations of Dallas. The Stewarts became great friends of our family and we welcomed Olva their daughter as our guest the following year. Skeet turned out to be the first American army officer sent to Bletchley Park to work on the Enigma code. On a subsequent visit to their home, I noticed an enigma wheel in his study and then we found out that he was the officer in charge at Canons Park and the eight WRNS officer I had known in our Officers Mess at Fighter Command all those years ago. It was only then I found out what work they were engaged in – code and cipher intelligence for Bletchley. What a strange coincidence to learn this in Texas!

It was time for Clive to continue his journey around the States. Tired of bussing and hitching, he used his remaining cash to buy a train ticket to San Francisco. In his usual manner, he made friends with two young men in the carriage who offered to put him up for his stay in their home city. He saw all the sights; Fisherman's Wharf, Chinatown, the Golden Bridge and of course a lot of the nightlife. Finally, a week later, he took the Greyhound bus south and arrived at my brother's home for a rest. After a week or so getting to know the area, he decided he would look for a job and decided to head for Palm Springs. Dennis gave him some cash and Clive left for the desert. During a previous visit, Peter and I had made contact with a namesake, Peggy Younghusband, who lived in the High Desert at Yucca Valley, about twenty minutes from Palm Desert. She suggested Clive stayed with her until he found a job. He paid for his keep by painting her house and helping her son build his bungalow whilst looking out for a suitable post. Within a month, he was appointed Manager of Indian Wells Hotel, the famous site of the Bob Hope Classic Golf competition.

On a visitor's visa, he was not legally permitted to work. This did not deter Clive. He soon put his stamp on the hotel and brought a little Savoy style to the menu. Then as now, there were many illegal Mexicans working in the hospitality industry. This meant there were frequent visits from immigration inspectors to the hotel, investigating the status of the employees. Clive would show them round. They would interrogate all the Mexicans but never once did it occur to them to ask Clive for his permit to work! He spent a happy season there but in the hot summer months, the hotel closed so he went to Las Vegas, once more looking for work. Before long, he was employed as road manager for the Platters, the well-known

Afro-American group, famous for the 1950s song *The Great Pretender*. He went all over the country with them and into Mexico. He had hair-raising times getting them to gigs on time when the band was stoned with drink and drugs. The tour lasted for three months. He had never taken drugs in his life and this experience made him even more certain he never would.

When the Indian Wells reopened for the following winter, he returned there once more as manager. The time came when his visa was due to expire. Returning to Dennis and Jill in Pasadena, he spent a little time there, repaying the money Dennis had given him as he had managed to save quite a bit from his earnings. He took them out for a final thank you dinner and then the following day, left LAX to return home. It was 1972; he wondered what would come next.

It may seem that Clive had taken many different posts during these early years but this is customary in the hotel and catering industry. It is essential to get as varied an experience as possible. The wider the experience one manages to have, the more useful one becomes.

Clockwise from top left:

Eileen as a Glaxo Baby (fourteen
months);
Eileen's father, Harlow Le
Croissette, a despatch rider in
the newly-formed Royal Flying
Corps;
Eileen's mother, Ethel Le
Croissette (nee Smith) during
world war one wearing her
husband's Royal Flying Corps
brooch

Three generations of the Le Croissette family; Eileen aged four at centre front.

Eileen and parents, including new addition, brother Dennis.

Clockwise from top left: Eileen's birthplace, 28 Radcliffe Road, Winchmore Hill, North London; Eileen as a girl guide; Champion long jumper!

Section Officer Eileen Le Croissette marries Corporal Peter Younghusband at Edgeware, 30th September, 1944.

Peter Younghusband and his Music, 1946.

Mine Hosts at the Duke at Bratton with Clive, 1960.

Christmas preparations at the Duke at Bratton.

Offering the stirrup cup to the Tetcott Hunt.

'Spycatcher' Smith (centre) warns us of the Profumo scandal.

Master Thatcher ridging the Court Farm House.

Raymond Baxter, Lieutenant Colonel Simon West and Eileen at
the Defence Academy, Shrivenham, Wiltshire.

Dr Dennis Le Croissette with the Surveyor space
craft prior to launch.

UNWINDING

During the first four years in our new home, we gradually built up a small catering and consultancy business. We took on only what we wanted to do, leaving some time we hoped for travelling and enjoying other pleasures. Ushers Brewery was sorry to see us leave the Duke as it had meant good business for them. They approached us to act as trouble-shooters for their managed chain of small hotels and inns throughout the West Country. This opened up an interesting sideline. Every month some crisis would occur in one or other of their hotels. They might have to fire a manager at a moment's notice and would need a temporary replacement. There could be a problem through illness or it might be a holiday relief; perhaps the right returns on food and liquor were not being attained. We would often go at a moment's notice and try to resolve some problem. This was interesting to do but also a challenge. We had to be careful not to bring in changes which the locals might not like or become too popular when temporarily replacing a manager. Meanwhile, we would also cater for a few weddings on our home ground.

In 1972, our solicitor, John Hodge, approached us with a proposition. He had a lady client who had died leaving considerable debts. He wanted to sell a small herb-packing business she had formed, trading under the name Susan Strong. Apart from a small amount of stock, there was the promise of regular orders from Fortnum and Mason of London for a gift pack of bouquet garni. We bought this enterprise for £400 and enrolled the help of friends in the village to cut small squares of gingham with pinking shears and pack the mixed herbs in attractive boxes. We then extended the range with marinating herbs, pot herbs and other packs suitable for gifts. This extension to our activities, although small, produced some welcome extra income. I had also some years before joined a fellow ex-WAAF in a small business, importing textiles from China and Spain. Vera Everatt was a great saleswoman and built up a large clientele with agents throughout the company. My contribution was a small amount of capital and the managing of the accounts and VAT returns. It was never very profitable but it did provide a necessary small income for Vera. Our company Younghusband Sales and Development Agency Ltd covered this variety of activities even though the scrap steel sales only lasted three years. Added to this we had made some wise investments so although our income was not enormous, it allowed us to travel abroad at least once a year.

Clive returned from his adventures in America and stayed with us for a few months before his appointment as general manager of the Balalaika Hotel in Sandton, South Africa. Once more, he was on the move.

After the death of my father, we were a little freer to take longer spells away. In May 1971, we visited my brother and Jill his wife in Pasadena, California. Many more were to follow in the years to come. Dennis with his usual generosity took us on trips to San Francisco, Las Vegas and the desert area around Palm Springs. For us the USA was a new world, new ideas, and a new way of living. Some of these I liked. I was not so sure of others. People seemed to move frequently and to make and drop friends and relationships so easily. It was very noticeable that Peter's inherent courtesy was considered as something extraordinary. When a lady entered a room, he immediately stood up. The other people present would invariably remark 'Gee, what a gentleman'!

We returned home after six weeks and took up our routine again. There was always plenty to do. Even if we had no consultancy appointments, the Court Farm House took a lot of maintaining. Built in 1490, there was always some painting or plastering to be done. Peter was great at these jobs. We soon realised that the roof would need re-thatching. This would be an expensive job but as we were a Schedule 2 historic building, we were able to get some financial help from the Historic Building Trust. It took nearly three months to complete the task. Our thatcher was a true craftsman. He would whittle the hazel wood pegs and tie the wheat reed into dollies before placing them on the roof. I had the pleasure of designing the ridging pattern, which finished off the effect. We kept a diary of his activities and it makes interesting reading of an amazingly skilled craft.

The garden covered almost a quarter of an acre and needed a lot of work to maintain. We grew much of our fruit and vegetables and enjoyed entertaining friends to dinner with our produce. Life went on at an even pace. Then late in 1974, my brother phoned and suggested we might consider moving to the States. He went on to say he could obtain the much-prized Green Card for us, through the Fifth Preference – a brother-sister relationship. This would allow us to work there. This was a possibility we had never before considered.

Peter and I discussed it at length and we decided to accept the offer. It was quite a decision to make. We were both in our early fifties by then. Three months later the Green Cards arrived. We had by then passed both interviews and medical exams at the US Embassy in London. We became American Residents. Rather than cut all our ties completely, we decided to rent out the Court Farm House for the time being until we had decided whether we really fitted in with American life. The house was leased for a year to a couple we knew. We left the Susan Strong business to be managed by a friend. Our bags were packed and we set off for Los Angeles.

My brother had an apartment ready and waiting for us in Pasadena. We were starting a new chapter in our life. I immediately researched the possibility of a post in hotel management. Try as I might, I had no success. The Hotel and Catering Institute was not recognised in the States and my exam results were not accepted. In addition, I was a woman and at that time, even in the USA, hotel management was predominantly a male preserve. I would have to think again. Both Peter and I passed our driving tests so at least we were mobile. It was decided that, as Peter was a very good handyman, he and Dennis would invest in a house where we would live. Peter would modernise and spruce it up and then as the market was buoyant, we could sell it for a profit. I could not see Peter fitting in to American work styles, far better he worked on his own and at his own pace. We found a charming house in Sierra Madre, a few miles from Pasadena and moved there. He soon found plenty to keep himself busy. I started looking in the press for catering advertisements. Almost immediately, I found that a company called Marie's Gourmet Catering was looking for a kitchen manager so I applied. Having convinced the owner I was able to manage and had catering experience and, in addition, I could speak Spanish, I was immediately engaged. Most of her staff were Mexicans. They were excellent workers but spoke little English. She had found great difficulty in making them understand her orders and was delighted I could communicate with them! This small concern prepared hors d'oeuvres and starters for both domestic and party use and cooked main courses and desserts for dinner parties. They arranged for waitress service but were only responsible for delivering the food to the venue. They had many clients amongst the film community. I recall going to Loretta Young's house in Hollywood with our products when she was holding a charity dinner. This was a typical engagement. It was an interesting and I imagine profitable operation for the owner, Joan Clarke.

146

Then we had some bad news. The tenants we had left in the Court Farm House left suddenly without paying the last two months rent. We were very concerned as to what to do as we could not leave the house empty and unheated indefinitely and we needed the rent money. We decided we must return to Britain to sort things out and find new tenants. We stayed in Bratton nearly five months trying to decide how best to deal with the problem. During that time, we managed a visit to Clive in South Africa. Our stay coincided with the Soweto riots when many schoolchildren were killed or injured in the homesteads there. The rioting spread and caused damage and injury throughout Johannesburg. Many houses of white families and their business were set on fire. Clive's hotel was the largest area of thatch in South Africa so you can imagine his anxiety. He spent every day and night, together with members of his staff, on watch armed with fire extinguishers. Amazingly, they were not targeted.

Life in South Africa at that time was a very false one. Apartheid caused much distress to the black population. The wives of the white fraternity lived a strange and useless life, mostly spending their time at coffee mornings and lunches with their friends. I found it difficult to accept this way of living. They did no work in the home, having African staff to do everything for them. These workers toiled from early morning until around nine o'clock at night, sleeping in a small hut in the grounds. They were allowed perhaps one day a month when they could leave the house and return to their families. I found the whole atmosphere unpleasant and was more than pleased when the time came to return to Britain.

Very soon, we found a suitable tenant and made certain this time the financial side was under control. We realised we had to return to the States and get on with the experiment of life there. I was still undecided. Having served in the Forces during the war, I was finding it hard to give up the country I had given five years of my life to help defend. I also had concerns about the cost of health care since we did not quality for any assistance and health insurance was very expensive.

Arriving back in California, a friend of Dennis approached me to come and work for him at Radio Shack, owned by the Tandy Corporation. He said 'You know all about radar. You'll soon get the hang of it'! I had never had any experience working in a shop but I decided to give it a go. Before they would employ me, Radio Shack insisted I pass a lie detector test. California State Law forbade this test as part of the requirement for employment but in order to work for Radio Shack, one had to sign a disclaimer and agree to the test. This seemed strange to me but I acquiesced. The test lasted about twenty minutes. A wire was attached to my hands and another to my stomach. I was then asked a series of questions, the reaction to my answers being displayed on a chart in graph form. As I had been self-employed for so many years, many of the questions did not apply and were difficult to answer. One example was 'Have you ever stolen more than $5 from any employer?' I was also asked if I had ever been a prostitute or had taken drugs. I passed the test.

Working at Radio Shack taught me a lot about American business methods, especially their high-pressure retail selling techniques. Gimmicks such as Back to School Offers, Two for the Price of One and many other devices to increase sales, now regular features in Britain, were being used in the States more than thirty years ago. It was interesting to see the effect the film *Roots* had on the Afro-American population. Many of them seemed to acquire a different air when they approached any white salesperson. They became prouder, sometimes even aggressive. This iconic story of an Afro-American seeking the roots of his slave ancestors gave them a confidence and a pride in their antecedents. What was interesting was that as soon as they heard my British accent, they would completely relax and become friendly. They forgot or never knew that many British ships were used to bring the slaves to the Caribbean and on to America. They also failed to realise that the Arabs were the ones responsible for enslaving their ancestors on the west coast and selling them to the traders.

Clive meanwhile was finding life in South Africa far from easy and even dangerous. He wrote and asked if we could get him a Green Card. This was not difficult. As the unmarried child of American residents, he qualified as a Second Preference category. Within eight weeks, he had received the necessary permission to enter and work in the USA. He arrived early in 1977, having travelled from Johannesburg via South America. He stopped in Rio de Janeiro for the Carnival and then he visited Cuzco and the fabled Macchu Pichu. He always said this journey was one of the most memorable he had ever done. Once in the States, with his Savoy credentials, he had no difficulty in finding a job. He was soon appointed to the opening team of the New Otani Hotel in Los Angeles and then later made reservations manager. This was the first venture in the USA of this well-known Japanese Hotel group.

By this time, I was seriously considering whether I wanted to stay in the United States for the rest of my life. I found Los Angeles a city without a heart. The work I was doing was not what I enjoyed. I missed my friends. Peter seemed undecided. He had not been exposed to the American working atmosphere as I had. He was happy for me to decide. I knew that I would be sad not to be near Dennis and, of course, we would miss Clive, but then Clive had always been somewhere else. In retrospect, I often wonder how we would have fared if we had stayed. At least I would have been near my family instead of having no-one close to me as I find now in my later years. Reluctantly, I told Dennis I wanted to return to the UK. I know he was disappointed. He had done a lot to help us settle.

Perhaps if I had gone when I was younger it would have been easier. If I had had a University degree then, it might have been easier to get a position that was more suited to my abilities. Above all, there was the problem of medical care. We could not afford to pay for private medicine at the sky-high prices they asked and at our age, we might fall ill any time. Public health care was well nigh impossible to obtain and if you managed to find it, the quality and conditions were poor. Weighing all these things up, we made our decision. In late 1977, we returned home to the Court Farm House. Fortunately, the last tenant had completed her agreed stay so the house was ours again.

HOME AGAIN

Home again; we picked up the threads of our old life. It was simple on our return to renew our business contacts with the Brewery. Susan Strong continued to prosper and Minifaldas still produced a small income. We resumed our contact with the Welsh Eisteddfod, working with Hamard Catering. For the next two years, we made several trips to Europe, visiting many of our old haunts in Spain and renewing contact with some of our boys from the Duke days. We would take the car and without making any prior bookings, go wherever the mood took us. We managed to live comfortably if not extravagantly. Peter had always seemed fit and well. He continued to enjoy maintaining the house and managed to find opportunities to enjoy his hobbies of fishing and shooting. He spent several weekends fishing on the River Wye and on one occasions caught his heaviest salmon to date, a massive 22 pounder! He was always the driver whenever we did any consultancy jobs. We were a good team.

After a year working at the New Otani Hotel in Los Angeles, Clive was offered his first general management post in the USA. He took over the Hotel Concorde in East Hollywood. It had formerly been a nursing home but recently an Arab family had purchased it and converted it into a luxury hotel. Once he was established there, he suggested we should visit him so in January 1979 we escaped the British winter and renewed our Californian links.

Clive had always taken lame dogs under his care and once again, it happened during our stay. A young Canadian nurse

Clive makes his first parachute
jump over California

arrived, the daughter of a family of Dutch emigrants now in Canada. She had been engaged to work with Kaiser Permanente; a private medical service based nearby and temporarily they booked her into the hotel. Having never left home before, she was very homesick and true to form, Clive decided to look after her. He would bring her to join us if we were having a meal together and obviously was becoming quite attached to her. Our stay lasted three weeks and we managed to see many of the friends we had met in the area previously. It was enjoyable to be a visitor to the USA but I did not regret deciding not to live there permanently.

Back in the UK, we resumed our normal life until one night in February. We had gone to bed as usual but at around two o'clock in the morning, I awoke to hear Peter making some strange sounds. Putting on the light, I could see he was suffering some sort of attack. Frightened, I phoned my doctor to ask his advice. That was in the days when doctors were prepared to come out at night. He arrived within a very short time and immediately summoned an ambulance. Peter was having a heart attack. I was not allowed to go to the hospital with him. I had to sit and wait for news. The hours crawled by until around, 10am, I learned he had been stabilised and I could visit him in the hospital in Bath, about eighteen miles away.

I arrived there an hour later, dreading the verdict. I was told it was a minor heart attack and, with drugs, he should be able to resume a normal life. However, there was one proviso; he was to give up smoking. This proved an enormous problem for Peter. Despite banning him access to them in the hospital, he still managed to cadge the odd cigarette off a friendly cleaner. I was very angry when I was told this and we had the worst argument we had ever had. We rarely argued but on this occasion, I was furious. I had never smoked and found it hard to understand why when one's life depended on it, giving up tobacco was such a problem. On returning home, I telephoned my doctor to ask for advice. Unfortunately, his wife answered. She acted like a guard dog for her husband. I was very worried about Peter and wanted to know how I could help him stop smoking. I was anxious and no doubt agitated. When I told her my worries, she replied 'Go and buy yourself a new hat. That will calm you down!' This only angered me and upset me even more since I never wore hats. In fact, I hated hats and furthermore had never had much interest in fashion. Most of my teenage years had been spent when rationing of clothing was in force or when I was in uniform. Prior to that, my mother had made all my clothes. After the war, clothes coupons were still necessary for some time. By then I was working in a remote country hotel in the wilds of North Devon, far too busy to do anything other than buy what was necessary to appear presentable! How could a doctor's wife be so callous? On his return home, Peter did his best to kick the tobacco habit but I am sure he would still have the odd cigarette when I was not about. He had always rolled his own and I occasionally found a stub of a cigarette in the garden.

Meanwhile Clive had been very worried as he and his father were very close. The two had often fished together and this continued to be their greatest pleasure, despite being a continent apart. Clive must have discussed his anxiety with Liz. She, as a nurse, had apparently used her knowledge to reassure him, explain the treatment and the chances of future attacks. Obviously, she was a comfort to him. He was by then almost 33 years old and perhaps realising it was time to settle down, on his birthday, 27th March, he proposed to her. He had only known her a couple of months. We originally felt she was perhaps not the most suitable wife for him. She was thirteen years younger than he was and unaccustomed to hotel life. However, it was his choice and he seemed very happy. We were pleased that he had found a mate.

They married in the following autumn. Peter by then was feeling fit again so we were able to fly over for the ceremony. This took place in Studio City in the catholic church, a building which had been built and partially subsidised by Bob Hope. We met Liz's parents and one of her three brothers and her sister. The hotel prepared the reception as a wedding present for Clive and many of our American friends as well as Dennis and Jill joined the party. The two newly–weds went off to Tahiti for their honeymoon. A little more than a year later on 4th July 1980, their daughter Tiffany was born, sharing my birthday with me.

The week she was born coincided with Clive being offered the prestigious position of general manager of the Chicago Athletic Association and Men's Club. As he was to be accommodated in the club temporarily, Liz decided to take her new baby back to Canada to her parents whilst Clive looked for a house. This led to a major problem as she was still in the process of obtaining a Green Card, allowing her to stay indefinitely in the States. She had not realised that applicants were not allowed to leave the country until permission had been granted so when she tried to return to Chicago, the US Immigration authorities, based in Toronto, refused her permission to board the aircraft. The baby could have travelled as she was born in the US but not the mother! Clive was distraught but finally a way was found to by-pass the problem. Liz, her mother and the baby booked to go on a shopping trip by bus from Stoney Creek in Canada to Buffalo, just over the American border. Apparently, such trips did not need a visa to enter the States. Clive drove down to Buffalo to meet the bus and his wife and new baby, then they all went back to Chicago and no one was ever the wiser!

The Chicago Athletic Association and Men's Club on the bank of Lake Michigan had existed for over ninety years and was regularly used by visiting presidents and other notabilities. Its members were the elite of Chicago. Clive thoroughly enjoyed the challenge of running this prestigious club and before long, he and his family became part of this fascinating and busy city. We were to have many interesting and enjoyable visits in the next few years to the Club and to our son's new home in Arlington Heights. Clive was to remain there for the next eleven years, bringing in new members and upgrading the restaurants. His greatest achievement was to organise the Centenary celebrations for the club in 1993.

During the next four years, we were able to include visits to other parts of America. One of our most interesting trips consisted of a journey through many different states on a Greyhound bus. This took nine days. We would stop each evening wherever the bus was

Chicago city centre from Sears Tower

155

around six o'clock, find a motel and then continue our journey the following morning. Our fellow travellers would vary from day to day. The first day 'Jesus freaks' tried to convert us to their form of religion, the second day a Native American showed us the beaver skins he was taking to the next big town to trade. Later in the trip, we met a young hippie, returning to his family after spending a year in the Mohave Desert, near Charles Manson and his tribe. Our journey started in Washington and we travelled through Virginia and Kentucky, stopping off at Memphis, Tennessee. Then we followed the Mississippi River to St Louis, Missouri and drove west through the plains of Kansas to Denver in the Rockies. Cheyenne, Wyoming, was our next stop before heading for the Mormon homeland of Utah. We spent some time in Salt Lake City, visiting some of the museums and the Temple there. Then going from the sacred to the sinful, we arrived in Reno and its slot machine culture. Finally, the last lap took us through the Mojave Desert south to Hollywood and Pasadena for a much-needed rest at my brother's home.

On a later occasion, we drove a car through Arizona and Texas to Houston and then on to New Orleans. There we stopped for a special treat for Peter. He had a great love of traditional jazz and he was thrilled at the thought of being able to visit Presentation Hall. This venue in the heart of the old city was home to a group of veteran traditional jazz musicians. Their grandparents, and in some cases parents, had been slaves. We made sure we went to one of their concerts. Each evening jazz enthusiasts would make their way down the back streets of New Orleans to this venue. Seating consisted of horsehair-filled cushions on the floor. The musicians would play continuously for about a couple of hours each evening, obviously loving every minute of it. Several of them were then in their eighties. The group usually consisted of a pianist, a bass player, both a soprano and alto sax player, a trumpeter, a clarinettist and a drummer. One of the sax players had lost his right knee below the knee. He sat playing his instrument, with his part leg jiggling to the tempo. The old man who played the trumpet took a fancy to me and during the interval, presented me with a long silvery chain. We were able to chat to them all and it was obvious they lived for their music. They had an LP for sale and naturally, we bought one. Then as we all left, they came round with an old trilby hat and asked for a dollar apiece! It seemed a very small sum for such wonderful entertainment and I am sure everyone there gave them more than they asked. We certainly did. I still have the chain. It think it is made from stainless steel links but I treasure it for the memory of that wonderful old musician who must have lived through the hardest of times and yet managed to smile and make great music.

I still enjoy my visits to America, especially now going to the area where Dennis and Jill retired in San Diego County. They bought a lovely home in Carlsbad on the Pacific Coastline. This growing city is just beyond the dangerous Californian earthquake zone and the San Andreas Fault. It is a beautiful area and the views of the backcountry range from the far-off San Bernardino Mountains in the north to the Mexican border in the South. Perhaps if we had joined them there, and not in the Los Angeles area, I might have settled better. Looking back, I am not sorry for the experience of living in the USA for those two years. We learned a lot and with the profit Peter shared with Dennis when they sold the house in Sierra Madre, we were not out of pocket. However, I still prefer living in Britain despite all the problems we see around us these days.

LIFE IN THE EIGHTIES

W e returned home and Peter seemed in fine form. We took on as much work as we felt we could do comfortably. Late in 1982, our old friend, Vernon Herbert, contacted us. He had bought the Norfolk Arms at Arundel and had continued to provide all the catering facilities for the Glyndebourne Opera season. During the previous season, he had fallen foul of the newly appointed general administrator. Apparently, when this man was a comparatively unimportant official there, he had had some problems with the catering department. He had remembered this and on taking over was resolved to find alternative caterers. He suggested that the lunchtime meals provided for the staff, the artistes and the orchestra were not suitable and not sufficiently varied. Vernon paid no fee for the privilege of providing the highly profitable meals and wine for the evening audiences. Not all of the audience took picnics in the grounds. Over half of their number ate in one of three dining rooms, named Upper, Middle and Lower Wallop! This was obviously a very profitable business for Vernon. However, to compensate, he agreed to provide all the daily meals for the many singers, dancers, musicians and other workers, during both the months of rehearsals and the performance days, for a minimal fee, just enough to cover the cost of the food. I remember the charge per head to be less than two pounds. Vernon had originally worked closely with John Christie, the founder of the opera and he had been told the contract was his for however long he wished.

The new administrator, however, had other ideas and wanted to put the contract out to tender. By then John Christie had died and his son George had now taken over the operation. Vernon realised he needed to give a new look to the lunchtime facilities. He knew we had been living in American and were accustomed to their type of service and were perhaps more up-to-date with current food preparation. He also realised he had to change his manner of operating. To our surprise, he proposed we took over the management of the lunchtime facilities, introducing something more suitable than the traditional lunch then provided. It was an interesting thought and a new challenge. We visited Glyndebourne to inspect the facilities available and we made a few tentative suggestions for improvement prior to the season starting. From April 1982, we moved into a rented town house in Lewes and worked from there. It was obvious there was a lot to do and barriers to break down.

We decided to get rid of the waitresses who had previously served there. These same girls worked in the evening restaurants and were very much the old school of waitress. They always wore the traditional black uniform with white aprons. We introduced some younger girls, gave them a modern uniform, with bright colours and a new look. We prepared a new type of menu, consisting of grills and fresh fish dishes, supplementing this with a blackboard menu that changed daily. Depending upon the nationality of the artistes performing, we introduced meals from that country. It could be from Italy, Spain, Scandinavia, Greece, the USA or many other countries. We then added an American type salad bar, with nuts, seeds and herbs in addition to all the usual items. We realised that singers did not want a heavy meal before performing and that the dancers would have special needs. We tried to cater for all tastes.

It was a great success. Of course, there were problems. The old waitresses resented losing some of their hours and their tips. The chef and kitchen staff had to learn new ways of preparation and serving.

159

However, the new management approved and George Christie was full of praise. There had been some original query whether the general administrator would accept us prior to our arrival but I managed to solve that by bearding him in his office right at the start. I had always believed the best form of defence was attack so I asked to see him. I entered and said immediately 'I have heard so much about you from Alison Browne'. Alison was a much-loved former member of staff who had recently left to take over a refugee children's home in Sussex. It so happened that her family lived in Bratton and I had prepared the wedding supper for her sister's recent marriage. It was a white lie since I had never discussed the administrator with Alison but I thought it might help to improve the situation. He asked how I knew her and added 'Alison was such a wonderful person, we miss her so.' From that moment, we got on like a house on fire.

Ultimately, he put the catering contract out to tender, as he wanted to get some additional income from the catering operation. Vernon's was one of the final two tenders but he eventually lost out to a large firm who normally did racecourse catering and who had enormous resources behind them. The interesting thing was that at the end of the season, Brian Dickie asked me to join this company and continue working there. However, I felt I could not possibly accept after all the years Vernon had been our good friend. Nevertheless, my season at Glyndebourne was most memorable. Dame Janet Baker performed her last operatic role during that summer. She played Othello in Othello and Euridice. We became friendly during her lunchtime meals and I used to protect her from too much unwanted attention. When she later performed in concert in St David's Hall in Cardiff, her husband contacted me, inviting me to the performance and afterwards he arranged for me to meet her again in her dressing room. She was a great lady and a superb singer.

I also met Maurice Sendak, the American author of the children's' book *Where the Wild Ones Are*. He was the producer with Frank Corsaro of the opera *The Love of Three Oranges*. The other joy of this operatic season was that I had permission to sit in the theatre during rehearsal time and see these wonderful operas being brought to life by such producers as Peter Hall. Added to this, I was able to listen to the music of Simon Rattle and Bernard Haitink conducting the London Philharmonic Orchestra. Despite a lot of work and initial problems, the season at Glyndebourne remains a happy memory.

GOING TO WALES

L ittle did we know it but the year 1983 would bring yet another change of direction for us. In the spring, we were undertaking a holiday relief in Salisbury when we received a phone call from Chris Pollard. He had been approached by a Frenchman who owned a perfume company and who wanted to expand distribution to Great Britain. Chris was living in Wales and had many business interests in the area. His name had been put forward as a possible partner to the French company. We had always kept a close friendship with him and his family since I first met him all those years ago at Hotelympia. He knew I had kept up my French and he suggested that perhaps I might be interested in joining him in this new venture if it got off the ground.

The company named Julian Jill manufactured perfumes based on many of the scents used in the well-known and classic names of the day. They employed a 'nose' who was able to identify the ingredients and blend them to sell at a much cheaper price than the famous names. The selling of the products was by the multilevel marketing method. It begins with main agents in an area who then recruit salespeople under them, each receiving a share of the commission. This is not the same as pyramid selling, which had gained such a bad name, as the agents do not have to purchase any stock before receiving orders. The French company had already recruited two main sellers in Britain, one in Wales and one in Devon. They were building on this base. However, they would need a distribution service working alongside and this was what we were to provide. Together with the

French company, three of us formed Julian Jill (UK) Ltd. We three held 51% of the shares. The intention was that I should take on the role as managing director and work from Bratton, receiving stock there, issuing it to the sales team as they sold. We would buy the perfumes from the French company and be responsible for paying the commission to the sales team, who would pay for their orders as they collected them. This would be in addition to my other activities.

We had no idea how it would grow. As we had a very large garden shed at the Court Farm House, there was ample room initially for storage from where we despatched the orders. I was able to manage the accountancy system and commission quite easily. Within a year, the business built up well and we made a net profit of around £32,000. It seemed to be growing rapidly and the sales team was expanding. Near the end of the year, Chris Pollard suggested that perhaps it would be a good idea to transfer the warehousing to Barry in South Wales, where the local Welsh Development Agency was encouraging new businesses by offering cut-price terms for the first year rental of warehouse facilities. My garden shed was getting too small for the volume of deliveries arriving so we seriously considered the idea.

We knew the area well since for several years we had spent Christmas there with the Pollard family. At the same time, we were finding the maintenance of the Court Farm House, due to its age and construction, an onerous and ever-ongoing task. Since Peter's heart attack, he was not able to undertake the many maintenance tasks he had usually done and we had found the cost of repairs mounting. We finally decided to take up the offer of warehousing in Wales. We immediately put our house on the market, with a view to moving to the Penarth area in South Wales. As soon as the storage facilities were in place, whilst we were selling the house, it necessitated our spending three days a week there. We were able to stay with the

Pollards for the time being. Finally, we sold our beloved Court Farm House in May 1984. It was a sad day for us both. I walked round the house touching the beams and the old doors. I went into the bedroom Clive had used and found myself crying. Peter walked round his garden that he had brought to life so wonderfully and said goodbye to his trees and his flowerbeds. Then we drove off.

We were not to find a suitable new home until some months later and temporarily had to rent a small house from a friend. It was necessary to get the business operating swiftly. We employed a warehouseman for the depot and he did all the packaging and posting that we had done in the past. We ran sessions for the growing sales team to encourage them to extend their leads. I continued to run the office and make regular stock checks. Having learned from my hotel days the importance of watching profit margins, I produced a monthly profit and loss account so we were able to monitor our progress. Obviously, there were many more expenses operating in Wales rather than working from home so this was an essential task. Sales would have to continue to increase in line with the additional expenses.

All seemed to be going well. We took a group of the sales team over to Marseille, visiting Grasse, the centre of the perfume trade, to help them understand the process and to encourage them to expand their sales. This trip was both exciting and educative. We saw the whole process from the way the 'nose' analysed the notes of the perfume and then created the recipe to produce it. We saw the fields of flowers growing on the slopes of the hills, which provided many of the basic perfumes. We watched the bottling process and the packaging and came home, decidedly more knowledgeable and more enthusiastic.

By July 1984, we were able to move into our new home. We had first seen it at Easter time in the coastal village of Sully on the outskirts of Penarth. Built in 1978, it was a complete change from the Court Farm House. The garden was considerably smaller. The modern house had large windows with wonderful views to the rear. On a clear day it was possible to see the Brecon Beacons due north of us. Looking to the northeast we caught a glimpse of the hills around Caerphilly and from the front windows, the Bristol Channel could be seen between the trees. The up-to-date kitchen led to an area where I established my office. We had four good-sized bedrooms, ready to welcome anyone who cared to visit. The dining room was joined to the sitting room by a large arch and was ideal for entertaining. We were happy with our choice. We called it 'Picquets' after the hill in Bratton where King Alfred defeated Guthrum the Dane.

In March of that year, Arthur Scargill of the National Union of Miners had confronted the Conservative government under Margaret Thatcher, bringing his members out on strike on 12th March. Initially the Welsh miners were loath to take part, as they had not received universal support from fellow miners on a previous strike. However, finally, they joined in and the business situation in Wales changed. We found the girls selling the perfume were becoming less motivated, the potential purchasers less willing to buy. Trade generally slowed down. This was disastrous to us with our increased expenses of the warehouse operation. By September, I could see the previous year's profits swiftly disappearing. We called a council of war. Alain Ouaki, our French partner, was becoming disillusioned with the British operation. I too was most disappointed especially having built up the trade so successfully during the first year and a half. Before all the profit was gone, we jointly decided to close down the operation. We paid all the commission due and any outstanding accounts. We returned the remaining stock to France for credit. However, we lost out on all the tax and duties already paid on its importation. By the end of January 1985, the company went in to voluntary liquidation and all debts were paid. We felt very bitter at the wasted effort.

The whole business was sabotaged by the strike, resulting in negative attitudes in both agents and customers. We were not the only sufferers. Many small businesses like ours had to close down at this time. What was particularly upsetting was the fact that the Julian Jill distribution business in Germany, started at the same time as ours, was flourishing with the current buoyant state of that country's economy. I was particularly upset, as I did not like being associated with any type of failure. What I did not realise was quite how much it had affected Peter. He had worked hard to support me in every way possible and he was equally upset to see the business having to close, after we had all made such efforts to succeed. He never showed his distress but it must have been eating away inside him. His nature was quite different from mine. He kept his feelings hidden and would never talk things out. On 3rd February 1985, Peter celebrated his 65th birthday and drew his government pension, for which he had contributed for forty-four years. I wished him many more years of happiness and especially more opportunities to indulge in his favourite sports of shooting and game fishing. That spring, we decided to re-plan our lives and take more time to enjoy ourselves after a lifetime of working.

In April, we spent a weekend with some old friends in Cirencester. We had met Squadron Leader Bob Hill when we were working at the Goddard Arms at Swindon. He was then president of the officers' mess and regularly piloting a transport plane out of RAF Lyneham. We had often organised functions for his fellow officers at the hotel. We became friendly and now that he had retired, we frequently visited each other. On the Sunday morning of our visit, Peter and Bob had gone to his sailing club to paint his dinghy. It had meant carrying the boat out of the boathouse and turning it over. It was quite heavy and the two had a hard job managing it. However, they returned apparently unaffected by the effort. We drove home that evening via the M4, in time to watch the final of the World Snooker Championship. This match (between Dennis Taylor and Steve Davies) remains a classic to this day. It was a marathon. Peter had been looking forward to the final all the week. We had a light supper and Peter got himself his usual pint of beer from the keg we kept in the garage. He had always been a beer drinker and it was an essential part of his diet! The match started and it grew more and more exciting as each player seemed to match score for score. It was within the last few minutes as the vital shots were being played that I became aware that Peter seemed to be snoring or at least breathing in a very strange way. I went over to him and said 'Wake up; it's the most exciting bit of all!' He did not respond so I touched his face and his tongue fell out. Something terrible was happening. I realised then it must be another heart attack.

This was the weekend in Wales when all the ambulances were on strike so I knew there would be no response from a 999 call. I also remembered that one had to keep the brain alive with oxygen and the first four minutes were vital. I had no real experience of what to do. I grabbed the phone and rang the first number I could remember; it was Chris and Vivien Pollard's. I yelled, 'Get our doctor to come at once, Peter is having a heart attack'. I rushed back to Peter; I could not move him from his chair so I tipped his head back and tried to breathe into his mouth. As I did so, I felt the air coming back out. I thought that meant he was breathing again but then I noticed his lips were turning blue. I really had no idea what else I should do. I had opened the door in anticipation and first the Pollards arrived, followed quickly by the doctor. I suppose only fifteen minutes had elapsed by then but it seemed an eternity as I waited. The doctor went straight to Peter, examined him and shook his head. Then he did something I will never forget. He gave me the thumbs down sign.

167

I am sure he did not realise that he had performed this inappropriate gesture. I will never forget it. I know he was desperately upset because not only was he our doctor but we had known him and been friends for several years before moving to Wales, meeting each year at the Boxing Day party at the Pollards' house. I stood by Peter's side in shock. They led me away to the kitchen. I insisted I must phone Clive. It was 12.30am our time and 6.30pm in Chicago. Clive was having a barbecue in his garden when I had to tell him the terrible news. I cannot remember much after that.

I still wonder if the exertion in hauling the boat in Cirencester had caused this terrible thing to happen or was it the disappointment at the closure of Julian Jill that had triggered this second and final attack. Ever since, I have thought it could have occurred during our return journey from Cirencester, on the M4. An even greater tragedy might have happened. At least Peter was at home and enjoying a happy moment.

Someone phoned the funeral directors and Peter was taken away. I never saw him again. I only wanted to remember him as he was when he was living. Vivien took me back to their house where I stayed for a couple of nights. I remember insisting on phoning everyone I should. Especially, I remember phoning Downside Abbey. Peter had been brought up as a Catholic and we had become good friends with two of the monks at the Abbey, Father Benet and Father Theodore. They had been great gastronomes and splendid wine bibbers, frequently visiting the restaurant at the Duke. Father Theodore had died a year before but we were still in touch with his colleague. The phone was answered by the Prior. I told him I would like Father Benet to take part in the funeral service for Peter. He did not answer me for a while. I wondered if he had heard my question. 'This is not possible,' he replied finally; 'Father Benet has had a brain seizure and now has only occasional moments of consciousnesses.' He went on to say

168

our friend was, at that moment, receiving the last rites. This was an added blow.

Clive managed to book immediate emergency bereavement flights and he, Liz and Tiffany arrived within 48 hours. He helped me get through the funeral service, first at the church and then at the crematorium. I can still see him touching his father's coffin as it passed him in the chapel. So many friends came to the service that day – people from far away and from all parts of our lives. Many of them said to me 'Peter was always a perfect gentleman'. He would offer help whenever it was needed. He would always back me up in whatever I did.

Chris and Vivien Pollard, with their customary generosity, offered to provide a reception after the service. It was a time to meet with many old friends, who offered comfort and help to Clive and myself. Clive was to stay only a few more days, since Liz, his wife, announced she wanted to go to Holland. She came from a Dutch family who had emigrated to Canada when she was only eight. Now seventeen years later, she felt as she was back in Europe, she must visit her relations in Hertogenbosch. It was so soon after the funeral and I did not want to be left alone so I asked Clive if I could come with them. Of course, he agreed. He drove my car and we had a pleasant journey to this old Dutch town. Liz's aunt and uncle were most hospitable to us all and made us very welcome. Tiffany was able to meet her great aunt and uncle, and some of her Dutch second cousins. I too formed a friendship with this family, which continued for many years until the death of both Ria and Jacques Houdijk.

I knew Clive would soon have to return to Chicago However there was one thought that helped me accept his departure. The previous autumn for our ruby wedding anniversary on 30th September, we had decided to escape the problems of Julian Jill and visit Clive in Chicago. This would be the last time he would see his father. They had always been such companions. Peter had taught Clive to shoot from the age of fourteen and they had spent many happy days together, fishing for trout or for salmon. This was what prompted Clive to ask me if we could put Peter's ashes in the River Wye where they had spent so many hours together. I agreed and we arrived at Green Bank where Peter had caught his first salmon; Clive gently spread his father's ashes on the quiet flowing waters of the river. We watched them being carried towards the sea. The following day I said goodbye to my son and his family. Now I really was alone.

IN MEMORIAM

They have told me, they have told me
You are gone, there is no more.
Stop the sorrow, and the weeping
Life is only here and now.

Yet I can see you in the garden
Where the lawns are neat and trim,
Where the tiny seeds were planted
Hoping for the flowers to come.

I can hear you in the music,
Music that you made your own,
In the singing, in the trumpets,
In the vibrancy of drums.

I can touch you by the river
Where the mayflies court and dance,
Where the hungry trout are rising,
Quiet at the daytime's close.

I can smell the nearness of you
As they burn the autumn leaves
And in the hayfields' summer drying,
In the rose's soft perfume.

I can feel you still beside me
As the night-time shrouds the sky,
While the sleeping yet eludes me
And the hours are dragging by.

Why then do they tell me, tell me
You are gone, there is no more?

TRAVELLING SOLO

After forty years of marriage, thirty-six of which Peter and I had spent working together as a team, the thought of facing an unknown future alone was hard to contemplate. I am a gregarious creature. I was now in a large house that seemed so empty, no conversation, no one to prepare special meals for, no one with whom I could discuss the news of the day or share the pleasures of the garden. At night, I would lie awake for hours, remembering the good times, the difficult problems we had surmounted together, the hardships and the successes. I thought how loyal Peter had always been, backing my every effort and providing the solid reliable support throughout our life together. I realised I had not always appreciated that and how much I would miss him. I knew too that I would have to find the inner strength to continue. I was in a new area of Britain, a Wales that was breaking away from England. I knew few people here and my close family were all living in the United States, miles away and on a different time zone.

I had to get on with my life. First, I had to get used to driving the car for longer distances. I had passed my driving test in 1948 in Devon but since then, Peter had been the driver for all our long trips, I had only driven locally. I had to get used to motorway traffic, as it was impossible to leave Wales without driving on the M4. I decided my first solo trip would be a visit to my oldest school friend, Doreen Hide in Overton, Hampshire. That was completed without any problems. Next, I went further afield and visited Vernon Herbert and his wife in Ringmer, Sussex. Although they had retired from the catering concession at Glyndebourne, they still had many contacts there. As a special surprise, they took me to a performance of a Richard Strauss opera. This was a delight and a complete change from only hearing the music relayed to the office, as we did when working there a couple of years before. I then travelled on to Peter's cousin Beau in West Hoathly. Later I went back to Bratton to renew old friendships there from our Duke days and look again at my beloved Court Farm House. All of this was nostalgia for the past but at the same time, I was gradually gaining more confidence in my driving.

I began preparing special meals again and having friends to stay. Together we would explore South Wales. I even managed to celebrate my birthday on 4th July with a barbecue, inviting the many people who had helped me through the last three months. Then the matter of obtaining probate of the will arose to get my finances in order. My solicitor in Wiltshire knew things were straightforward and he suggested I should complete the process myself. He said 'You are quite capable of sorting out the paper work – so get on with it'! This I did and found it comparatively simple.

Summer was coming to a close. Taking advantage of some fine weather, I decided to visit my WAAF friend in Totnes. Kay Tanner, known as Willi, had been my Watch Leader at Fighter Command and someone I admired tremendously. She was a great officer and everyone respected her. She had overcome so many difficulties in her life – abandoned by her mother when very young and brought up by a so-called uncle in Malvern. On her sixteenth birthday, her guardian announced her mother was arriving that afternoon. This was the day when she had to decide whether she was going to live with her mother and stepfather for the future or stay with his family. He threatened her that if she chose to leave, he would never give her another penny. She would have to make her decision within a few hours. This was difficult, as she had not met her mother since she was an infant. This 'uncle' must have been an unpleasant man. As he gave her this ultimatum, he looked out of the window of the hotel he owned and pointed below to a passing 'rag and bone' man and wife, in their horse and cart, overflowing with scrap metal. 'That could be your mother for all you know' he said.

Her mother finally arrived. She greeting Kay warmly and seemed charming. Meeting her after so many years, Kay was forced to make a swift decision. Her mother and stepfather seemed pleased to see her and anxious to get to know her after all this time. They offered her a home with them in Sussex. Life had never been all that happy in Malvern. She had always felt an outsider in that family. She made the decision to go to live with her mother. She moved to Birdham where her mother was running a hotel. Sadly, this relationship was never a happy one. Within a year, Kay had taken a job in London and supplemented her small salary at John Lewis's by acting as a life model at the Slade. The final break came when her mother decided to tell her, years later on her wedding day, that this 'uncle' was really her father. Her mother phoned her on the night before her wedding 'I have to tell you, you are illegitimate and that was your father who brought you up, not your uncle. But you *were* conceived in Claridges and born in the London Clinic.'

Later Kay had married her stepfather's brother, a man much older than her. She always seemed to be attracted to older men, perhaps because she needed a father figure. Subsequently, she lost her only child at birth, strangled by its own cord. Her marriage sadly was not a success. Despite being an ex-naval officer, her husband Eric was idle and somewhat of a waster, dragging her into debt. Eventually he got a job as an entertainment officer on a cruise ship going to Australia. He made several voyages and then he became involved with another woman over there and never came back. She never knew to the end of her life whether he was still alive but she still never divorced him. Kay's WAAF service record was impeccable however. She was sent in 1944 to Colombo to open up a Filter Room and later became personal assistant to Air Vice-Marshall Goddard, who was Commander in Chief of the Air Force in the Far East. She was the first British woman to enter French Indo-China after the Japanese army left. Few people experience a life of such sadness, yet despite this, are capable of performing such a life of service to her country. She managed to overcome all her difficulties and at the time of my visit, was serving as a volunteer with the Samaritans. Her own experiences gave her a special ability to understand other people's problems. The times I spent with her were always inspiring.

These visits to friends gave me no time to feel too lonely during that first year. I seemed to be in overdrive. I was told that in the first year of widowhood, I would get a lot of support and I did. However, I was also warned that I must be prepared for it to tail off after the first twelve months. This advice encouraged me to join a yoga class. I thought it might increase my independence. I found the discipline of the exercises and the practice of meditation to be a calming influence. It brought back memories of the first time I experienced the art of meditation at the International Guide Camp, in a field in France, on the slopes of Mont Blanc when I was only fifteen years old.

By now, I had decided to relinquish my partnership with Vera Everatt in Minifaldas. Her husband had joined us during my stay in the USA. Since he was an accountant, he had taken over most of the work I had been doing. Vera did all the purchasing and selling and organised the manufacturing of the linen goods we were now marketing. I felt they should have the benefit of the meagre profits we made. We had suffered a serious problem whilst I was living in California. The purchasing officer of Chinese table linen that Vera had found in Hong Kong was, unknown to us, importing the linen goods illegally from China. At that time, Chinese products could not be imported into Great Britain. The agent had stated on his invoice that the goods were made in Macao but unknown to us, in reality, they had come from China and smuggled over the border into this Portuguese enclave. This led to us having a major confrontation with Custom and Excise officials and we were forced to pay a large fine. As I had little to do with the organisation these days, I felt it time to retire gracefully.

I subsequently agreed to take on a holiday relief management at the George Hotel, Grantham to allow two old friends of mine to visit their family members, spread around the globe. As usual, something unforeseen always happens in hotel life. On this occasion, we intercepted a phone call by sheer chance between a resident and a fellow conspirator. The assistant manager and I came to the conclusion that they were planning a fraudulent deal of some sort. We notified the police and they followed it up. It turned out to be something they had been investigating for months without success. We were heroes! I do not believe that the public realise how frequently hotel managers are able to help the police to uncover criminal activities

Meanwhile the demand for Susan Strong products continued to increase. I extended the range of products to include marinating herbs and potherbs. My WAAF friend, Vera Everatt, regularly took a stand at gift fairs in the Home Counties, selling the imports and other goods from Minifaldas. She agreed to include the herb range in her activities. I was not making a fortune but at least managing to cope both financially and psychologically.

It was now autumn; I had survived so far. Then came a delightful surprise. I received a phone call from the small island of Gozo, one of the Maltese group. 'Charles Minardi here, pack your bags and come and visit me next week. It will do you good!' Charles, a gay bachelor, had worked over many years with me at the Hotel and Catering Exhibition at Olympia. We had served together on the committee

176

of the Junior Salon Culinaire both as members and as judges. The Committee of the Cookery and Food Society organised the many cookery competitions for both hot and cold dishes, in which young students in the various catering colleges in Britain took part during the biennial Hotelympia exhibition.

Charles thought I could do with a break. How right he was! I booked a flight for the end of September from Heathrow and flew to Luqa in Malta. I had once spent a holiday in Malta and although I found its history interesting, with the many invasions it had suffered and its mixed cultures, I had never felt a great urge to return. However, whilst there, I learned one very interesting fact about this island. It was formed almost entirely of solid rock with very little soil. In order to grow crops, soil had been imported from Italy many generations before. Consequently, the Maltese government passed a law that when a dwelling was built on agricultural land, the soil must first be removed and then transferred to another area of bare rock, as it was such a valuable commodity. This ensured that there was always land to cultivate.

I was interested to see what Gozo had to offer. Charles met me at the airport on Malta and we travelled to the port, taking the ferry to Marsalforn. The sea trip took about an hour, passing on the way the small third island of Comino famous for the cumin spice grown there. Arriving at our final destination at Xlendi where he had his home, I could see that many of the buildings were constructed from sandstone, giving a honeyed tone to the town. Charles lived in an old three-storied house, built on the cliff overlooking the fjord-like bay of this small town. The scenery of Gozo appeared quite different from that of Malta. Its foliage was greener and more lush, with many hills and deep valleys as well as rugged cliffs. Its farmers grew many different vegetables, especially tomatoes and beans. In addition, there were vineyards, providing some reasonable local wine. The island was still unspoiled by tourists and life was tranquil. At that time, things moved at a leisurely pace, revolving around farming and fishing. The local markets sold homegrown food and the island produced many textiles. It was still living in the past but offered a wonderful atmosphere in which I could relax and find myself. I had a room on the third floor, overlooking the bay. As I awoke each morning, I could see the fishermen packing the fish they had caught in the early hours into baskets ready to sell on the quayside. Already there were locals waiting on the beach, anxious to get first pick of the day's catch.

Charles was an expert cook and fed me most delicious meals. One day we visited a nearby village where we found all the available men rebuilding their church. They were constructing a much grander one around the old edifice. When it was completed, they would dismantle the old building and remove the debris. They were using enormous blocks of sandstone, cutting them with saws to shape the blocks. Their craftsmanship was outstanding. The dome of the church when finished would be one of the largest in the world. The money for this great feat had been contributed by the women of the village, saved over the years by selling eggs from the chickens every household kept. The islanders were fervent Catholics and their churches were full for every service.

My stay on this small island will remain in my memory as a special occasion, both for the kindness shown to me by Charles and the fortitude of these island dwellers. One special experience will always stay with me. Looking out of my bedroom window one early evening, a dozen swifts flew past at eye level. I watched them settle amongst the stones in a nearby field. I realised this could be the winter destination of our own summer swifts who had been gathering on the telephone wires as I left Wales. About ten minutes later, an enormous flight of more birds followed exactly the same

178

path as before and came to rest in the same field as the 'pathfinders'. Then a further half hour later, the tail-enders arrived. I imagined they were perhaps this year's fledglings. I marvelled at the ability of these small birds to follow the same route as the rest and arrive safely at their destination.

I returned home, feeling more able to face the future. That winter, I enrolled in an Italian class and another in Chinese cookery, which kept me occupied two evenings a week. I did not manage to learn much Italian unfortunately, as the teacher was not only not very good at teaching a class of adults but also had such a strong Scottish accent, that the Italian we were able to speak after a term or two was almost unintelligible! I fared better with the Chinese cookery. Meeting people in the area and making new friends encouraged me to make plans to spend Christmas with my family in the USA. Travelling there for the first time alone would need a great effort, especially as I would be going to Chicago as well as California. However, I knew that I needed to see them all. I decided I would spend Christmas with Clive and then travel on to visit Dennis and Jill, by then retired to Carlsbad in San Diego County. I made the bookings.

PICKING UP THE THREADS

Setting off in mid-December, I was a little apprehensive and sad. I remembered all the travelling Peter and I had done together in the past, the interesting and happy times we had spent in so many places around the world. The first leg of the journey to Chicago via Atlanta went well but then there were problems. The connecting flight was cancelled due to a heavy snowstorm and it was four hours before a replacement flight arrived. Finally, I arrived at O'Hare airport only to find there was no Clive to meet me. He had been checking on the flight arrivals and mistakenly was given an incorrect time for my revised flight. In desperation, after waiting for an hour, I finally had to persuade an airline official to phone Clive at his office to tell him I was waiting. He could tell I was upset. He insisted that they made certain I was looked after and taken to the VIP Lounge to wait for him. By then I was very tired and tearful. However, after a reviving brandy and a further half-hour wait, I met up with my son, only for us to find my luggage had been lost in transit. This finally turned up two days later.

The winter weather in Chicago is freezing. Regular snowfalls make driving hazardous. When the wind from the North blows over Lake Michigan, the temperature can drop to twenty degrees below zero with the wind chill factor. No one stays outside for very long. I certainly did not. However, it was good to see Clive and Tiffany again. Tiffany had started school and was lively and entertaining. We celebrated a traditional Christmas, my first one with my granddaughter. Then early in the new year, I flew to San Diego. This time the journey went well and before long, I was enjoying the Californian sunshine and a comfortable 72 degrees Fahrenheit. Seeing my family again recharged my batteries.

One evening during my stay with my brother, he said, 'You're used to looking after people – after all those years running hotels. Why don't you write to the *Los Angeles Times* travel editor, Jerry Hulse, and say you would be happy to show visitors coming to Britain some of the beautiful and interesting corners of Wales?' There and then, I sat down and composed a letter. To my amazement, Jerry Hulse quoted it verbatim in his next Sunday column in that widely–read newspaper. He mentioned both my address and that of Dennis. Before I returned home, I had received eighty enquiries and a further thirty were waiting for me on my return to Wales. They arrived from many different states as this travel column was syndicated to other newspapers. I was overwhelmed at the response. I answered them all. I quoted a price for accommodation and meals whilst offering escorted tours in my car or acting as a guide in the visitors' rented vehicles. American visitors, I knew, planned whistle-stop tours whenever they came to Europe, cramming as much as possible in a two-week trip. And so it turned out. Most wanted a three-day stopover in Wales, en route for a visit to find their long-lost relations in Ireland or perhaps to trace their clan in Scotland.

That first summer of 1986, I arranged to accommodate twelve sets of visitors. This kept me busy from May to September, planning the routes, arranging visits to special centres and working out the meals I would give them. I had suggested there would be one gourmet evening meal during their visit. Getting out my numerous cookbooks, I would produce something spectacular for my guests. This kept my cooking skills up-to-date. It all worked successfully. Every arrival was a surprise and a guessing game. I had no idea who my next guests would be. They came from all over America, many born outside the States including several whose parents had emigrated there after the last war, from war-ravished countries. The visitors ranged from a couple of elderly academics, wanting to see the museums and the churches, to four young girls who wanted to get to know the youth scene in Cardiff. There was a particularly obnoxious party of two very 'nouveau riche' scrap dealers together with their daughter and her maitre d' husband. This group arrived equipped with one of the then new video recorders, an enormous machine that the husband had permanently hoisted on his shoulder. They were the most embarrassing of my guests. I took them to Llantwit Major, a nearby village that was celebrating their annual Victorian weekend. On arrival there, we had to jettison the car and drive around in a pony and trap. When we alighted in the middle of the village, my four guests made a beeline for the mayor and mayoress, elegant in their robes of office, who were mixing with the crowds. Of course there had to be a photo of them all together and an onlooker had to be instructed how to use the video recorder. My party exclaimed in very loud voices at everything they saw 'Gee, ain't she cute!' Or 'Can you believe that!' The final straw was when we passed the local butcher's shop, which had several chalked notices on the window. When my visitors saw the sign FAGGOTS FOR SALE, their highly audible comments were unprintable.

Fortunately the next group to arrive was a mother and daughter of a much more quiet and placid disposition. On the whole, most visitors were easy to get on with and seemed to enjoy living in a private home. They had the advantage of meeting my friends and seeing parts of Wales, which formal tours never visited. At the end of the first season of hosting American visitors, I realised that all these activities had helped restore me to an active life. I knew that I would have to fight loneliness which, after a busy career in the community, would be difficult to cope with. However, I was feeling more able to face the future. My confidence was restored.

That year of 1986 was memorable for the three large catering events I undertook. This would be the first time without Peter; we had always worked as a team. I attended my eighth Welsh Eisteddfod, now working for the new contractor, Carter Catering. Robert Carter had taken over the outside catering division from the Pollards' company Hamard when they sold their management services group to Grand Metropolitan Hotels. I also worked with Robert at the Aldershot Army Show in June of that year and then later when he obtained the catering concession for the American company, General Electric, at the prestigious Farnborough Air Show in September. This was an important hospitality operation run on American lines and I was appointed manager in charge. My previous USA experience with Marie's Gourmet Catering in Pasadena came in very useful.

It was a difficult assignment. The majority of my team of Welsh part-time kitchen assistants and waitresses had no idea of American eating habits or what was required for business hospitality purposes; so important to this major USA company. It was a steep learning curve for them and a hard teaching experience for me. The menu preferences were very different, as were the time meals were required. Americans are accustomed to taking early lunches from 11.30am. The company's managers were very demanding. Of course, they had every right to be since they were the paymasters but I admit it was one of the most difficult management posts I had ever undertaken. However, it must have been successful since on the strength of my efforts there, the American company asked me to take on the organisation for the company's operation at the Paris Air Show four weeks later. I had to refuse as I was already scheduled to entertain a group of Americans in my home at that time. I was not sorry, as I would have had to drive myself around Paris and set up the operation beforehand. I was not sure that I would have been able to face that, knowing the Paris traffic!

Despite all this activity, I managed to fit in a Mallocan holiday with the Pollard family in their senorial house in Palma. They had turned it into a bijou hotel. Its situation in the older part of this lovely city was ideal. The terrace overlooked the garden of the bishop's house and nearby was the beautiful cathedral. Only a short walk away was the busy port and the city centre. Mallorca is much maligned. Other than a few of the coastal resorts, beloved of the mass tourist trade, this lovely island is a beautiful place. Its varied countryside of mountains and small bays offers a great variety of scenery. Palma, its capital city, is one of the most unspoiled in Europe.

MALLORCAN SCENE

The breeze stirs.
Almond blossoms like confetti
Fall upon the warm earth.
Around the trees
The lime green oxalis grows,
 Its shamrock leaves
Framing sun-awakened blooms.
Dry stone walls edge the terraced slopes.
Since ancient conquerors tamed this land.
They made the island bloom, then
In turn, themselves became the conquered.
The jagged coastline, frilled with endless coves,
Courts the flirting sea.
Whilst through the grey Aleppo pines
The setting sun tinges the mottled waves.

Christmas again saw me travelling to Chicago, followed by a New Year visit to California. That is when my brother and I started investing in US old gold dollar and half dollar coins. The market was very good for a while and the investment sound. This changed when the government issued a new ruling on coinage and we were lucky to get out without too great a loss.

My sister-in-law, Jill, after a strictly academic life in library science was now retired. She had taken up seriously a new hobby in textile art. After batik and silkscreen printing, she was now concentrating on art quilting. In her early days in Australia, she had learned to sew and this had always been a favourite pastime. Now she was applying this to art. During my stay in Carlsbad, although no seamstress, I joined her in attending her quilting club and we went to several excellent exhibitions. I was amazed how popular this hobby was. Over three million adherents belong to quilting groups in the USA. It is an enormous sub-culture, producing items ranging from bed quilts in traditional designs to abstract wall hangings. Other quilters concentrate on making clothing including skirts, waistcoats, bags and even hats. It surprised me to learn that the price for some of the speciality wall hangings could range from $1,000 to $5,000.

Spending January and February in the mild weather in San Diego County is a great way to get rid of the winter blues. By March, I was home in the UK, ready to face whatever 1987 would bring. Of course, I missed Peter but I was making a life on my own. By then in my sixty-seventh year, I did not need to fill it with too much work but I would continue welcoming several more American visitors during the summer months for a further two years, gradually reducing the number of guests I accepted. I was becoming accustomed to my solo life. I found other ways of spending my time but I enjoyed the challenge of making sure my guests enjoyed themselves and learned as much as possible about Wales whilst they were with me. Some of these visitors remain friends to this day and each Christmas I receive their traditional newsletters telling me of their doings and their travels to other more exotic destinations.

Later that year I decided to join a few classes to polish up my French, anything to keep my brain working. I even joined a painting group. This was a revelation. I had never had the opportunity to attempt any form of art since I had been in a fast stream at grammar school that did not have time for such extras. Suddenly after all these years, I found that I could draw, left-handed of course. I did most things with my left hand; cutting, stirring, gardening, everything except writing. The story goes that if left-handed people are forced to write with their right hand, it would destroy their confidence. I never found this and cannot remember being pressed to change hands when I was a child, learning to write. In fact, I consider that if one writes with the left hand, it is easier to write mirror writing. I am adept at that! Learning to draw and paint with watercolours was amazing. It opened a whole new world, as well as acting as a wonderful therapy. I could lose myself for hours and forget the sadness. I will never be a Monet or a Goya but I have produced several paintings, fit for *my* walls at least!

Despite all the activities, the weekends were always the worst times. They still are. With my son and his family as well as my brother so far away in the USA, I dreaded Saturday and Sunday. I would see all my neighbours going out together with their children or I would hear them in the garden laughing and enjoying a drink together. These were the difficult days. I had only been in Wales for a short time and all my old friends were so far away. I decided it was time I indulged in some beneficial exercise as I was spending a lot of time in the car. I enrolled in a health spa located in a Trust House Forte hotel in the east of Cardiff. I enjoyed the exercise and especially the chance of an invigorating swim in their pool. This led to a brief dalliance with a fellow exerciser. It started with a coffee together and went on from there. It did my ego good to attract the interest of a younger man at my advanced age but this was a brief interlude as I soon found him both boring and self-obsessed as well as being married, although on the verge of divorce.

Very soon afterwards, an old acquaintance, from our days at the West Country Inn at Hartland, surfaced. We had originally met when he arrived with his Territorial Army unit for their regimental dinner. Our paths had crossed intermittently since then, as he was also involved in the hotel industry. He had seen the notice of Peter's death in the *Daily Telegraph* and had telephoned with his condolences. We met subsequently for lunch during which he surprised me by saying 'If I had not done what I did, or had done what I failed to do, you would have had a broken marriage.' This made no sense to me. Then he explained. His regiment had taken part in one of the Lord Mayor Show's parades years ago and both Peter and I had been invited by the regiment's colonel to come as their guest to watch the procession. This was during our time at the West Country Inn. Only one of us could leave the hotel so I was the one chosen to go. I was then persuaded to spend the weekend at the home of the colonel who organised a riotous dinner party for his fellow officers and consorts. It appears that after over-imbibing, this man had decided to come to my bedroom after I had retired. He had entered the room and approached my bed, he said, with amorous intent, and then had second thoughts and retired smartly!

When he related this incident to me, he asked, 'Surely you remember me coming into your room.' I thought back and then vaguely remembered hearing the door open all those years ago, someone come in and then leave again. I replied, 'I do just remember, I thought it was someone so drunk they had forgotten which room they were in!, At the time of this meeting, he was about twelve years older than I was but obviously still very fit. I laughed and thought no more of it.

He lived on the south coast. He had told me he had friends in the north of Wales and visited them every autumn. Subsequently he phoned and asked if he could call in on his way north. I agreed and suggested perhaps as it was a long journey, he might like to stay the night. All went well. He was entertaining company, we had an enjoyable dinner and reminisced on hotel life and the next morning he went on his way. This happened for two or three years. I always imagined he had a lady friend somewhere on the North Wales coast as he constantly referred to 'Josie'. However, as time went by, it became obvious he wanted more than an evening meal and b and b! It became quite difficult to ward him off. Then the following year, he wrote to me, inviting himself to stay and saying there was no need for him to have a separate bedroom! By then he was over eighty and I was more than surprised. On receipt of the letter, I immediately dismantled the other bed in my room, taking the legs off and hiding the mattress. On his arrival, I made it abundantly clear that I was not interested in his suggestion and that our friendship was purely platonic. That was his last visit although I still do get a birthday card!

The whole thing made me realise that the sexual urge may remain until very late in some lives. I felt sympathy for him and others like him. This sentiment encouraged me to write a poem entitled 'The Widower'. I have written poetry all my life, mostly after experiencing strong emotions or unusual incidents. This poem has proved to be one of my best and in 2007, United Press chose it for inclusion in their anthology for that year. Few people realise why I wrote it but I am sure there are those who can understand the emotion.

Thinking back on my own sexual experiences, I am convinced that the beliefs I grew up with were not helpful to young people but were even harmful. They reached the age when their hormones were becoming active without any knowledge of how to cope with the condition. I entered marriage without any experience, not realising the many pitfalls there would be in finding a happy and successful sexual relationship. We just found out by whatever experiences came our way.

THE WIDOWER

How long before it stops,
the loin pain, the ache for union?
Not only youth's prerogative to mate
in lust or love.
The old too need the jigsaw feel,
two parts fitting close
that gives the flesh a meaning
the touch a thrill.
What measure in life's span
will halt the memory
of desire arising, passion grown
in lust or love?
Pity the old whose bodies still
respond, yet are despised,
whose hearts desire
and know no peace.
They are the living dead.
the loving lost.

My original Baptist chapel teaching encouraged the belief that being a virgin at one's marriage was an ideal preparation for happiness. I accepted that belief. During the war, so many of my generation married after a very short acquaintanceship, barely knowing their partnet. No one knew how long any of us had. We could be killed on the home front as well as on active service. We grabbed at happiness when we found it. Having made our choice, we made the best of it.

I certainly do not believe there is only one person destined to be the love of one's life. Peter and I were very good companions, a good working team and we spent many happy times together but our sexual life faded over the years. Neither of us could be blamed. These things happen. The French blood of my ancesters must still have survived. I had a strong sexual drive. I found it difficult to cope with frustration. When I spoke to my doctor on the subject, his advice was instant. 'Go elsewhere' he said 'and soon!'

KEEPING GOING

Looking back over the last years of the 80s, I realise how restless I was. It seemed I was escaping from something and I did not know what it was. Losing one's partner affects us all in different ways, especially when there is no family support. I have seen so many women rush off looking for a replacement, another man or perhaps a sudden close friendship with a similarly lonely woman, often ending in tears. In my case, instead, I involved myself in as many activities as I could and accepted any hotel reliefs or consultancy projects that might present themselves. If anyone asked me to join something or take on a voluntary job, I would do it. This is how I found myself secretary to the Marie Curie League of Friends. They were very active in fundraising and had contributed many valued extras for the patients in Home Towers, their hospice in Penarth. I soon realised it was the wrong thing to have done as I had been in contact with so many cancer sufferers. Having lost both my parents to this terrible disease and already being low in spirits from the death of Peter, I found it impossible to continue. I went on for eighteen months and then resigned. It was completely the wrong choice on my part.

I made up my mind to travel as much as I could. I knew it would be harder on my own but unless I started, I would never make the effort, so from the first year, I visited both my brother and Clive regularly. In order to retain my American residency and Green Card, I was legally bound to return to the USA within a year from my last visit. I was lucky enough to manage side trips to many other cities and sites in that enormous country. In fact, I have now visited thirty-two of the fifty states. Santa Barbara, Seattle, Portland, Phoenix and Houston were towns added to my list. Death Valley and the Grand Canyon and the Arizona Desert soon joined them. My Houston visit took me to the home of the family who had befriended Clive on his first trip to America. This visit was memorable for the quantity of bay oysters I consumed, coupled with trips to the Space Centre and to the Lyndon Johnson Memorial Library in Austin. I learnt that all presidents at the end of their term set up such libraries and fill them with their memorabilia and documents.

During the coming year, there would be only four American groups staying with me. I started making more travel plans. It was then that I had a surprise call from Dennis, suggesting I meet him and Jill in Paris in May. He was contemplating a leisurely visit to friends in Scandinavia, an area new to all of us. I was delighted at the idea. Only a few weeks later and I was on my way. After several days visiting various friends in Paris and sampling delicious meals in newly found restaurants, we set out for our trek eastwards. Taking the motorways through Belgium, we stopped off at Hertogenbosch, allowing me to visit once more the Dutch relations of my daughter-in-law. Sadly, it was the last time I would see Jacques Houdijk, her uncle, who had become a great friend. He was in hospital and died a week later. He was a quite a character. During the German occupation, he had been a member of the Dutch Resistance. Early in 1944, his cell of the Dutch Resistance was betrayed to the enemy. All thirty-eight members were captured and sentenced to death. They were imprisoned together in the days before the sentence was to be carried out. He and a friend were the only ones saved. Early that morning, Jacques and this friend were able to hide themselves in a dirty linen basket as it was being taken out to a waiting lorry. They were successful in escaping and they both reached a detachment of British troops. He then served with the Allied Forces for the remainder of the war. The remainder of the cell were shot two days later. He used to tell me of his unending sadness at the fate of his colleagues and the guilt he felt at being able to get away.

After Holland, we made a quick journey through Germany to Hamburg and from there a ferry trip to Denmark. All the countries so far were remarkable for their cleanliness. There were no signs of the rubbish left in the streets that we see in Britain. The main problems were the hotel and restaurant prices, almost double the cost of French hotels. However, the choice of fish, especially smoked varieties, was outstanding. After a visit to the Tivoli Gardens in Copenhagen, we moved swiftly on to Sweden. There we stayed with an old colleague of Dennis, from Southampton days. Dr Tom Robinson had met a Cambridge-trained Swedish chemist, Britta. After they married, he moved to Sweden and worked for the Swedish atomic centre. They lived near Upsala, a most interesting town. Whilst there, we visited a centre where replicas of the old Viking ships were being reconstructed with great care and accuracy. We saw these skilled workers, shaping the planks for the boats, using the same tools as their ancestors before them. Most Swedish families seem to have a second home near the sea or lakes. We spent three days at the Robinsons' wooden chalet on the Baltic Sea coast. The weather was delightful and the wooded area around the house full of interesting birds. It was also memorable for the wild raspberries and bilberries growing in profusion. As you can imagine, we took full advantage of this harvest.

After this enjoyable break in our long journey, we continued on to Stockholm and then by ferry to Norway and Oslo. Time was getting short so we only managed one trip to a nearby fjord. Once again, we found many Norwegians had second homes. This time they were situated on the small islands in the fjords. We had noticed from various signs during our journey that many words in Scandinavian

193

languages resembled ours. We saw in the restaurants, 'Barns Menu', listed as the menu for children, similar to the Scottish word, 'bairn'. We passed many houses offering rooms for visitors with the sign RUMS, in large letters on their walls, as our 'rooms to let'. It made us realise how much of their culture the Vikings had left behind in Britain.

Now it was time to return to France and this time, we headed south to Toulouse, to visit the pen friend my brother had been writing to since his school days. The two had never met until this moment. I, however, had met him when I was in Paris during my wartime duties with SHAEF. This was the same young man who had been a member of the Resistance in Paris. It was a lovely reunion for us all and Roger and Jacqueline Sirdey spoilt us with great French hospitality and the wonderful home cooking of this very skilful French lady. Finally, after six weeks of crossing and re-crossing Europe, I took the train from the French capital and headed home, leaving Dennis and Jill in Paris.

It was a beautiful summer that year, made even better with visits from many friends and a short but welcome one from Clive, on a business trip to London. I was beginning to feel almost human again. I found a French class to join and started a friendship with a group of people, all keen francophiles. This friendship has continued throughout the following years. Our tutor had retired from the local grammar school but was anxious to continue teaching, which was lucky for us. She had, a few years previously, been on the twinning committee, joining Penarth with the northern Brittany town of St Pol de Leon. This French port would become well known to us all as we subsequently visited there on many occasions. I met and became friends with the dentist Paul le Rumeur and his family and this has formed a wonderful ongoing friendship, visiting each other at yearly intervals.

Perhaps it is as well that we do not know what the future holds. I passed the autumn, enjoying the French classes and evenings with the Writing Circle. Little did I think that immediately after Christmas, I would be in hospital undergoing an urgent hysterectomy operation. This common operation usually passes without a hitch – not so in my case. An infection started and I remained hospital-bound for over three weeks. This was not the first operation I had undergone and I had faced it with equanimity, knowing I usually recuperated swiftly. However, on this occasion, I came home weak and depressed. It needed a lot of effort but eventually, I got back to my energetic self and looked forward to a busy New Year.

Like many grammar schools, Southgate County, my alma mater, was converted into a comprehensive in the Fifties and never regained its academic excellence of previous years. However, during 1988, some of the old scholars decided to organise a reunion for those who had attended between the years 1928 and 1952. My brother decided to come over from California to meet up with old friends and together we returned to North London for the occasion. Dennis and I thoroughly enjoyed ourselves on the day. The event was a great success. Despite the many years since we had met, I managed to renew acquaintance with around twenty of the Old Boys and Old Girls of my schooldays. It was interesting to see how the years had treated them and to learn what careers they had pursued.

There were over two hundred old classmates there, many from our era. It seemed that most of them had remained within the confines of London suburbia. Dennis from California and a couple from Australia had travelled the greatest distance just to catch up on the lives of their old friends. Looking around at these mostly retired fellow students, their characteristics did not seemed very different from how I remembered them. The hair may have changed colour or even disappeared, the body become a different shape but the same idiosyncrasies remained. The class comedian still cracked his corny jokes, the shy girl was still self-effacing, the class flirt continued to smile at the men and the brainy ones had made good in the big world. Some of the masters and mistresses from the school had made the event. Now they did seem to be changed characters, the muscular gym teacher now shrivelled and bent. The maths teacher I feared most was now a gentle old lady and even pleased to see me! I enjoyed the event immensely and we all agreed we should try to meet again in a couple of years.

I had not visited the London suburb where I grew up for very many years. I was delighted to see that Winchmore Hill had not deteriorated like so many of the London suburbs. The Green, a relic of when it was a village before London overtook it, had been spruced up; its old cottages were painted and bright with flowering baskets. Our house at 28 Radcliffe Road looked well cared for but the front garden had changed its use. It was now a car park for two expensive looking cars.

On my return home, my thoughts turned to George, my first boy friend and my once fiancé. We had met at school and had stayed close during those early wartime days. I wondered what had become of him and how the enforced marriage had worked out. I thought he might be interested to learn about the reunion. I am good with a telephone and although I did not know where he was now living, I soon found out. I managed to contact his brother's widow who gave me his current phone number. I learnt his home was in the Newcastle area so I phoned him to tell him about the school reunion. My phone call obviously came as a surprise but he seemed pleased to hear from me. He did not say much and spoke very quietly. Perhaps he did not want his wife to hear. Had he ever told her he was already engaged when he met her? Did it matter? After all, it was over fifty-seven years since the broken engagement. He asked for my number and

196

said he would call me later. I wondered whether I would ever hear from him again.

Later this year I had an unexpected opportunity to visit briefly another city on the East Coast of America. This time it was Boston. The Pollards' daughter Rebecca, who I had known from a baby, had studied at Wellesley College in Massachusetts and was graduating this June. I joined the family to celebrate her success. The American graduation ceremony was straight out of a Hollywood movie – champagne bottles popping, balloons, effusive parents, gushing girls and the flash of hundreds of cameras – but nevertheless a thoroughly enjoyable experience. Next morning, a walk through the Boston Heritage trail took us back to the days of the Plymouth Brethren and the first days of the Brits in America. The Americans are very good at re-creating the atmosphere of the past. They may not have a long history but they make the most of it. Footsteps inscribed in the pavement take the visitor from the quayside of the original landing of the Pilgrims around the city to all the points of interest.

After a beautiful summer entertaining more Americans in Wales and visiting a very hot Chicago in July, I finished the year with a memorable visit to the House of Commons. I was invited to a lunch, hosted by Chris Pollard, together with members of the Cardiff Business Club. We had the privilege of meeting Douglas Hurd, the then Foreign Secretary in the Thatcher government. Sitting next to him, he told me that sometimes he had fifteen different meetings in a day. He had already had five that morning! I was very impressed with him. He seemed a safe pair of hands for our foreign relations.

At the end of 1988, Chris Pollard was nominated as High Sheriff for South Glamorgan for the period May 1989 to May 1990. This was a great honour for a non-Welshborn resident. The Office of High Sheriff is at least 1,000 years old, having roots in Saxon times before the Norman Conquest. It is the oldest continuous secular office under the Crown. The High Sheriff is the sovereign's representative in the county for all matters relating to the judiciary and the maintenance of law and order. He takes precedence in the county after the Lord Lieutenant except when deferring to a Lord Mayor on special occasions. High Sheriffs are responsible for duties conferred by the Crown including attendance at Royal visits to the county. It includes ensuring the well-being and protection of Her Majesty's High Court Judges when on duty and attending them in court during the legal sessions. They have duties at election times and proclaim the accession of a new sovereign.

The procedure of nomination for High Sheriff is an old and interesting procedure. Three nominations are put forward for each County at a meeting of the Lords of the Council in the Queen's Bench Division on 12th November each year. Subsequently the final selection is made in a meeting of the Privy Council, by the Sovereign when the custom of 'pricking' the appointee's name with a bodkin is perpetuated. Eligibility for nomination is quite severe and precludes peers or members of parliament, Custom and Excise or Inland Revenue officers, officers of the armed forces currently on full pay. There is then an installation ceremony and sworn declaration in terms dictated by the Sheriff's Act of 1887, prior to the period of taking over the office.

I was to learn more about the office in the forthcoming months. Meanwhile Chris and Vivien Pollard were to have a busy year. Their daughter Rebecca was married during 1989 and her reception was held in the garden of their newly built house on the cliffs of Penarth in the grounds of the old mansion, once owned by the Plymouth family. This house would see many interesting and exciting dinners that year, when the High Court judge of the moment would be entertained and have the opportunity to meet important people of the County. This entertainment is part of the duties of the High

Sheriff. During this exciting year, Chris also received the Order of the British Empire for his services to tourism and business in Wales. His drive and ingenuity had brought extra trade as well as much-needed employment to South Wales in the past. I am not always in favour of the way such awards are given, especially when it is to civil servants who are only doing the job they are paid to do, or when it is given to pop stars. On this occasion, however, the award was fully justified.

The new year of 1989 was spent in Andalusia with the German pen friend I had corresponded with for so many years. After becoming the pen friend of her brother Werner in 1933, when I first began my German studies, I had continued after his death writing to his mother briefly and then his stepfather and finally his sister. Having met her for the first time in 1980, and then welcomed her to Bratton for her first stay in Britain, I was happy to accept an invitation to join her in a holiday flat near Marbella. Since she spoke no English, it needed quite an effort to drag up what German I could remember. I have to confess that post-war I had little interest in the language and much preferred improving my French and Spanish.

Gea had suffered as well as her brother, during the Nazi regime, by being labelled as a second-class citizen. The bloodline from her Jewish great-grandparents was not strong enough for her and Werner to wear the yellow star but enough to prevent her continuing her career as a nurse. She was sent as a clerk to Auschwitz and she witnessed the terrible deeds there. Her job was to record the belongings of the prisoners as they arrived. She told me that because of the supposed taint of her small amount of Jewish blood, she had suffered greatly. On my return home, I thought a lot about the trials of Jewish and part-Jewish families in Germany during the Hitler regime and I was stimulated to make my first attempt at writing a radio play. The Writing Circle had challenged us to submit an entry.

I found it very difficult to get the dialogue right. I based it on a coach trip by an English woman who meets up with a young German boy in the early 30s who tells her of the problems he has with his trace of Jewish blood. Although this was based on Werner's fate, I did not consider my effort very successful and I concluded play writing would not be my forte.

The spring was full of activities relating to the installation of the new High Sheriff at the beginning of his duties. I was fortunate to attend the inaugural luncheon in Cardiff County Hall and subsequently I was invited to several of the dinners for the visiting judges, hosted by Chris. I found these century-old formalities an interesting part of our history. As each High Court Judge took up duties in the Cardiff Courts, the High Sheriff would give a dinner. The purpose was for the incoming judge to learn more about the area and its problems. As guests, we were given instructions on procedure. We would be introduced and then had to say something about ourselves. We were expected to provide interesting conversation during dinner and of course behave with propriety. Finally, we could not leave until the judge had departed.

You can imagine my surprise on the very first occasion, when on my best behaviour, to find the visiting judge and his wife were neighbours from when I lived in Bratton. By now knighted, Sir Peter Webster and his wife April greeted me with 'Hello, Eileen, lovely to see you again', followed by a warm embrace. I must say it surprised some of the local celebrities invited for the occasion, who had never met me and, I imagined, were wondering what I was doing there! I had the privilege of attending several of these dinners and meeting some most charming members of the judiciary. On one occasion, I recall spending most of the meal discussing salmon fishing with the visiting judge.

These occasional dinners continued into the New Year until Chris finished his term of office in May 1990. It was an interesting time, and I was privileged to attend many of the official functions. One particular highlight was lunch at the House of Lords, hosted by one of the Welsh lords. We were told that Lord Longford would be present. As we all knew, he was a confidante of the child murderer, Myra Hindley and had supported her after her apparent conversion to Christianity. We were warned not to mention the subject. However, to our amazement, the first topic of conversation the venerable Lord brought up was just that! At these luncheons, a number of lords have to be present and amongst them was Lord Lyle. He was one of the few lords retained when the present government cut the number of non-life Peers down to 85. This charming gentleman was seated next to me and on learning my granddaughter lived in America, he insisted on taking me to the parliamentary bookshop and buying some interesting memorabilia, which he inscribed, to remind her of her British heritage.

It was agreed by all that Chris's period of office had been excellent. Apart from his Shrievalty duties, he will always be remembered for renovating the office of the Law Courts. In addition to obtaining copies of the coats of arms of many of his predecessors and displaying them on the walls, he had the old dingy and dirty curtains replaced and the room took on a whole new look. It was beholden on the current High Sheriff to obtain a coat of arms and I was able to introduce Chris to Sir Colin Cole. He was once a Territorial Army Colonel who had visited the West Country Inn, and he was currently the Garter King of Arms. Despite the prestigious name and position, I was surprised to learn that the officials of the College of Arms receive yearly salaries from the Crown but that these are decidedly meagre! Garter King of Arms: £49.07, the two provincial Kings of Arms: £20.25, the six heralds: £17.80, the four pursuivants: £13.95. These salaries were fixed at higher levels by James I but reduced by William IV in the 1830s. The work of the heralds is otherwise unassisted from public funds. However, in addition to their official duties, they have for many centuries undertaken private practice in heraldry and genealogy, for which they are allowed to charge professional fees.

A special lunch at the law courts in Cardiff allowed me to meet George Thomas, the then Speaker of the House of Commons. This Welshman, a Labour supporter throughout his life, performed his office as Speaker impeccably, maintaining impartiality throughout, unlike some of his successors. The office of Speaker dates back to the fourteenth century. The Speaker presides over the House's debates, determining which members may speak. The Speaker is also responsible for maintaining order during debate, and may punish members who break the rules of the House. Conventionally, he remains non-partisan, and renounces all affiliation with his or her former political party when taking office. He does not take part in debate nor vote (except to break ties, and even then, subject to conventions that maintain his or her non-partisan status). Aside from duties relating to presiding over the House, the Speaker also performs administrative and procedural functions, and remains a constituency Member of Parliament. Historically, the Lord Chancellor presided in the Upper House of Parliament, the House of Lords. However, more recently this function devolved to a separate person, the Lord Speaker, under the Constitutional Reform Act of July 2006.

After all this initiation into the ancient customs of our country, I returned to more mundane pursuits. This would be the last year when I would be hosting American guests. My diary was becoming too full of other pursuits. A local wine tasting group was added to my activities. Together with a few keen neighbours, we pursued the drinking and analysis of wine. At our monthly meeting, in turn, we would choose a region or a grape variety, submit three samples for tasting and then judge on taste, quality and price – a very pleasant way of spending a Monday evening once a month.

The year had begun sadly. I learned in January that my old friend, Major General Christopher Man had died. On his retirement from the army, he had moved to Pitlochry to work for the Duke of Atholl, running his shooting lodges and other activities. Peter and I had visited him early in his stay there and were pleased to find him happy in his new occupation. General Man had been a good friend to me, especially at the time of the burglary at the hotel in Bratton, when Peter was ill and I was coping on my own. Chris Man had had an illustrious career. He served as a major with the Middlesex Regiment and during the war in the Far East, was captured and imprisoned by the

Major General Christopher Man en route to the Army Commissions Board, Westbury

Japanese. Suffering harshly in the prison camps, he kept morale going for his fellow inmates. His wife, a Red Cross nurse, had gone with him to Hong Kong when he was drafted there with his regiment and she was also captured and imprisoned. On their release, neither knew whether the other was still alive. The amazing story was that on the ship returning released prisoners to Britain, Chris Man after three weeks at sea, rounded a corner on deck of the ship, to find his wife who also had just been released.

Sadly, she later developed a brain tumour, which although treated, left her severely handicapped.

On their return home, Chris Man volunteered for the Parachute Regiment, undertaking intense training in his mid-thirties. He gained promotion after promotion and was the only ex-prisoner of war to be appointed general. His last posting was as major general in charge of the Army Commissions Board in Westbury, Wiltshire. The official residence was in Bratton. There we became friends.

This too was the year Clive would decide to leave the Chicago Athletic Association and Men's Club after eleven years, for pastures new. The Club, by now, was very profitable with a large and active membership. The restaurant and kitchen was operating efficiently, the staff well-trained and everything running smoothly. He was ready for a new challenge and this came when he was headhunted by the Fort Worth Club in Texas. This old-established club in the pioneer town needed a new look. Its finances were in a poor state and its membership diminishing. The Board members had learned of Clive's reputation and asked him to join them, offering a three-year contract on an enhanced salary. He decided to accept. In the years to come, he admitted to me it was perhaps the wrong decision but he was eager for a new challenge. This approach had come at the opportune moment or so he thought at the time. By March, he had sold his house, found a lovely new one, installed Tiffany in a new school and set about getting the Fort Worth Club in order.

The club was situated in a large building, which they owned. Many of the floors consisted of offices, which the club rented out. Apart from running the club, Clive was also responsible for these leasing arrangements. He had under him a building manager, responsible for the maintenance, who appeared initially an asset and a friend. However, Clive had not at that time learned that Texans in the long run prefer only to employ other Texans. He was being used. The membership consisted of many mega-rich Texans, including the Bass brothers, many of whom had made their money first in cattle rearing and then in oil and precious metals. Amongst these members, Clive also was to meet the famous pianist Van Cliburn, who took him under his wing in the initial days. Van Cliburn became famous after becoming the first American pianist to win the famous Tchaikovsky Award. I was looking forward to a future visit to this new part of America and perhaps meeting him.

During the spring of this same year, Southeby's announced a special sale of Russian wines, ports and sherries in London. The Russian government was in need of hard currency and decided to dispose of stocks of wines, which had been stored in underground cellars in the Crimean region since the years of world war two. This area was famous for centuries for wine growing and had the facilities to conserve these old wines. Vivien Pollard invited me to accompany her to the sale as she thought it would be a good idea to buy a small supply of port as future presents for special occasions, such as christenings or twenty-first birthdays. We had to reserve seats. Entering the auction hall, it was noticeable there were many very foreign-looking people already there. Their dress seemed different from the usual London buyers. They all looked rather solemn and slightly ill at ease. The bidding was brisk. There were Russian ports and sherries dating back to pre-war. The varying years were sold in batches. Vivien was cautious and waited until there seemed to be fewer bidders for each lot. She finally acquired a case of 1939 and 1945 port at a reasonable price for wines of that age. I was curious about the many bidders amongst the foreign contingent there until it all made sense when I spoke to one of them. These were émigré Russians whose families had left Russia at the time of the demise of the last Tsar and the revolution. Some had come from France and other European countries with the sole intention of buying something to remind them of their homeland's past history. I realised why they looked sad.

Living near Cardiff, I was able during the summer to introduce an American visitor from Cardiff-by-the-Sea in Southern California to the Welsh capital's Lord Mayor. Irene Krazler, President of Friends of the American Cardiff-by-the Sea, was visiting and brought a collection of memorabilia from the smaller sister city. She was overwhelmed with the grandeur of City Hall compared to her local mayor's office!

Heading for my seventieth year, I realised I was lucky to be fit enough to travel alone without too much difficulty. After a trip to France and to Mallorca, I planned my first visit to Clive's new Texan home in October. Continuing onwards to visit my brother in Southern California, I would be away for two months. The journey would entail getting to know the new airport at Dallas. Arriving there, I found it daunting; it was enormous. Built comparatively recently, it seemed to spread for miles. There were self-driving trains between different points, which I found totally bewildering. However, I soon realised everything in Texas would be bigger. Fort Worth was very close to Dallas. It was a much older city based on cattle rearing and considered itself superior to the brash new town, born out of the financial dealings of oil.

Clive's new home was spacious and full of the most up-to-date devices. It had an attractive garden and a large pool and terrace including an enormous barbecue area. It was in this garden or yard as the Americans call it, that I saw my first praying mantis. I was surprised how small it was and very green. Fortunately, October temperatures, although hot, were tolerable. Even the sky seemed bigger and filled with more stars than anywhere else I had been. Clive took me around the historic part of town and I attended a typical Texan cattle show. What amazed me was the size of the animals. As one particular class of entrants, entitled Cotswold lambs, entered the judging ring, the animals looked more the size of a pony than the creature I knew as a Cotswold lamb. The calves were even larger. I believe this is due to the steroids introduced into their feeds.

The Fort Worth Club dated back many years to pioneer days. It definitely needed up-dating. This Clive was now doing. He introduced new ideas, new menus, he imported a French chef. His knowledge of Spanish, retained from his year training in Torremolinos, was particularly useful. Many of the staff were Mexican. Initially, he did not let them know that he understood and spoke their language and thus learned about some of the problems besetting the club. Finally, when he addressed them in their own tongue, he gained not only their respect but also their co-operation. Most Texans employ them on their ranches or in their homes but few of them bother to learn Spanish.

Clive soon realised that he would have a tough task on his hands. The Texan character was quite different from the character of Chicagoans. Texas to them is its own country. I found my visit interesting but I would not have wanted to live there. I found they were not very friendly, especially the women. These ladies all seemed to have 'big hair' and were rather arrogant, sporting flashy clothes and flashier jewellery. Returning via a more congenial California, I arrived home in time for Christmas and another new year.

THREE SCORE YEARS AND TEN AND THEN SOME

The days of our years are threescore years and ten; and if by reason of strength they be fourscore years, yet is their strength labour and sorrow; for it is soon cut off, and we fly away.

Heading into 1991, and looking forward to my seventieth birthday in July, I found the above quotation from Psalms 90 rather daunting. I did not feel very different from last year. Of course, I could not run the 100 yard sprint as I did when I was sixteen nor could I lift as much as I could ten years ago, but all in all, my brain seemed to work fairly well and my memory did not fail me too often. I had to be satisfied with that but we all, as we reach the supposed allotted span, must think seriously of the problems in store. Having reached this milestone year, I decided to do as much as I wanted to do, travel as often as both physique and money allowed and stretch my brain as long as I enjoyed doing so. That was the formula I intended to adopt.

Since arriving in Wales, life had become more challenging. Living alone in a large house for only one person, the chores became onerous. Not having any close relative anywhere in the vicinity and the very nearest and dearest all living in the United States, I needed to call on my inner reserves to fight the waves of loneliness, which occasionally overcame me. I realised that to keep close contacts with friends, one had to work at it. Fortunately, I still enjoyed cooking so it was no hardship to entertain. By chance, my next-door-neighbour ran a successful bed and breakfast business. Sometimes, she would overbook and call on me for help. This resulted in several temporary residents staying with me. In fact, Alan Beattie, a Midlander, here to commission new equipment for a chemical company in a nearby industrial estate, spent almost a year with me. Since he worked all day and often late into the night and went home most weekends, it was no problem and provided a little financial bonus.

Visits of friends were numerous. My oldest school friend Doreen and her husband Jim came frequently. My brother and Jill spent three months in Britain, visiting Yorkshire for a brief trip and then stayed with me. We were invited to spend a week on the south coast of England, in the holiday home of a farmer friend of mine from my old village of Bratton. This delightful spot at Sandbanks allowed Dennis to renew contacts from his days at Southampton University. During the summer, I also enjoyed visits from several of my American friends including Ed Chandler. He was one of the engineers who had worked on the Surveyor space probe with Dennis and I had worked with him at Radio Shack. His wife was a delight. She was half American Indian and half Tennessee country lass. She taught drama and literature and was herself an actress of renown.

However, the great joy of the year 1991 was a three-week visit by my granddaughter Tiffany. She shares my birthday so we planned a joint celebration, my seventieth and her eleventh. Her arrival in late June was a great event. She soon made friends with twins living close by and with the daughter of Vince McNabb, Chris Pollard's finance director. Amazingly all the four youngsters had birthdays within three days of each other so there were plenty of celebrations to be planned. Thanks to the kindness of the Pollards, I was able to use their London house, in a Mews just off Knightsbridge to introduce Tiffany to London during her visit.

Her new experiences started with the train journey to London. Like so many Americans, she had always travelled everywhere by car or by air so a railway journey was something special. We were to spend three full and delightful days in the centre of the West End. I booked a Harrods bus tour, which took us around the main sites of the capital, to Buckingham Palace and Parliament, past all the museums in Kensington and through the City. Tempted by what she had seen from the top of the bus, Tiffany's immediately request was to visit the National History and Science Museums. I had not visited them since my own childhood in London and the improvements and attractions were manifold. I saw how children were stimulated with hands-on exhibits and challenged by machines and computers. She loved it and so did I. Then a visit to The Tower of London and Madam Tussauds, coupled with frequent visits to McDonalds and Pizza Hut, filled the mind and the stomach of my eleven-year-old granddaughter. It was an exhausting but very worthwhile experience to see her reactions to all these new sights and experiences. I hoped too she would learn and appreciate her own British heritage.

Home again, it was party time – a pre-birthday party for Tiffany and her new friends at my neighbour Rae's house. Rae had a big garden, an enormous pool, and many grandchildren. Having had six children of her own, she knew just how to plan a children's party. Then my own special day arrived. Unbeknown to me, Vivien and Chris had convinced Clive to come over for a few days to join me in the celebrations on 4th July. I saw him so seldom and missed him so much that it was the best present I could have had. My doorbell rang two nights before my birthday and there he was, straight from Texas. From then on, my house was filled with visitors, all coming to the party that the Pollards had arranged in their big new house. For my seventy years, there were seventy visitors, a wonderful buffet and a vast choice of wine. It was one of the happiest evenings of my life, only missing Peter's presence to make it perfect.

However, I found that even in South Wales, there are people for whom those of us from England are unpopular, despite so many people from outside Wales living in and around the Cardiff area. In North Wales, feelings are even stronger and the use of Welsh as a first language prevalent. I try to remember we are all British but I realise too that it is essential to enter into all parts of life here to be accepted. Since the devolution, speaking with a London accent, even if it is not Cockney, often causes adverse comments. It is such a pity. So many of us who volunteered for the Services in world war two thought we were doing it for Britain, never dreaming that this small island would be broken up. I find it very sad. I often remind those who are in favour of partition that none of us really know what bloodlines run in our veins. After all, the Romans, the Normans and the Vikings have invaded this land. Wales, especially, had an influx of workers at the time of the industrial revolution from the tin mines of Cornwall, from Devon and Somerset, from Liverpool in the north and from Ireland and even from Italy.

By now, I had enrolled in a creative writing class in nearby Penarth. This encouraged me to go back to one of my early loves, writing poetry, but it also encouraged me to try other forms such as short stories, articles and reviews. Above all, I found that I had so many experiences to draw upon that article writing was the most appealing. It was then I started writing about some of the interesting and unusual war experiences I had undergone. It opened up a new interest and several of these articles now appear on the internet.

My French group was very active, especially jointly with our twin town, St Pol. This would be the year when many of the class, learning English, would pay us a visit. I would renew my friendship with Paul le Rumeur and subsequently visit him and his family in their summer cottage on the Brittany coast at Pors Guen. This small village was a microcosm of French life. The baker called each morning with freshly baked baguettes. The local fishermen sold their night's catch from the beach. There were few foreign visitors, only friends and relations of the local inhabitants. This led to many future annual visits to this small community. I came to know so many of the residents and soon became part of many of their social activities.

During wartime, one of the houses on the North Brittany headland was the site of a German gun unit. The house always fascinated me since it never seemed occupied. The windows were always shuttered and dark. On the wall surrounding it, there were still the signs of the gun emplacements. I called it the haunted house; it seemed to bear the scars of its wartime history. This bit of coastline had also suffered greatly from the disaster caused by an oil tanker, the Amoco Cadiz, which loosed its oil over the beaches here and for several kilometres distant. The locals still talk of the hours they spent, cleaning up the shore and trying to restore their beautiful beach. The entire cargo of 1,619,048 barrels spilled into the sea creating a slick 18 miles wide and 80 miles long, which polluted 200 miles of the Brittany coastline.

With frequent trips to France and Spain, I was able to practise my French and Spanish but I realised I had never had much Spanish tuition, so with the coming academic year, I decided to do something about taking some serious lessons. After a few weeks private tutoring at home with a young man from Peru, I decided that I should enrol at Cardiff Centre for Lifelong Learning where lessons at all levels were available. This led to a wonderful new entrée into the academic world. I enrolled in Marta Sanchez' class. She had come to Britain as a Chilean refugee from the Pinochet regime and I continued studying with her for many years. The University brought me in touch with both interesting fellow students and tutors. I have continued studying there up to the present day with both Spanish and creative writing classes.

In the future, it would lead to me gaining the Diploma of High

Education in these two subjects. This new award is equivalent to the first two years of a bachelor's degree study. It took a long time to get there as it required 450 hours study for each subject. However, all those years of effort were not wasted, as later, I was able to use this diploma as credits that enabled me to complete further study with the Open University, leading to my eventual graduation with a Bachelor of Art degree. This had been a long-standing desire of mine since wartime when my WAAF service prevented any chance of going to University.

I filled my days with so many interesting activities that I had no time to feel sorry for myself. I was comparatively fortunate with my health, perhaps suffering a couple of bouts of bronchitis each year. This was a relic of my days in the WAAF, caused by working underground, but a dose of antibiotics usually seemed to control the problem. I had a right knee replacement in 1994. We had always had private health insurance when working, to ensure treatment was available as soon as possible. However, this finally became too costly as the annual premium increased horrendously at the age of seventy. From then on, I was in the hands of the National Health Service.

Meanwhile by 1994, at Fort Worth, Clive was coming to the end of his three-year contract. He had brought the club back into profit with a now thriving membership. He inaugurated the Fort Worth Outdoor Sport Club with hunting parties and fishing groups, which were very popular. The French chef had upgraded the restaurant service and the banqueting reservations were the highest ever. During his stay in Chicago, when the end of a contract period was approaching, the board, well in advance, had discussed its extension and the future pay scale they would be offering him. The Texans did not work that way. Three weeks before his three years contract in Fort Worth terminated, he still had heard nothing. He approached the president and asked what was happening. He was assured all

213

would be well and he was not to worry.

The date came and went and he still heard nothing. Meanwhile, a new president was elected. The buildings manager, who Clive had regarded as a loyal friend, had been canvassing behind his back to replace him. This man had no catering experience, no hotel know-how but he was a Texan and the new president was a buddy of his. Suddenly Clive was informed they were replacing him with this man, at a much lower salary because after all, the Club was running well now. They would save money and above all, the Club's supremo would be a Texan. Clive was given three months salary and that was it. The news was a tremendous shock.

During his entire career, he had never been unemployed. This meant he also lost his health insurance. There were only around a dozen club management posts of a similar level to the one Clive held, in the whole of the United States. Vacancies were rare. He was under a lot of strain. The family would have to move again, house prices were falling, and at the same time, the economy was slowing down. After selling the house at a loss, he looked everywhere for an alternative job offer. It took him two years to find one. In the meantime, he put some money in a business with an English friend living in Portland, Oregon, who was involved in taking school tours to Europe. They started to explore the possibility of running gastronomic tours, to be led by Clive, to famous European restaurants. Clive with his family moved to Oregon. Before the business could get going, he had a further setback. His partner Steve's wife left him and demanded a large financial settlement. The money Clive had loaned to the business was lost. This was a very worrying two years for him and his family. I imagine the stress was enormous. Finally, in August 1996, when he had turned 50, he was appointed general manager of a charming golf and country club in Florida. He was content with this. The pressures would be less than those of a city club and there would be a chance for a little more free time.

He started work on 26th August. The salary was less than before but the demands were fewer. Running a country club with golf facilities would be a new experience. The venue was attractive and the atmosphere friendly. He was looking forward to his tenure there. On the Friday night, at the end of the first week, he planned to take his wife and Tiffany out for a celebratory dinner. It never happened. When he arrived home, he seemed more than usually tired. He sat down and asked for a drink of orange juice. Almost immediately and without any warning, he fell to the floor. He had had a seizure. Liz, his wife, being a nurse, did what she could whilst waiting for the paramedics. They arrived very soon and worked on him for over an hour – but in vain. My wonderful son Clive died in hospital.

That night of 30th–31st August 1996, around 3.15am, I was awakened by the sound of the telephone ringing. My heart stopped. I knew something awful had happened. It was my brother calling. 'I have some very bad news,' he said. Then he had the terrible task of telling me my son was dead. He later said that it was the hardest thing he had ever done in his life. I was in shock and alone. My brother phoned my friend Rose and asked her to come round. At five o'clock that morning she arrived at the door, but what could she do? I re-live that phone call every night of my life.

I spent the weekend trying to get a flight to Florida. Finally, I found one for the next day with Laker's Airways. It seems a few seats were always kept in reserve as bereavement flights. Freddie Laker himself was a passenger on the plane that day and knew why I was booked on this flight. I will never forget his kindness. During the flight, he helped people with their luggage and once we were in the air, he came and sat next to me and stayed with me for two hours. He brought me a glass of wine and really helped me through the flight. As I left the plane, he gave me his phone number and asked me to call him. He had learned I was ex-RAF and as he had flown on the Berlin airlift, he felt a fellow interest. What a wonderful man!

Arriving in Sarasota, I learned that Clive's body had already been sent for cremation. Liz, his wife, told me she had decided to donate his eyes, his bones and his skin to give some other person a better life. I was happy about that. It seems at that time in the USA, it was not customary to have a cremation service, as would be the case in Britain. After cremation, the ashes were returned to the next-of-kin and then arrangements would be made for a memorial service. But the worst part was that the cremation company sent a demand note for a certified cheque in payment before they would consider dealing with the body. My brother organised a bank credit note and Liz finally received the ashes ten days later. She did not know what to do and was so distraught that I suggested we try to arrange a service in the Chicago area. Clive had once told me that the two places where he had been happiest in his life were Bratton and Chicago.

I wondered how I could arrange something to commerorate the life of my beloved only child, whose life had been so vibrant, so full. His closest friend in Chicago, Dave Sauer, came to the rescue. He and Clive had spent many happy hours fishing together for salmon on Lake Michigan. He arranged a Catholic memorial service at a little church in a village by the lakeside and invited Liz, Tiffany and me to stay with his family. To my astonishment, two hundred of the Chicago club members came to the service to honour my son, even though he had left the club five years before. Finally, together with Dave and his family, Liz, Tiffany and I set out in the boat Clive used to go fishing in, on Lake Michigan and we cast his ashes in the water together with his favourite fishing rod. Dave dropped into the waters of the lake a six-pack of beer, remembering the happy times they had spent together. We laid a dozen roses on the lake surface as I read a farewell to my beloved son.

MY FAREWELL

As we give you back to the elements that created you – the air you flew in, the waters where you loved to fish – we say farewell to you, my son, who brought love and joy to those who knew you. You touched the lives of many people in many lands, with your generosity of heart, your love of life, with your caring.

Those of us, who are part of you and of whom you are a part, say farewell – your lovely wife Liz, Tiffany, your beautiful daughter, both so loved by you, and I your mother. I say farewell too for those who love you and who are not here, Dennis and Jill, Quentin and Rusty, Beau and Di, Doreen, Vivien and Chris, Jim and Tina, Rebecca, Martin, your friends in Wiltshire and in Wales, at the Savoy, in Canada and in Spain, those of your adopted country, especially Chicago which was a beloved place, of Oregon and of Florida.

May your spirit join with your father, my Peter, and be at rest and your memory remain with us and help us in the dark days to come. Be strong for us, my son. I love you.

I was heartbroken. I could not believe that my lively gregarious Clive would never again telephone and say, 'Hi, Mum, what's cooking?' I would never hear him singing the latest song or taste the meals he had prepared for me – never again. Nothing worse can happen than for a mother to lose her only child, at whatever age.

The tragedy was made even more heartbreaking because a year later, on the very same day and at the very time that I had received that terrible phone call, unable to sleep I turned on the television. There was the breaking news about Princess Diana. She had never been a favourite of mine. I had met her twice and she had not impressed me very much on either occasion. Yet to this day, I am constantly reminded of her death on the night of the 30th August, bringing back the time when I heard the worst news of my life.

How does one cope with the news that your son has died, your only child? No one had taught me how to face such a tragedy. I returned home. I lived each day as it came, not thinking about the future. It was the past that consumed me, night times especially. I would sleep for a few hours and then lie awake, thinking, remembering. I recalled every incident in his life, every moment good and bad. By the morning, I would face the next day with dread. That year of 1996 seemed interminable until finally in December with Christmas approaching, I collapsed. I found myself in hospital. A blood test proved my blood count was so low that it was life threatening. No one could find a medical cause for it. I knew what it was – utter sorrow and heartbreak. Several days later, having received five packs of blood, painfully injected, I returned home to try to find some reason for living.

FACING THE FUTURE

It would have been easy to feel sorry for myself. Losing an only child at whatever age is one of the worst experiences in anyone's life. Without close family nearby, it seemed impossible to continue living any sort of worthwhile existence but I realised I had to make a great effort and find a way to keep going. Fortunately, considering my age, my health was reasonably good. By then in my seventy sixth year, I could still drive and walk a reasonable distance. I continue to exercise and garden but above all, I tried to keep my mind occupied. I was able to invite friends to stay and I would cook special meals for them. My French and Spanish classes kept my brain turning over. Painting acted as a therapy when I felt depressed. I was still able to travel alone without difficulty.

Since Clive had always loved living in the village of Bratton, I decided to erect a seat in his memory and many of his friends both in Britain and overseas asked to contribute. A beautiful oak seat was placed near our old hotel in Bratton, in the children's play area on the village green. Together with some of his friends from Wiltshire, we had a dedication service in the spring of 1977. It was good to feel some memory of him would remain in his homeland.

I knew that it would be impossible to fill the place in my heart my son had filled. My life seemed pointless. Then in the autumn, Marta, my Spanish teacher, asked me if I would help a Venezuelan friend of hers, Mari Mantilla. They had taken master's degrees in education at Cardiff University together more than eighteen years previously. Later that same year, Mari's husband, Lucho Mantilla arrived to pursue a course at The Royal Agricultural College in Cirencester. This was in preparation for him joining the family business of cattle rearing on the Llanos. A year later, whilst in Britain, their daughter Marysol was born, thereby qualifying for British nationality.

She was now seventeen years old and wanted to return here for a year, to learn to speak English fluently. Marta asked me if Marisol could stay with me. Having plenty of spare room and welcoming the idea of sharing it with someone who spoke Spanish, I agreed without question. This decision was to bring me great pleasure and a lasting friendship with the Mantilla family. Marysol arrived in late September and joined the sixth form of a nearby Comprehensive school. By a stroke of luck, a nearby neighbour with twin daughters of the same age as Marysol, also going to that school, befriended her. The three girls travelled together daily. In no time, my visitor had made many friends and was feeling at home with life here. She was extremely intelligent and very popular. In fact, at the end of the school year, her fellow pupils voted her Queen of the Prom during the end of term celebrations. Her command of English improved rapidly and she ended her studies with a Cambridge certificate in English language. I considered myself fortunate to have met Marysol. She had become very dear to me and was a joy to have in the house at a time when I desperately needed affection. I knew the house would feel very empty once she had left.

Her parents and two brothers arrived during that following summer of 1998 to meet her and take her on visits to both France and Spain, in addition to spending some weeks here in Wales with me. We all became great friends, so much so that the following January, I visited the family in San Cristobal in Venezuela and gained my first experience of life in South America. I was surprised to learn I needed yellow fever inoculations and a course of malaria pills. Marysol's hometown is situated at 3,000 feet in the Andes in the west of the country. The border with Columbia is a bare ten miles away and in those days was causing much anxiety for the people of San Cristobal. The guerrilla fighters of this nearby country were making frequent forays into the area, kidnapping some of the richer residents and demanding high ransoms. There had been several occasions when the unfortunate victims were killed if the ransom was not paid promptly. One of Marysol's uncles had been ambushed but fortunately was returned safely to his family, after they paid the equivalent of £30,000.

My visit coincided with the town's feria and as it was summer in the southern hemisphere, every day I would lunch at a relative's home with the Venezuelan version of paella, consumed 'al fresco'. This was a prelude to a week of corridas, bullfighting being most popular there. It was also just at the time of the country's election when Hugo Chavez was elected president. This was the beginning of great changes, many for the worse, in this country, rich with oil from the Maricaibo region. Over the subsequent years, the situation has continued to deteriorate. Despite saying the poorer would get richer and the richer poorer, there are more poor than ever and many international companies have left the country, causing disaster for the economy. Chavez now assumes almost dictator status and has annexed much of the land owned by the ranchers and farmers to be handed over to his supporters. He is virulently anti the United States and has formed a quasi-communist bloc with Cuba, Bolivia and Ecuador. Many young talented people from Venezuela have emigrated to the United States or to Europe, finding the current political regime a deterrent to any worthwhile future.

In February 1999, I concluded my Venezuelan visit by journeying on to Carlsbad and San Diego County. It was an excellent way to start the final year of the twentieth century. On my return, I decided to celebrate and buy myself a new computer. Having been involved

221

with a basic knowledge of technology in my days in the WAAF, at the beginning of the radar era and having a brother who was both a physicist and an engineer, involved in space travel instrumentation, I had tried to keep up with the times. I bought an Amstrad as an introduction to word processing and by now had moved on to a more modern computer, bought secondhand from Marta Sanchez's son who was employed in the IT industry. Like so many people, I was learning by trial and error but I managed so far to do what I needed. I took a knowledgeable friend with me to PC World and bought myself the most up-to-date model.

Home again; I missed the cheerful company of Marysol. And so the sad months passed, punctuated with phone calls by my brother and Jill, both of whom, despite living so far away, were a constant support to me. Each year, I could visit my friends in Brittany and perhaps manage a visit to Spain. Having American residency and holding the much-valued Green Card, I was bound to return annually to America and would plan to spend the worst weeks of the winter in Carlsbad in the warm Californian sunshine. This was no hardship. I had many friends there and my brother always was most welcoming.

That Easter I found myself entertaining another overseas visitor. This time it was Virginie, a friend of Roger Serruys, Dennis's French pen friend. She was aiming to get a post as an English teacher in Paris. To be successful, it was necessary to take a special exam and reach a high position in the results. The expected number of applicants would be around two thousand and to obtain a post in Paris, it was necessary to be in the top hundred. I was asked to give her some concentrated tuition in English. Virginie was a delightful young Parisienne and obviously very bright. Her knowledge of English was excellent but her accent was very French. Therefore, we concentrated on improving that together with introducing her to

222

some of the many idioms and phrases we use in everyday speech. I had only two weeks in which to succeed so the lessons were very concentrated. My French group were most supportive and invited her to various meals so she was able to meet several families in their homes in South Wales. On her return, all went well and her examination results justified the efforts we put in. She came thirtieth in the final exam and secured a first class post in one of the better schools in a pleasant Paris suburb.

On a sadder note, our beloved French teacher, Evelyn Allen died, suffering a brain disorder. She had been instrumental in the twinning between Penarth, South Wales and St Pol de Leon in Northern Brittany, and after teaching generations of grammar schools students, she had helped so many of us maintain our interest in the French language by running informal classes in our homes. Her influence remains and even now, the residue of her class continues meeting each Wednesday for conversation and translations of newspaper articles in the language so beloved by her.

The month of May saw a general election, resulting in a Labour victory. We wondered what changes were in store. To cheer myself up, I bought a new car, once more a Nissan Micra automatic. I have never been a car addict. For me, a car is the means of getting from A to B, safely and in reasonable comfort, but then I am not a man! I like something small, not flashy but comfortable, reliable and easy to maintain. I once vowed never to buy a German or Japanese car but since reliability is a 'must' and previous Nissans had never let me down, I have had to change my mind.

That summer and autumn, my diary seemed permanently full. My next-door neighbours continued to fill me up with their overflow of B and B visitors. Friends from my school days and from the WAAF visited. I had no time to look back at the past. I kept myself busy. As well as a visit to Mallorca once more, Dennis and Jill met me in Paris and we visited their favourite resort on the south west coast of France at Arcachon, continuing on to visit the Serruys family in Toulouse. Later in the autumn, I managed to cram in a week's painting tuition with the well-known artist Trevor Waugh in the Cotswolds. What a delight that was! He had the ability to make us all produce a picture worth hanging on the wall and wowed us in the evenings, playing his guitar. The year and the century ended.

MEETING THE TWENTY-FIRST CENTURY

As 1st January 2000 and a new century dawned, I was looking out over the backcountry of Carlsbad, California, once more visiting my brother. It did not seem any different from any other day. Little did I know what the following years would have in store. I was in my seventy-ninth year, reasonably healthy, physically and mentally active and by now, accustomed to undertaking long journeys by air on my own. I did not think or feel old.

Back in Wales a few weeks later, I took up my usual activities. I rejoined the French group, which by now had reduced to nine from the fourteen original members. Two had moved away and three older members had died. I still went to painting classes and even sold a few watercolours. My great love of the Spanish language was nurtured with classes at Cardiff Centre for Lifelong Learning, still under the auspices of Marta Sanchez. Together with her family, she was forced to leave Chile at the onset of the Pinochet regime. I learned that she and her husband had been lecturers at the University of Santiago and, being socialists, strong Allende supporters. For a while, her husband had been imprisoned in the infamous Santiago stadium. With support from universities in Britain, they had been able to come to this country and obtain their Master of Education degrees and both were now employed as academics. Marta was an excellent teacher but very demanding. You could not get away with any indifferent work!

Early in the year, I found walking becoming difficult. Some years previously, I had a small repair operation on the cartilage of my right knee. It was now starting to give me more trouble and by March, I was suffering intense agony. I returned to my friendly orthopaedic specialist, a fellow Hispanophile. He took one look and said, 'It's time you became bionic – you need a new knee.' I recall the day of the operation vividly. After a mild sedative and an epidural injection, I was wheeled into the operation theatre. I remembered chatting to the anaesthetist all through the operation and listening to the talk between the surgeon and his assistant. In the recovery room, I was able to raise my leg and show my surgeon how well things were going. I felt fine. Returning to the ward, I found I had some visitors waiting to see me. They were amazed to see me looking and feeling my normal self. It was then about six in the evening. Later I must have fallen asleep. All I can remember is hearing voices and feeling rather strange. There were two doctors by the side of the bed. I heard someone say, 'Don't worry. We are taking you to the Intensive Care Unit where you will be looked after.' I realised something was very wrong. I was having difficulty breathing. I could hardly speak. Then I must have passed out because the next thing I remembered was lying in a different ward, breathing through an oxygen mask. There were a few other beds around me, all occupied, with very ill patients. Where was I?

It was some time before I found out what had happened. It seems that around 9 o'clock that evening, a patient in the bed opposite to mine noticed I was gasping for the breath. She called to the nurses who were all chatting at the other end of the ward. I am sure she saved my life. It seems that in that short time after the operation, I had developed aspiration pneumonia and if she had not called the nurses, it would have been too late. How or why it happened is a mystery to this day. Next of kin were advised. My brother was making plans to fly over from the States. He had been warned there was a possibility I would not recover! The danger period lasted three days and then I pulled through. The fact that I had never smoked was the turning point in my recovery.

I spent my birthday in hospital and after a further ten days returned home. A friend stayed in the house with me for a week until I was able to cope on my own. It was a great shock and it made me realise that one never knows what is round the corner. Recovering quietly at home, I soon became bored so I decide to plan a new kitchen – out with the canary yellow melamine doors and in with a new Moben pear wood look. I called the company and seven thousand pounds later, I had a wonderful state of the art kitchen as a memorial of my near death experience!

The first year of the new century came to an end. It was 2001 and in July, it would be my eightieth birthday. I was trying to decide how I would celebrate it. Meanwhile it seemed that once more I was going to mark the New Year with yet another medical problem! On 12th March I fell and broke my nose! I was visiting a fitness centre with the intention of possibly joining. Whilst being shown around by a personal trainer, he indicated something over to my right. I turned my head and tripped over a heavy exercise mat. I leapt in the air and was catapulted straight on to a metal piece of exercise equipment, which had not been returned to its correct place. It shot up and hit me in the face! Looking extremely bloody, I went off to the nearest Accident and Emergency department for repairs! I decided my new fitness regime would have to be postponed or better still, forgotten.

Undaunted, in June I visited Madrid for a week, invited to stay with a lovely Andalusian couple I had entertained the previous year. I had visited many places in Spain since my first holiday there in 1958. Peter and I had travelled from north to south, from east to west through the country by car on many occasions but we had never visited Madrid. This would be a great opportunity to remedy the omission. My hosts were wonderful. We visited the Roman aqueduct in Segovia, the Escorial and the Valley of the Fallen. This last place, where Franco is buried, seemed to me a place of doom. Erected to commemorate the fallen in the Civil War, but only those who fought for the Falange and Franco; it was built in its immensity by the nationalist prisoners. Their dead had no memorial. Many of these prisoners, working long hours in terrible conditions, died during its construction – a large number of them falling from the high roof of the building or collapsing after long hours of working in intense heat.

Back home, it was time to finalise the plans for my eightieth birthday celebrations. I decided it would take the form of an Open House – American style, since I was born on American Independence Day! I invited sixty-five guests, to arrive as it suited them, between midday and eight o'clock in the evening. My brother and Jill would be staying with me and would help with preparations. Jill's brother Rod and his wife Miriam, from Australia, whom I would meet for the first time, would also be staying with me. Several others would be arriving and would stay in my neighbour's bed and breakfast establishment. I planned a continuous buffet meal to be available all day and wine, beer and soft drinks for all to help themselves. I decided to serve wines from all the countries represented by my international list of guests. This meant there would be Australian, Californian, French, Spanish, German, Chilean and Welsh wines on the list!

Neighbours loaned me additional garden furniture and since I could always count on a fine day for my birthday, we would eat al fresco. It had never rained on my birthday to my memory. Things were going well on the evening before the event. The guests from far away had arrived. The food was all organised and the drinks in place. The garden looked welcoming with all the furniture in place and the flowerbeds full of blooms. We went to bed on the evening of 3rd July, content in the knowledge that our *mise en place* was ready. Around one o'clock in the early morning, I awoke to the sound of thunder and heavy rain assailing my windowpanes. That night we had the heaviest and longest storm I have ever experienced. It continued hour after hour. The lightning seemed to circle around the house continuously. The thunder would lessen and then return at an even higher volume than before! Would it ever stop and where would I feed sixty-five people, if not in the garden? No more sleep for me – that was certain!

We came down to breakfast and viewed the scene with apprehension. It was still raining. The tables with their bright cloths were soaked. The garden itself did not look as if it had suffered too much but the lawn was sodden. What could we do? Then a miracle happened – at ten o'clock, the sun came out and was hotter than ever. We wiped the garden chairs and tables. We threw the tablecloths into the tumble drier, everything dried out and we were back in business. The first guests arrived around midday and did not go home until teatime. The afternoon arrivals stayed on to the evening and those coming straight from work stayed on to almost midnight! It was a great event, mixing old friends and new ones, visitors from Spain and France, Venezuela and Chile, Scotland and Australia, America and England. I doubt I will ever have another more successful party.

Life seemed rather dull after all my guests had departed. I took up the threads of everyday life again. One afternoon, whilst working in the language laboratory at Cardiff University, I met a Chinese visitor. He was visiting the Professor of Architecture with whom he was doing a joint study. Based in Xi'an University of Architecture, he specialised in 'build'; all the technology found in buildings such as air conditioning, heating and insulation. He was using the language laboratory to improve his English. I noticed he seemed to have a good vocabulary but his accent was almost indecipherable. We started talking and I learned he was Professor Li Angui of X'ian

University of Architecture. He told me he had learned his English from the BBC Overseas programme and from books but had little or no opportunity to practise speaking.

I asked whether he had had the opportunity to converse with any British people. He said that he had not but practised with a Japanese colleague. I did not think this could have helped his accent much so I suggested perhaps he would like to come to my house and I would help him. His response was 'How much you charge?' I assured him I did not intend to charge him anything. It was a just friendly gesture, my small effort to improve international relations! From then on Angui would visit me each Saturday and stay all day. His written English was excellent but he had great difficulty in mastering the accent especially the sound of the letter V. However, after several months and a lot of hectoring on my part, he definitely improved. I ended up proofreading his papers, written in English, on 'build' and we became great friends. He reciprocated by showing me how to make Chinese dumplings, a speciality of his region! One Saturday he made 150 of them – they lasted me nearly a year! He finally returned home early in 2002 but assured me he would be back. This was the beginning of my Chinese adventures!

EIGHTY PLUS AND GOING STRONG

I was determined not to be intimidated by the 'eighty' word but having learned from experience that I could never know what the next day would bring, I resolved to go on travelling whilst I was able and to keep my mind as active as possible. I kept up my learning activities and steered clear of too many TV soaps! The days seem to slip by so quickly that I vowed to make as much of them as I could.

I spent my usual ten days on the Brittany Coast at Pors Guen with my dentist friend and his family. Whilst there, I was invited to attend the wedding of the daughter of his neighbour. I was interested to see how the French organised such an event. I soon found out that on this occasion it was very different from our more formal affair. In the church, a rather haphazard procession formed with the bride and her father somewhere in the middle. The small bridesmaids seemed completely out of control and darted in and out of the line. Meanwhile, the latecomers amongst the congregation pushed their way through the procession, anxious to reach their seats before the bride reached the altar!

The service was extremely long and being a catholic mass, there was a lot bell ringing and incense spraying. Finally, as the bride and groom left, they set out, with all of us following them, to walk round the town and then headed for the venue where the vin d'honneur was to take place. A large number of the congregation, including myself, had been invited to this. However, prior to getting any refreshment, we had to arrange ourselves on the tiers of seats outside the building for a mass photo. There were about a hundred of us. The seating arrangements took a very long time, as people kept changing places and then space had to be found for the late comers! However, finally, the photographer was satisfied and we entered into the hall where we were plied with copious glasses of excellent champagne and offered a vast choice of tasty 'bonnes bouches'. Two hours later, we left and made our lurching way back home.

During the summer, I heard once more from my Chinese friend, Li Angui. He said he was returning to work with the School of Architecture at Cardiff University for a further six months and was intending to bring his fourteen-year old son, Nan, with him. He asked whether I could organise a place for his son in a secondary school somewhere near the University. He warned me that his son spoke virtually no English. Not being a resident of Cardiff, I did not know much about the school system there. However, with the assistance of a helpful Cardiff Council officer, I managed to get him into a school in the centre of the city. I contacted the school personally to let them know a little about their prospective pupil. I spoke with the deputy head teacher and explained how he would need special help with his English and asked if he could work with a group of native British speakers. My intention was that he should learn the language correctly. I was swiftly rebuked and told this was a multi-cultural school. I was made to feel I was a racist! I was only trying to ensure the lad acquired a reasonable accent and a good knowledge of grammar from the start. Black mark, Eileen – but this was political correctness taken too far and I was both angry and upset.

Angui and Nan stayed with me for nearly two weeks until they found a suitable flat near the University. His wife was to follow in a few months' time, as she was only able to obtain a visa for a three-month stay. Whilst the two of them were with me, I managed to teach the boy a few useful and necessary phrases and most important, how to use a knife and fork. He even came to like my cooking. Nan was a great 'computerologist' and spent hours at my PC, sending emails to his friends in China. After he left, I found to my astonishment that as well as being able to use the French and Spanish keyboard and spell-check, I would now be able to write in Chinese characters! Angui was most grateful for my help and hospitality and was always extremely polite as I find the Chinese always are. I now have an open invitation to visit him in Xi'an.

I was still enjoying my creative writing classes and only wished I had started them years before as I found how much I enjoyed writing both articles and short stories. I had always loved writing poetry but now prose became a favourite pastime. I managed to write several articles about my wartime activities, which I sent to the BBC when they compiled their online collection of people's memories. It was then that the School/History website approached me for permission to include the articles in their collection. This would lead to an exciting contact with the military in the near future.

By now, December was approaching and I was preparing for a very special visit to America. My granddaughter, Tiffany, was to graduate on 16th December from the Florida International University with special honours, *summa cum laude*. It had been a long hard journey for her to reach this final day. Clive, her father, had died so suddenly and unexpectedly just after her sixteenth birthday, Her mother, unable to be alone, had remarried less than a year later and after twelve months, had moved to Jersey, in the Channel Islands. Tiffany had been alone for her initial years at University in Bradenton in Florida. My brother and I had done our best to support her. On her mother's return to Canada, Tiffany joined her and spent her third academic year at Brock University. Then, after deciding to change her main subject, she moved south to the Florida International University at Miami. She found that accountancy was too boring and wanted to combine it with something more exciting, so she chose Hotel Management! Thus, she became the third generation in my family to follow in that career. In the States and Canada, it seems it is easy to move from one university to another since the courses are interchangeable and follow the same guidelines.

I was immensely proud that despite the pressure and heartache, she had come through it all successfully. Throughout her studies, she had worked long hours in a restaurant, in order to supplement her finances; consequently, she had only a comparatively small student loan to repay. Added to that, she had already received the offer of a job in Georgia with the Marriott Hotel Group in the financial control department. So two days after her graduation celebrations were over, she would head straight off for her new job.

The day of her graduation was a memorable one for me. Later that evening together with her mother, stepfather, a few of her friends and Clive's best man, John Layzell and his wife, we toasted her success with a celebration dinner in a nearby hotel. I only wished that Clive could have been there. He would have been so proud of his daughter. The following day I left to continue my journey to California, to pass the New Year there. Carlsbad is almost a second home for me as I have visited there many times. I am welcomed at the writers' group where Dennis was a member. Knowing several people in the area, I always feel comfortable when I am there. In addition, of course, the weather is a bonus. Even December there feels like a British day in June.

However, it was back home in Wales in May that my Chinese adventures continued. Having finished a pleasant dinner with Chris and Vivien at their house in Cowbridge, I was about to return home when there was a knock on the door. It was quite late, around 10 pm. We wondered who it could be. Closing the inner door, Chris went to investigate. We could hear him talking to at least two people. He

234

came in laughing. 'They must have known we were all once in the hotel business,' he said.

It was a young Chinese couple looking for a room for the night. They had seen this house all lit up, with flower-filled window boxes and had mistaken it for a bed and breakfast establishment. He called them into the house and then tried ringing B and B's in the area to see if they had a room. He had no luck at all, as they were either closed, full up or not answering. So knowing I had several spare rooms, I said 'Come with me. I'll put you up for the night'. They were delighted and explained they were on an exchange with Sheffield University. The husband was head of the section for foreign students at Heilongjiang University and his wife taught English in a secondary school. That was when the fun started. They said 'But there are seven of us!' I thought quickly, working out how I could fit them in, and then replied 'That's OK, I'll take you all'. So finally, the young wife came with me in the car and the other two carloads followed. I had no idea who the rest of them were.

It was a journey of twelve miles home. Whilst we were driving, I asked the girl, who had adopted the English name of Emma, how they had got on with the students at the University. She admitted that initially there had been some difficulty. I asked her if she realised why and she said she had no idea. So I explained about the TV scenes we had

Enjoying lunch with Dennis's writing group, Carlsbad, California

all seen of students being killed around Tiananmen Square. She sounded surprised and told me she knew nothing about it. They lived in the far east of China and I realised that the details of the students' massacre had never been publicly revealed. I explained what we had seen and she insisted I should tell all the others when we finally arrived at my house.

Once home, they asked me if they could cook their supper! It was 11pm by now and I had already had an enormous meal. However, I agreed and they brought in a pot of soup and pre-cooked spare ribs to be heated. They soon boiled a saucepan of noodles and one of the men moulded meatballs, dropping them in the soup to cook. Finally, around midnight, we all sat down for supper! I rustled up some chopsticks and Chinese bowls I had bought years ago and we started talking. I soon realised that they were short of cash and were travelling on a low budget. I remember that Li Angui told me he was only allowed to bring a small amount of currency to last him a whole year.

Most spoke reasonable English. They were all either lecturers or professors from various universities around China. Once they had relaxed, I told them the story of what we had seen on television during the student riots in Beijing. They appeared not to know anything about it and the professor from Beijing Institute of Civil Engineering vigorously denied it had happened. I wondered if like the Russians, there was always a Party member present, checking on the others. I did not push the issue and we had a very interesting and pleasant meal together. Eventually, by moving the mattresses from the beds on to the floor in my three extra bedrooms, I managed to accommodate them all comfortably.

Next morning they asked for some eggs. I gave them fifteen and these together with the leftovers from their supper were cooked and served for their breakfast. It seems they had set out the previous morning from Sheffield, intending to drive to the Gower Peninsula. However, they had first driven north to see Liverpool and then Manchester and realised they were too late to make the Gower in time to find accommodation. After profuse and grateful thanks from them all, they set off again on their journeying. After visiting the Gower Peninsula, they intended to return via Bristol and Bath, hoping to see Stonehenge on their way back to Sheffield.

Before leaving, they signed my guest book; Zjiming Wang from the University of Shandong wrote, 'I'm from Confucius's town and he said 'All the world are brothers', then he continued 'I am so lucky to meet you. You are so kind, clever English lady. It worth me to remember all my life.' The young couple I first met added 'It is a lucky day on 15th May 2003 I will remember it forever. I meet Mrs Eileen.' I treasure these entries and would love to visit China and meet up with some of them again. Perhaps the whole episode will do some good in helping the people in China to understand us. My friends were aghast that I had invited seven strangers into my home. The thought of any danger had never entered my mind. On reflection, it was probably safer with seven than with one!

This new year was to see more globetrotting. I joined Dennis and Jill in Paris in the spring. We travelled south to San Tropez and spent a week exploring the French Riviera. We were intending to return to Toulouse to catch up with Dennis's pre-war pen friend, Roger Sirdey. However, I asked if we could make a slight detour to Apt. This meant heading north, through

My Chinese university guests

237

the more mountainous region. I had a special reason for this as my fellow French group had been translating into English a book written by a member of the French Resistance, Monsieur Jean Fernand. I had already contacted him and asked if I might call and meet him. He had readily agreed and this was the reason for our detour. This is how I remember that visit

Golden fields flecked with scarlet poppies, cherry orchards studded with ruby fruit, isolated villas with pantiled roofs and always the backdrop of stark granite mountains – that is how I saw Provence on the last day of May. It was a warm sunny morning as we left the Côte d'Azur, choked with traffic and seething with tourists. We headed into the hinterland for a rendezvous with history – destination Apt, a town of about 12,000 people and an appointment with the honorary mayor, Monsieur Jean Fernand.

Some months before I had read a book entitled *J'y étais* (*I Was There*) written by Jean Fernand. It told the story of the Resistance fighters in this region of France. The author explained in the preface his reason for writing it: 'I wanted the truth to be known of the bravery and of the loyalty – and sometimes the treachery of the little people in this unknown part of France'.

My French class, consisting of dedicated Francophiles, decided that, as a special project, we would translate this book into English. As we read it, we were captured by the stories of courage and cruelty, of bravery and tragedy. Then by chance, I had this opportunity to travel to the very part of France where all these stories had taken place.

Now I was to meet the author. I had made the appointment by telephone. The voice at the other end was that of an old man, his accent clearly not the clipped French of the Parisian. I wondered if I would manage to understand him when we met and whether the meeting would merit the long journey. As we approached our

238

destination – 'Apt 20 kms' the signpost said – we started to climb. The road zigzagged its way as the open countryside changed to thick woodland and then tangled maquis. This area of rough scrub had given its name to a branch of the Resistance fighters, men who had been brought up to face a tough life, making their livelihood from a difficult terrain.

We crested the mountain and below a panorama lay before us; a vast plain dotted with villages, each dominated by a tall church steeple, with fields of intense cultivation and lush orchards. It was a scene of tranquillity and peace. In the middle of the plain lay the town of Apt, an ancient town, renowned for its main industry, the luxury production of preserved fruits. The town had now been overtaken by so-called progress, with new villas, apartment blocks, industrial zones and a vast military establishment.

As I entered the old town and crossed the river, I wondered whether my journey was a wasted one. Would I understand this old Frenchman? Was he still able to communicate? Could he even remember? I need not have worried. No sooner had I rung the doorbell of the small villa on the outskirts of the town, than the front door opened and there stood a man belying his eighty-three years of age. He was tall and fresh-faced, his silver hair combed neatly over a high forehead. He wore a formal dark suit and a crisp freshly ironed blue shirt. His matching tie bore the cross of Lorraine, the sign of the Free French and under the knot, I spotted the flash of the Order of the Legion d' Honneur on his lapel.

'Bonjour, Madame, bienvenue – welcome.' He greeted me with great courtesy and immediately showed me into his sitting room. This room told me everything about him. New files lay on the table; a tray with two glasses and a bottle of Muscat had been prepared. On the wall, I immediately noticed framed photos of President de Gaulle and our Queen, alongside an array of medals, which included

239

the King's Medal from George V1 and the Freedom Medal of the USA. This was the home of a disciplined military man, who even at eighty-three years of age, maintained order in his household, despite living alone.

'My friends and I meet weekly to talk in French. We are attempting to translate your book into English,' I explained. 'We will do it honestly and accurately, leaving nothing out and putting nothing in.' He was obviously delighted. 'Madame, I would be honoured,' he said. At first, his open-vowelled Provencal French was difficult to grasp but before long, I was able to understand him well. He continued, 'I will give you any help you may desire.' He went on to announce proudly he had published the book himself, 1500 copies, and had sold 1200, retaining 300 to give away as gifts. 'I retain the rights but you may have them for the English version. I have the original illustrations, these you may also use.' Then he looked at me, his blue eyes twinkling, 'You and your friends are very brave to attempt such a task!' I was inclined to agree with him. His smile seemed to show how touched he was.

'Come, join me in a glass of pastis,' he led me to the prepared table. 'I wish you *bonne chance* with your task.' As we sat in his charming sun-filled sitting room, he told me his story. At the outbreak of war, he was a soldier in the elite Parachute Regiment but when France fell, he had been discharged and sent home where he started a garage business in the then unoccupied part of France. Restrictions and rationing limited his work and his income but he earned just sufficient to keep himself, his wife and their small son. Then as the war progressed and the Allies threatened to become strong enough to invade the Continent, the Germans gradually took over unoccupied France to safeguard the southern coast from invasion by the Allies.

'Life was very difficult for us then, when the Boche came.' he said. It was at that time he made contact by radio with London.

240

'Together my friends and I formed a Resistance group. At first, we made false papers and helped Frenchmen escape from forced labour in Germany. Then later, as the Maquis became stronger and started sabotaging enemy installations, we prepared landing sites for the dropping of supplies.' He paused in thought. 'We helped several Allied pilots to reach the Pyrenees and cross to Spain, and safety.' He took a sip from his glass. 'Many British agents landed here too. Sometimes, I would hide them in my home.'

'But surely that was very dangerous for your family?' I asked. 'Of course,' he shrugged, 'but they needed our help and my wife and my son were pleased to do anything they could.' He paused and picked up a photo which was lying on his desk. 'This was one of them; she was a Polish countess and spoke many languages. We had to get her out of the country very fast. The Gestapo was looking for her.' He stopped talking for a few seconds and a sad look came into his eyes. I sensed he was overcome by his memories. 'I kept contact with her after the war for many years until she died. She was very beautiful,' he sighed.

He sat down and poured another glass of pastis for us both and then he continued his story. 'One day a Wellington bomber was trying to land – it crashed in flames nearby. My friends and I went to the plane and hid the bodies of the three airmen who had died in the crash. Then we looked for any secret equipment so that the Germans would not find it. The Gestapo never found out whether those pilots had escaped or had died.' He opened the drawer of his desk and took out a file of letters. 'After the war, we buried them in the military cemetery in Marseilles. I still write to the families of those boys.' He went on to tell me how each year, he goes to put a wreath on their graves on the anniversary of their death.

'Come, you must see my museum,' he rose and led me out to his garage. He walked with a firm step, his figure upright. 'I have

241

tried to keep all these things together so people will not forget.' The place was laid out methodically and was full of memorabilia of the occupation. He pointed out the posters that the Gestapo had pinned all around the town.

WARNING, THOSE WHO HELP THE ENEMY WILL BE SHOT

There was an RAF parachute, torn and bloody, false passports, a small radio transmitter he had used to contact London, a pilot's compass given to him by a pilot officer he had helped to escape to Spain. So many more things to see and every one with some history attached to it. They merited a much longer visit than I was able to make.

Monsieur Jean took my arm and led me back in the house. 'You know,' he confided, 'my son, and his son, my grandson and I have all served in the Parachute Regiment. Next year, when I will be 84 years old, we hope to make a parachute jump together'. He stood erect and proud. I looked at him and nodded, 'Monsieur, I am sure you will.' What a man!

By now, it was late afternoon. 'Monsieur Jean, I have to go now,' I said in my halting French, 'My brother is waiting for me outside in the car. We have a long journey. But I will stay in touch and let you know how the translation gets on. Thank you so much for your welcome – and merci.'

As I left, this charming old gentleman said 'Permettez-moi?' and courteously kissed me on both cheeks as he led me through his delightful garden of roses and pomegranate trees to the waiting car. 'Au revoir, Jean Fernand and bonne chance!' This meeting I will never forget.

It seemed that this year of 2003 would bring a resurgence of wartime memories. I realised how those six years of conflict had affected my life and the lives of my generation. Recently, there has been an awakening in interest of these events and my connection with radar has provoked several requests for talks on the subject. It was during this year that I was first asked to give talks to schoolchildren who were studying this period of history. The first one was for nine-year-olds at the Cathedral School in Cardiff. The questions they asked afterwards were both interesting and sometimes amusing. Many of them told me proudly about their grandfathers who had served during the war. I found it profoundly touching to be able to give these

Jean Fernand from the French Resistance presents
Eileen with his book, *J'y étais*.

youngsters some idea of what their grandparents had undergone to preserve the independence of their homeland.

Our own family history took a great leap forward during 2003. Someone, seeing the name Le Croissette on my brother's website, contacted him by email. Gwyneth Cheeseman was a brilliant and keen genealogist and had recognised the name as part of her own heritage through her father's family. Both families stemmed from the Huguenot named Jean de Croissette who had escaped from Picardy after the Revocation of the Edict of Nantes. This Act, which had previously protected those of the Protestant faith in France, when rescinded, once more brought about great persecution, reminding one of the Massacre of the Innocents in a previous century. The story handed down through the family tells how Jean escaped by hiding in the breadbox on a vessel heading for an English port. Gwyneth eventually made contact with me and I passed on to her copies of all the research my mother had painstakingly carried out during the war years in London. With the further work Dennis and I did when visiting the Beauvais archives, Gwyneth has managed to produce a family record of the many branches, going back to 1430 to a small country manorial estate in a village in Picardy. Her web site gives a comprehensive background to this immigrant family. In addition, I have acquired an interesting new second cousin.

The wartime theme continued with my making a memorable visit to Bletchley Park, the home of ENIGMA, and learning more about the work done there to intercept Hitler's orders. It was interesting to see from where the important intelligence information that we received in the Filter Room at Fighter Command originated. We would receive advance warning of Luftwaffe plans of mass bombardment or of changes to German radar procedures. Additionally, whilst at Bletchley, I was able to see the famous Hut 6 where a cousin had worked as interpreter. He had taught German pre-war but in addition had studied German mythology. This particular knowledge enabled him to identify the code names Hitler allocated to his generals. They were all given names of German gods, appropriate to their individual characteristics and work. He recognised the character traits appropriate to each of the gods.

As the year was drawing to a close, once more an unexpected illness struck. This time it was to a very close friend whom I was visiting just prior to Christmas. She unexpectedly stumbled and found great difficulty in walking. It happened so suddenly. Rushed into hospital, she had many different tests but the cause was not apparent until an overseas doctor with a specialised knowledge diagnosed it correctly as Guillain-Barré Syndrome. This disorder causes weakness or tingling sensations in the legs. In many instances, the peripheral nervous system is affected. Then weakness and abnormal sensations spread to the arms and upper body. These symptoms can increase in intensity until the muscles are affected and the patient is almost totally paralyzed. The occurrence of Guillain-Barré Syndrome is rare. My friend was in hospital for many weeks and then had to learn to walk again but she is a very strong person and with her usual tenacity and resolution, she regained her health and strength. However, once more I realised we never know what each new day may bring.

A VOICE FROM THE PAST

On a particularly cold and depressing day in January 2004, I had an unexpected but most welcome phone call. It was from my once fiancé George, a voice from the past. He was calling from his home in Newcastle. He said he had wanted to phone me often since we had made contact over two years previously. I gathered things had been difficult at home and his wife would not have approved. I thought after more than sixty years that I did not represent any threat! However, by now sadly she had suffered a serious stroke and was unable to do anything for herself. She was unable to speak more than an odd word. He would not consider her going to a nursing home, but had been looking after her himself. At the age of eighty-three, this was quite a task. After years of separate rooms, he had moved in with her once more. Nightly with the help of care workers, she was lifted by a hoist from her wheelchair to the bed, and the process reversed each morning. His only daughter, Jean, who had never married, had also had been suffering from cancer and was very ill. She too needed his care.

His main pleasures were his continued close contact with the Dunkirk Survivors Association of which he was the local branch Chairman and his Masonic Lodge. His life sounded very sad. It was obvious he was a kind and caring man but it was a heavy burden. He seemed anxious to talk and I felt perhaps this long-distance contact might help him. This was the beginning of a renewal of our friendship via the telephone. I realised I might never see him again but from then onwards, he rang frequently and talked over his problems and told me of his few pleasures. I realised I was still very fond of him.

The year proceeded like the ones before. I continued with a few courses at Cardiff Centre for Lifelong Learning to challenge my brain. I made my usual visit to California plus an essential visit to my beloved Spain. By now, I had come to expect the sadness we must all face as we age. We lose so many friends as the years go by, some after months of illness, others so unexpectedly that we find the shock hard to overcome. Things happen we never expected and disappointments occur. This year seemed especially hard. Things were not to get better.

High summer, I was hit by a special disappointment. Tiffany, my granddaughter, whilst working at the Marriott hotel in Georgia, had met and fallen in love with the executive chef, Don Messina. She was now working as finance officer in the company's airport hotel in Miami. They fixed their wedding date and I received my invitation. We were all to rendezvous on the tropical island of Saint Lucia in the Caribbean. The ceremony was scheduled for Friday 12th August. My ticket was booked, my bag packed. Then disaster struck. On the very morning the happy couple were due to fly out from Miami, the Saturday before the event, Don learned his brother in Minnesota had been injured in a serious motorbike accident and he was now in a deep coma in hospital. The news was

George laying a wreath for Dunkirk veterans

very bad; he was not expected to survive. The bridal couple cancelled all arrangements and flew to his bedside. I too had to cancel my trip. By the Tuesday, the situation changed, he had come out of the coma and the chances of him surviving became more probable. Once more, the wedding plans were revived and Don and Tiffany flew out on the Wednesday and joined her mother at the island resort. For me, it was too late to reinstate my trip so I had to miss the wedding of my only granddaughter.

A further upset occurred. Despite all the arrangements for the wedding supposedly having been reinstated, the resort manager forgot to book the registrar. There could be no wedding. Don and Tiffany returned home, obviously heart-broken, and arranged a quiet ceremony locally with just two friends in attendance. What a disappointment for us all!

It seemed this year was destined for bad luck. On 30th September, the sixtieth anniversary of my marriage to Peter, I was quietly gardening, gently pruning a hibiscus bush and putting the trimmings into a bag at my side. All the action needed was to turn my body and knees to the right, without moving my feet. Suddenly I heard a loud pinging sound and then I was on the ground, crying out in agony. I was unable to stand and the only way to get help was to shuffle on my bottom backwards into the house, up two set of steps. One hour later, I managed to reach the phone and dial 999. It was three o'clock in the afternoon. In no time, the ambulance was at the door and the paramedics were encasing me in leg supports, deciding my leg was broken. I kept insisting that it was more likely that it was a ligament or tendon problem. In order to support both legs and lift me from the floor, they had to enrol the assistance of one of my neighbours who had noticed the ambulance and rushed over to help.

The A and E department as usual was full of rugby casualties. After a long wait, the duty doctor sent me to the X-Ray department. I was left to await the result. Once more turning to the duty doctor, I insisted that it was probably not a broken bone but perhaps a ligament or tendon. No one took any notice. Five hours later, I was informed, 'Your leg is not broken. If you can walk, you can go.' Struggling to

248

get off the bed, I got to my feet and managed to walk but I was still in great pain. I know now that I should have had an ultrasound scan. By then my knee was badly swollen and black and the pain intense. I asked if I could have a stick or a crutch but this was refused. My neighbours fortunately had arrived to see how I was and they offered to drive me home. They pushed me in a wheelchair to the car.

From then on, I struggled to continue with my daily life. Finally, five weeks later, still in agony, I saw my GP. She immediately advised me to contact my orthopaedic specialist. 'You will manage to get to see him far more quickly than I can arrange,' she assured me. Two weeks later, I turned up for the appointment. He took one look at my leg and immediately diagnosed the problem. 'Ruptured quadriceps tendon,' he said 'emergency operation next week.' He dictated this into his cassette recorder and told me to be ready for an operation within seven days. However, it was not to be the next week but a month later before I received instructions to report for treatment, three days before Christmas. In the meantime, my leg kept collapsing and I had a further two falls.

Two days before the appointed time, a second letter arrived, notifying me that my operation had been cancelled, as there was an emergency operation required for someone else! I was furious and so was my surgeon. He must then have pulled a few strings because finally on 5th January 2005, I was operated on in a BUPA hospital, paid for by the NHS. In the meantime, whilst shopping on New Year's Eve, I had a further spectacular fall in the town centre. Once more, the ambulance was summoned. This time I persuaded the paramedics to take me home. I did not want any more A and E experiences.

When the time came, I was conscious throughout the operation as I had only had an epidural injection and I remember clearly hearing the surgeon exclaim, 'My God, it's gone up so far!' He was referring to the quadriceps muscles attached to the snapped tendon that he had to reconnect to the lower muscles and kneecap. It took several weeks and a deal of physiotherapy treatment before I could walk properly. I did not then know that the delay and original wrong diagnosis would cause me so much difficulty in walking any great distance in the future. Neither did I realise the significance of the surgeon's comments during the operation. I only learned several years later that the delay had caused the muscles to waste, causing permanent damage.

Returning home, I had my bed brought downstairs for the first week whilst a friend stayed to help. My brother immediately flew over from the States to take over. It was wonderful to have his support. My leg was incarcerated in a metal brace, which I had to wear for six weeks. Fortunately, it was on my left leg so having a car with automatic gears, I was able to manoeuvre myself into the driving seat and was able to drive after the first fortnight! I was independent again; I even managed a dinner party for my brother to meet some of my friends before he returned home.

Recovery was speeded up with some good news. After all the years of study with Cardiff Centre for Lifelong Learning, the senate had decided that the standard of exam results of we older learners, was commensurate with that of the students studying in the main faculties. It was decided that those of us who had gained 120 points both in level 1 and also in level 2, provided it was in two different subjects, would be awarded the new Diploma of Higher Education. This would be equal to two years of University study and accepted by any other university in the United Kingdom. There were five lifelong learning students eligible for this award during this first year. I received a letter notifying me that I was one of them, having completed examinations in both Spanish and creative writing. I was so excited because it meant I could now study to earn a further sixty points at level 3 and perhaps gain a degree. This had been my ambition since a child but the war had, I thought, put an end to that. Male RAF Officers post-war were offered the opportunity to study at a university and all their fees paid. This did not apply to the WAAF officers, another example of the sexism I have so often encountered. Here was an unexpected opportunity and I vowed I would do everything possible in order to accomplish my long-held ambition.

Rather than travelling daily to the University in Cardiff to study, I decided to approach the Open University. The local Cardiff branch gave me all the help and advice I needed and my accreditation was accepted. I enrolled for a course which was due to start in February 2006. The nearest subject offered to creative writing was 'The Art of English', based on the study of sociolinguistics. After enrolment, I was surprised to receive my student number – A02052422. This was the same number I received over forty years previously when I had enrolled in a foundation mathematics course in the first year that the Open University was founded. I had been unable to complete that course due to the serious illness of both my husband and my father who was then living with us in Bratton. I hoped that I would succeed in completing it this time. Meanwhile the year continued happily with visits from American friends and an interesting visit to the Albujarra region in Southern Spain where my Spanish teacher had purchased a holiday home. My weekly conversations continued with George who had spent a short spell in hospital but who assured me he was now fine. These chats seemed to help him face the many difficult days he was facing as a carer.

This was also to be the autumn when I met Lieutenant Colonel Simon West. He was then a member of the directing staff at the Army Defence Academy at Shrivenham in Wiltshire. One day I received a phone call, telling me he had come across the three articles

I had written on my WAAF experiences when he was browsing the School/History website. He wanted to know if he could visit me and discuss how I had used radar. He suggested 14th September. He explained he was organising a thirty-eight week special course for four hundred army majors and one week would be dedicated to the history of radar. He proposed making a video of the interview, which would be incorporated into his presentation, together with a further one with Raymond Baxter, the long-time presenter of *Tomorrow's World*. He too had served in the RAF as a Spitfire pilot, involved in operations against V2 bases. After my interview with Lieutenant Colonel West, he suggested that I should spend two days at Shrivenham in mid-November for the presentation and that during my stay, I would be available for discussions with the course students. It sounded interesting.

My brother and Jill paid a second visit to me whilst on their way to visit the fellow professor from Southampton University who we had visited in Sweden. I was always delighted to see them, Dennis had been there for me at all times and having lost the rest of my nearest family, we were especially close. Then it was time for my visit to Shrivenham. Early on the morning of 14th November, an army car drove up to my door complete with a smartly uniformed corporal driver. Once over the Severn Bridge I felt at home. Despite many years in Wales, I always feel more welcome back in England. We drove through the Wiltshire countryside and in through the gates of the Defence Academy. Once more, I was in a Services atmosphere. Having been signed in at the guard room, we moved on to the camp. I could see that this training establishment covered a vast area. There were many large and important looking buildings; it resembled a university campus. Everywhere was immaculately maintained with well-trimmed lawns surrounding the living quarters of the resident personnel and their families. Entering the Officers' Mess, the first thing I noticed was the vast array of regimental silver on display. Polished and gleaming, there were items symbolic of past battles and famous victories of many regiments. Since the current course was for the Royal Artillery, their regimental silver was prominently displayed.

After officially being checked in, I was shown to my quarters, which consisted of a single bedroom and adjoining bathroom. Everything was army issue. The bed was neatly tucked in with grey blankets, the furniture strictly utilitarian, not much sign of glamour here but warm and comfortable. Returning to the anteroom, I was introduced to the brigadier and his adjutant and then to several of the officers on the course. They were all interested in my history and asked many technical questions. Raymond Baxter arrived with his personal assistant who had driven him from his home in Berkshire. We were introduced. Raymond was a friendly and most charming man, a little frail but still with a wonderful speaking voice.

The two of us were treated as honoured guests and escorted to a special dinner table. Our fellow guests had been specially chosen for their connection with radar. They included an RAF squadron leader for our benefit. Raymond and I sat on either side of the brigadier and enjoyed an excellent dinner supplemented with some first-class wines. Simon had suggested that I should go on night

Raymond Baxter, presenter of
Tomorrow's World

ops with the gun crews but in the event, the weather turned very stormy so the exercise was cancelled. I was not sorry! Instead, we all adjourned to a side room for coffee where we had the chance to talk with some of the students once more. After a few more glasses of wine and feeling like a VIP, I finally went to bed and slept like a log.

After an early breakfast in the Mess, we were taken to the large auditorium. The four hundred majors were already seated in tiers of seats, rising high in the hall. After a quick cup of coffee, Raymond and I were escorted to the centre of the front row, once more seated on either side of the Brigadier, to hear Lieutenant Colonel West's presentation. Imagine our surprise when the screen displayed enormous pictures of both Raymond and me. We were then introduced to the assembly and Simon gave a brief history of our usage of radar during wartime. Then the main presentation started. It began with our video interviews followed by the history of the creation of radar by Watson Watts and its many uses, especially as far as artillery and gun laying were concerned. Simon West would stop the video now and again and explain the significance of anything special. Then to my amazement, a film of the Filter Room came up on the screen and suddenly I saw myself, aged twenty years old, filtering the many tracks as I had done, more than sixty years before. I grabbed the brigadier's arm and said, 'I can't believe it – that's me!'

I remembered so clearly when that film was made. It was during an extremely busy night watch in 1943. Nettlefold Studios were asked to film a typical night in the Filter Room, for training purposes and for war records. The director was Bladon Peake. He worked with us for a week, looking for a watch with the most aerial activity. On several occasions he took me out to dinner in the West End. I never thought I would ever see this film and now it had turned up all these years later. Simon's lecture was a great success and there were many questions, the majority of which either Raymond or I were asked to answer. The session ended successfully for Simon West and interestingly for me. After a congenial lunch in the mess, my driver drove me home. This began a great friendship with both Simon and Raymond. Sadly, Raymond became very ill the following year. He would not be the only one.

Christmas came and went. Surprisingly a promised phone call from George never arrived. I wondered why.

BITTERSWEET

New Year's Day, 2006 was a Sunday, the day my brother would always call me from America. He had done this for many years. Promptly at 6pm, the phone would ring and we would talk for an hour, exchanging news of the week. It was an hour I treasured – when I knew I was part of a family that cared. This evening was different. Dennis sounded worried. He had never had any medical problems other than hypertension caused by the problems he inherited when he took over management of the Surveyor instrumentation programme, prior to the Apollo Moon landings. The previous manager had been relieved of his post and Dennis had to sort out the many problems left behind. This had been a particularly stressful time for him but that was a long time ago in the 60's.

Retired since 1983, Dennis had always led a healthy life, He had never smoked, he ate sensibly and exercised regularly. He was now in his 81st year. This evening he sounded anxious. He had a cough that was troubling him and it would not go away. I insisted he saw his doctor. A week later he phoned again with the news that a scan had revealed he had lung cancer. To get the same horrible disease that had killed my father, a life-long smoker, seemed so unfair when Dennis had never smoked.

He told me it was impossible to operate and the only alternative was chemotherapy. He started the course immediately but had a very bad reaction. The treatment was altered with equally dire results. My brother was a brave man. He had a good medical knowledge, as he had been involved with biomedical engineering for many years. He decided he would cease treatment as he felt it would only postpone the inevitable. He would go into hospice care in his own home and let the disease run its course. This care in the home is made easy in the States. A doctor and nurse are permanently on call when needed to ease the pain. A team of carers would cover the daytime and Dennis's wife Jill would be there for the night.

He continued to ring me each Sunday for the next few weeks. He was philosophical. He had no religious beliefs and as a scientist, like so many others, considered there was no afterlife. Each week his voice became weaker and the length of the call shorter. I wanted so much to go to Carlsbad to visit him but he was adamant in his refusal. He did not want me to see him as he was. Finally, on the last Friday in April, Jill phoned to say he wanted to speak to me but he was very weak. I could hardly hear him; his voice was so faint. 'This is my final call.' he said, 'This is the end.' I said a few words to him in reply. I cannot remember what they were – I was too stunned. The following Monday, 1st May, Jill rang to say he had died peacefully during the night, eleven days after his 81st birthday.

There was to be no funeral service. He would be cremated and his ashes, as was his wish, taken by boat and cast into the Pacific Ocean, the ocean he loved to watch from the coastal road in the town in California he called home. I wanted to send a message to be read from the boat but I learned no one would be there other than the crew of the vessel. I wondered if anyone would remember all the experimental work that he had done in space research and ultrasound diagnostics now he was gone. I was glad that some weeks before I had written to him, telling him how much I loved him and thanked him for the help and care he had given me over the years. Jill told me he was very touched by it. I knew how much I would miss him, the last link of my closest family.

This would not be the only sadness in those early months of the year. January and February had passed without a phone call from George and I had never heard from him at Christmas as he had promised. I had tried twice to phone him but there was no answer. I sent a birthday card for 3rd February and later a letter but still no reply. I wondered what could have happened. Finally, on 9th March, I phoned once more. This time there was an answer. A strange man's voice said, 'I am answering on behalf of Jean who is in hospital.' I asked to speak to George. There was a long pause and then he said, 'George died on New Year's Day.' I tried to explain who I was. At first, I said I was an old friend of his from schooldays then I explained the closer connection. The man told me he was a close friend and neighbour and that George became ill in mid-December. This must have been very soon after his last call to me. He was taken to hospital with pulmonary fibrosis and never came home again. This was the second bitter blow in this New Year. I deeply regretted I had not tried to visit him. I realised how despite the past, I still had a great affection for my once fiancé. I wondered who had opened my letter.

I tried hard to overcome the melancholy thoughts and my memories of the past. It was not easy, but I focused on my decision to study with the Open University. By February, I received the schedule and books for my final course towards a degree. I had chosen sociolinguistics as this was the closest I could find to my creative writing studies. The discipline of twenty-three hours study a week, mastering the software necessary for the course and preparing the five required essays, which I had to send monthly to my tutor for assessment, helped take my mind off the sadness that overwhelmed me.

The Open University very soon impressed me with its efficiency. There was always someone ready to help and advise whenever I phoned. The tutor I was allocated was excellent. As well as arranging face-to-face tutorials at the Cardiff branch, she was prepared to offer help over the telephone whenever I called. I enjoyed the course even though sociolinguistics was a completely new subject to me. The work I was doing would lead to the final exam, which would be in the form of a long essay to be submitted in triplicate by mid-September. I very soon realised that to reach the standard necessary to pass, discipline, accuracy and a lot of study would be needed.

This year would not only be filled with Open University activities. I continued my Spanish class at Cardiff Centre for Lifelong Learning, this year covering the history of Spain during the Musulman occupation. I fitted in some painting sessions and my meetings with the French group. By now, my Spanish teacher and her husband had retired to Southern Spain in the Albujarra region. I spent a ten-day break there and learned more of this region, which was in the heart of the Arab occupation of Spain in the fifteenth and sixteenth centuries. There were still signs remaining of El Andaluz, especially in the small hill towns with their white houses.

In July, I spent a week on the Isle of Wight, together with Peter's cousin, Beau Younghusband, and it was arranged that we would visit the Jessie Younghusband School in Chichester. This school had been named after my husband's aunt who was one of the first governors and who had contributed greatly to the success of the school. We were the first of the family bearing her name that had visited there and the children gave us a great reception.

One of my favourite poems has always been *The Highwayman* by Alfred Noyes and I intended using this poem as the theme of my final exam for the OU. Many years before when we were running the Winter Gardens, I had taken part in one of the Springtime Festival concerts. I had recited this same poem. I had not realised that the poet himself lived nearby at St Lawrence, and to my surprise, he was seated in the audience in the front row. It seemed he was both surprised and pleased that I had chosen his poem for the performance. Imagine my delight therefore, during this visit, when I found that his son Robert still lived on the Isle of Wight at St Lawrence in his father's old home. Hoping I would not be rebuffed, I phoned and explained my interest in his father's work. Robert Noyes was most charming and immediately invited me to coffee at the house. There I was able to see many items of his father's memorabilia and in addition, he presented me with a copy of the original manuscript of *The Highwayman*, of a photo of his father which I was able to include in my final essay. On my return home with poetry still on my mind, I decided to attend a talk to be given at the Sherman Theatre in Cardiff by the current poet laureate, Andrew Motion. I was not terribly impressed as it was difficult to hear him. I had not read any of his poems previously and found that the ones he included during his talk did not appeal to me. Nevertheless, it was an interesting experience although it made me realise I preferred the poetry of Keats and Gerald Manley Hopkins and those of the poets of the Great War rather than the work of the modernists.

September was the time to gather the apples from my only fruit tree. It was heavy laden with large golden apples and by the time I had filled the basket, I had difficulty in carrying it. To add to my problems, I stumbled and fell heavily, this time managing to damage my right shoulder, leaving it frozen. The previous garden accident had ruptured my quadriceps tendon, leaving my muscles wasted and my left leg weak. I decided it was time to give up gardening duties; I would have to ask for help. However, this month too brought a great pleasure – the return to Britain of Marysol, the young Venezuelan girl who had made her home with me a few years earlier. By now, she was married to Carlos and had a new baby, Carlos Junior. Having studied intelligence technology at university, she had been employed in Caracas by a well-known German software company.

Her job was to instruct potential buyers in the use of its products and to troubleshoot any operating problems. Her excellent English had meant she had travelled to the USA frequently. Under the dictator Chavez, life in Venezuela was becoming very difficult for many of the middle class and since she had British nationality, she decided to relocate to London. Although only recently arrived there, she already had obtained an excellent post in a similar position. She brought her new family to meet me and it was a delight to welcome them all to Picquets.

It was at this time, I heard once more from Lieutenant Colonel Simon West. He was planning another training session, this time in North Yorkshire. He wanted Raymond Baxter and me to join him, when once more on 5th October he would present a training session on radar in world war two. He arranged that his Army driver would drive me there; we would spend a night on the camp and then return home. Raymond Baxter planned to join us but this was not to be. Just prior to the planned date, Raymond had been presenting a commentary on a series of road races at Goodwood. The weather was terrible, very cold and wet but he insisted on attending although by then he was quite frail. Whether this was the cause, it is difficult to say but a few days later, he was taken ill and died in hospital. I was very sad. Since our previous meeting, we had spoken frequently on the telephone and had become good friends. The visit would not be the same without him.

So it was that on 5th October, a young Army corporal drove me from Wales to Thirsk. It was a beautiful autumn day. I had never visited this part of the country and the scenery in North Yorkshire enchanted me. When we reached the camp, I found the Army had taken over a pre-war RAF site. The officers' mess was magnificent and once more, the regimental silver of the Royal Artillery was on display. The training session here was much less formal that the one at the Defence Academy. The officers on the course were more junior ranks, mostly captains or first lieutenants, and the whole atmosphere was more informal and friendly. I thoroughly enjoyed my time there. I was able to talk to many of the students and they were very interested to hear how the Filter Room had contributed to our wartime defences. It was a short visit and the following morning my driver and I set out on the homeward journey. I was fortunate that we were able to deviate via Doncaster and pay a visit to my cousin May, who had just lost her husband. It was good to meet her again after so many years.

A visit to a second old school reunion with my brother's close friend, Peter Stevens, a bout of bronchitis and some necessary home repairs brought the year to its closing month. I planned a party for mid-December to repay some of the hospitality I had received through the year. I invited 25 guests. By now, it was a little harder to do my own catering but with ample planning, all went well and nobody wanted to go home. I wondered how many more parties I would give. Late in December, I heard I had passed the examination, which should give me enough points for a Bachelor of Arts degree. I was ecstatic that I had at last fulfilled a long held ambition. But then came the disturbing news that as this was the only course I had done with the Open University, they were insisting that all students must earn a minimum of 100 points with them. I wondered if this was based on a required monetary target. This would mean that I had to gain a further 40 points. It was a huge setback and I would swiftly have to decide what subjects to study to make up the deficit. After a lot of thought, I decided I would take a week's summer school the following June in philosophy, at Bath University, under the auspices of the OU. This would give me 10 points. The final 30 would be in a completely new subject – Perspectives of Complementary and Alternative Medicines. This programme would take me the whole of the next year to complete.

I decided I needed a break before embarking on another year of study. I felt it was time to visit Jill in California. Naturally, she too was missing Dennis as they had been through so much together. I started making plans for a New Year visit.

RELIVING MY AIR FORCE DAYS

Octogenarians become accustomed to bad news, especially losing friends and family. However to learn of a friend's husband dying on Christmas morning is particularly sad. The first phone call I received in the new year was to tell me that Tony, the husband of my friend Liz had died. Tony was always the first person to greet us when, as keen hispanophiles, a group of us would meet every Friday at their home. We would practise our Spanish whilst consuming excellent coffee and the homemade cakes we contributed.

For many years, he had been a lecturer and teacher at the Royal Welsh College of Music and Drama in Cardiff. He was an organist of renown and for some time had been the Deputy Organist at Llandaff Cathedral He had also accompanied such well-known singers as Dame Janet Baker and Harry Belafonte in their concert careers. He was an avid cryptic crossword compiler and a charming man; I knew we would all miss him greatly.

Thus, the new year began with a funeral, a little different from the usual ones I had attended. Tony had requested a Humanist service. I found it very moving. The presiding representative spoke well, relating episodes in Tony's life and introducing the music, which had meant so much to him. I hope Tony was able to hear it in his after-life, if there is such a thing. By now, I am beginning to doubt this.

A few days later, I put these dismal thoughts aside and set off on my visit to California. This would be the first time since Jill had been widowed. I wondered how it would be. I was welcomed as usual and Jill had taken comfort in her work as an art quilter, putting her sorrow into her creations. I was conscious of the absence of my special brother. For me, as usual this visit was a recharging of the batteries. The benign climate of North San Diego County is the best medicine for an old body and a troubled spirit. However, after three weeks of sunshine, it was back home to a cold and wet February and the challenge of tackling the alien study of Perspectives of Complementary and Alternative Medicines. Again, a series of essays would be required but also a report on the facilities available locally for the various different types of complementary and alternative practices (known as CAM) and a discussion on their usage and worth before the final examination essay of 3,500 words.

My only experience of these practices had been the more accepted one of chiropractic. I would have to learn about such esoteric ones as the use of crystals or the practice of shiatsu. I realised that I had a lot of research to do especially as there were so many different techniques coming under the heading of CAM. As the weeks went on, I found myself becoming more and more interested in the research necessary to prove or disprove the validity and success of many of these treatments. I interviewed friends to find out their experiences. I contacted several NHS practice managers to learn their views. Most were interested in the more accepted forms such as osteopathy, acupuncture and chiropractic. A few were adamant that they would never consider recommending any CAM practice. It was obvious this course would not be easy and would certainly be controversial.

In April, Probus in Sully asked me to give a talk on the use of radar during wartime. I would be able to show the DVD of the 1943 film found at the Imperial War Museum. Due to the complexity of the Filter Room operation, it is essential to explain in detail all the symbols and actions shown prior to seeing the film. This takes around twenty minutes, the DVD a further twenty and allowing for questions and further explanations, I estimated the talk would last an hour. This branch of Probus was an all-male organisation; many of members retired and from a professional background. The presentation went well and since many present had spent some time in the services, either during the war, or for national service, they showed a lot of interest and asked many searching questions. I could see me doing more of these talks.

Three days later, the memorial service for Raymond Baxter took place in the RAF Church at St Clement Danes in The Strand. Having received an invitation to attend, I was once more driven to London by Colonel West's driver. Raymond's PA, who I had previously met, greeted me and we joined Simon West in the church. There were many representatives from the BBC, honouring Raymond's well-remembered programme, *Tomorrow's World*. Also present were colleagues from Goodwood and his motor racing activities together with members of the organisation of Little Ships. This was a society dear to Raymond, as it commemorated the rescues made at Dunkirk in 1940 by the owners of the many small ships who took part in the evacuation of our troops from France. Each organisation spoke of his work with them. His children took part in the readings during the ceremony. Later, many of us were invited to a reception at the RAF Club where I had the opportunity to meet his daughter and her family. It was a very moving occasion and showed how much Raymond was respected and loved.

During that spring, I decided to write a letter to the *Daily Telegraph*, which they published. There had been much discussion at this time as to which of the Armed Services had saved Britain from invasion by Hitler's forces. The Army, Royal Navy and RAF each laid claim to it. I put forward the theory that it was radar that had saved us. The early warning it was able to give ensured our then pitifully small number of pilots and aircraft to be used to their full capacity. It allowed them to delay take-off until the last minute rather than patrolling constantly on the lookout for enemy aircraft. This finally resulted in Goering's bombers being defeated. The fact that his bombing strategy failed convinced Hitler to delay the planned invasion of Britain and open a second front against Russia.

Its publication had an amazing effect. I received letters and phone calls from former RAF and WAAF Officers and airwomen who had served in the Filter Room, all saying that at last the work they had done had been recognised. One especial pleasure came out of this. Flight Officer Grogono, with whom I had served, contacted me and we both now get pleasure in our bi-weekly telephone conversations. She is now ninety-one years of age and almost completely blind. She had joined up right at the outset of the war and was posted to the Filter Room in those early days. There was no training at that time; one learnt on the job. The procedure was new and was evolving as events occurred. From these early days, the organisation grew to its efficient operations of 1941 onwards. She reminded me that in the first months of the war, no WAAF had uniforms. They just wore a band on their arm with WAAF on it.

This year of 2007 was to deal me an unexpected and bitter blow. I had always had good eyesight and only in the latter years needed glasses for reading. In June, I decided it was time to have a check-up so I made an appointment with a well-recommended optician in Barry. After extensive tests, he told me I had the onset of Age-related Wet Macular Degeneration or Wet AMD. I learned this was the major cause of blindness in Great Britain. It seems that with advancing years, a filter tissue known as the macular becomes damaged, allowing blood vessels to enter the eye and bombard the retina. This eventually causes scarring, destroying central vision and leaving only some peripheral sight.

I was given an early appointment with the ophthalmology clinic in the University Hospital at Cardiff. During the following week, I underwent a further series of tests and Wet AMD was confirmed. I was still getting over the shock of the news. The ophthalmologist I was referred to informed me that there was a new drug; approved only during the last two years, which when injected would counteract the damage caused. However, each dose of this drug would cost £750 and its use would be continuous. Because of this, the National Institute of Clinical Excellence, NICE, would not recommend its use on the NHS for the first affected eye. This meant I would have to go blind in one eye and then hope the other eye would not become infected. I was horrified at this apparent indifference to all the suffering for those affected, together with the subsequent cost to the community for the future care they would require.

I realised how my life would change. I had managed to remain independent until now. Would I have to stop driving? Could I continue to live in the house in which I felt so comfortable? Would I ever be able to travel abroad again? Thought after thought came rushing into my mind. I asked if there was anything that could be done. I was told, yes if I paid for it. The injection could be given at a private hospital but the cost would be very expensive, about £2,000 each time it was needed. I thought rapidly. Could I manage to pay for it at least to begin with? Perhaps the National Institute for Clinical Excellence (NICE) who had made the recommendation for treatment only to the second eye or the NHS in Wales could be persuaded to change their ruling. I said I would consider it. I was referred to an eye specialist who happened to be at the clinic at the time. This was the best thing that could have happened. He explained everything clearly and I realised that initially I would have to find the funds to be treated privately. This surgeon became an advisor, friend and supporter in later months. As speed is essential since the damage can occur very rapidly, within a week I was undergoing my first injection

268

of Lucentis at the BUPA hospital in Cardiff. Meanwhile, I resolved I would do everything in my power to fight this wicked and inhuman ruling by NICE and the local NHS boards. Little did I know how this fight would take over my life for the next eighteen months.

The procedure for the injection takes several hours. Initially a nurse would give me three sets of drops every fifteen minutes for one hour; one antibiotic, one anaesthetic and one to dilate the eye. Then when on the operating table, the area around the eye would be painted with iodine. A protective gown would be placed over my face and shoulders, leaving an open gap over the eye. I would be under a very strong light and able to see the large needle as it was inserted and the drug entered the eye. And so it was. The injection itself took only a very short time. After a rest in a nearby room and a cup of coffee and a sandwich, (I would always insist on smoked salmon!) the ophthalmologic surgeon would come for a final check and he would instruct me to apply antibiotic drops four times a day for the next week as the main danger was from infection. I soon got used to the procedure.

Initially there was an injection each month for the first three months. Every four weeks I would undergo a prior Ocular Coherent Tomography, (OCT). This is similar to a CT scan for the eye and it showed what damage was there and whether the treatment had been successful. After three monthly injections, the treatment appeared to be working at least temporarily. There was then a pause in injections as the scan, after a further four to five weeks, showed an improvement. Then four weeks later the next scan would show the damage to the retina had started once more. The injections would start again. This went on for a year with a total of six injections. The cost was mounting up but to save my sight, I would have to do all I could to find the money. However, I resolved I would also fight for it to be available for all on the NHS.

Everyone reacts differently to the treatment, dependent on one's genes. It had been hoped that as I had an early diagnosis, I might only need three injections. This had been the case for one lucky patient but unfortunately it was not so for me. As the use of the drug was so new, it was impossible to judge each individual's reactions nor is it yet known how long it would continue to be effective. I felt I was on a roller coaster; I would feel optimistic and then back to being despondent. On one occasion, my surgeon told me 'It is a war of attrition.'

I had tried to find out as much as possible about both the disease and the drug. I monitored the NICE website and learned they might be having second thoughts on their recommendation to use it only for the second eye. The phrase 'cruel and inhuman' was mentioned. I could see that this would be a long drawn-out process as other drug companies were putting their cases forward. I realised too that time was of the essence for those of us needing Lucentis and there were so many who could not afford to pay for this chance to save their sight.

I thought of several of my WAAF friends who were already blind in one eye because Lucentis was not available to them when they needed help. I resolved I would try in every way I could to get the treatment for everybody. I started by writing letters and emails to the Health Minister of the Welsh Assembly, the local member of parliament, even to Gordon Brown, the prime minister. The replies I received were evasive. I appealed to the Local Health Board and despite the support of one official there, I was told there was no chance of the NHS locally providing the treatment.

In the meantime, news came in that other areas were now offering treatment for the first eye. I found that in Scotland and in some counties in England, Lucentis was offered for treatment of the first eye. This was when I realised that I had become a victim of the so-called post code lottery in today's National Health Service. It was at this moment, that the Welsh press came into the picture. I had recently featured in the *Western Mail* magazine in an article relating the story of my WAAF activities, coinciding with the VE day memories. It was an extremely well written article by their senior features writer. We became great friends and she learned of my strong emotions regarding the poor treatment in Wales for sufferers of Wet AMD. She passed this information to a colleague, the Health Correspondent of the sister paper, *The Echo*. Greg Tindle took up the cause and after a series of articles, we managed to make the headlines. By then the Welsh branch of the Royal National Institute for the Blind was asking for letters in support. It seems the publicity in the Echo helped and they received more than 1400 letters. I started a petition in my village and in two days obtained 200 signatures.

Meanwhile, Jonathan Morgan, a Conservative Assembly Member, also Shadow Health Minister, added his support and was given time to put forward a motion to the Welsh Assembly, asking for the NHS in Wales to fund the treatment. This motion was scheduled for hearing on 25th June. Whether it was the 1400 letters, which landed on the desk of Rhoddri Morgan, the leader of the Assembly, or the constant press coverage by Greg Tindle that did it, I do not know but the day before the motion was to be heard, Edwina Hart, the Health Minister announced she was funding the treatment. The problem was she would not give a specific date for its implementation, only 'in the autumn'. Her announcement covered the following items:

Treatment of Wet AMD for both first and second eyes using the drug Lucentis;

Review of all drugs for the treatment of Wet AMD currently undergoing clinical trials so that they may be provided for treatment as soon as they are licensed;

271

Gradual phasing in of treatment centres across Wales to provide appropriate delivery meeting the prerequisites of best practice and equity of access;

Development of an electronic record system not just to accurately record data but to use as a teaching tool for ophthalmology;

Appraisal and reappraisal of the treatment protocols to ensure the service delivers the best outcomes for patients; and

Appropriate referrals from primary care optometrists – working to strict protocols – to ensure that patients are referred urgently.

Because treatment is essential as soon as a patient is diagnosed, I continued my emails to Edwina Hart asking her to give a date for the treatment to be available. By then we were on a first name basis! I reminded her that some months previously, I had suggested she started planning for both the training of operators and the provision of suitable centres for treatment. Finally, in October she announced treatment would be available from November 28th for those fulfilling the necessary requirements. I wondered how many people there were for whom this date would be too late. At least all our efforts had finally borne fruit.

After her announcement in June, my surgeon managed to find a space in his appointment list and I received my first NHS injection at the end of August. He was putting his reputation on the line. He said that as the money was there and he had the capacity, ethically, I should have it. By then, NICE had given their ruling that they now supported the use of Lucentis for the first eye. They had come to an arrangement with the pharmaceutical company providing the drug that after fourteen injections had been received per patient, the drug company would provide further ones free. What was not made clear was that each hospital had to register for this benefit. The frustration I felt over the delay of many months before NICE finally changed their ruling made me angry. I hoped that now many ex-service men and women would get the treatment they deserved.

Meanwhile in the months following June 2007 when I first learned I might go blind, I had been sending in my OU assignments and I had also spent a week at Bath University, attending a summer school on philosophy. This summer school, I hoped, would earn me ten points towards the extra forty I needed for my degree. Around one hundred and fifty of us turned up on the opening day. As the residential access on the campus was quite a way from the lecture rooms and since I have difficulty in walking a great distance, it was suggested I learnt to drive one of the electric scooters available. This was a great experience. I practised on the car park and having been declared proficient or at least safe, I set off for my room, accompanied by a student aid, carrying my luggage. This means of transport was great. I would go from lecture room to restaurant accompanied by a friend who would then open any necessary doors for me. It helped make the whole week a great experience.

The students were divided into three groups, each studying a different aspect of the subject. It was either Liberty and Justice, Mind and Action or the one I chose, Knowledge and Value. This covered the evaluation of the difference between right and wrong and whether it was possible always to evaluate what was right in certain circumstances. Each tutor had around twelve students. We were lucky to have an excellent tutor with a great sense of humour. We students were a motley lot, aged from very old (me) to the very young. The mixture of backgrounds was amazing, ranging from an ex-nursing sister now an editor with a medical publishing company, a Physicist who was a lecturer for the Open University, a practitioner of aromatherapy, a rampant communist and others from a variety of different spheres of life.

The study of philosophy was completely new to me but I

273

thoroughly enjoyed this introduction to the subject. There were debates, discussions and arguments, some heated but throughout the course, our tutor made learning a pleasure. We had several tests, which went towards our marks, and then there would be a final examination to be completed on our return home. Despite being a novice, I passed; I had ten more points towards my total.

Back home I pressed on with the assignments for CAM and sent in my final essay in September. Then I waited for the result, not due until late December. An October visit to Mallorca to the home of my friends Chris and Vivien raised my spirits. Finally, on 14th December, the result came through. I had passed my final exam with a distinction and the Open University notified me that from 31st December 2007 I could use the title Bachelor of Arts. It had been a long journey. The news was some compensation for all the trials and sorrows

A coffee break during a philosophy course at the University of Bath

of the months before. I started the new year of 2008 knowing that I would have a graduation ceremony to attend.

This was fixed for 17th May to take place in St David's Hall, Cardiff. About a month before the event, I received a letter from NIACE, the National Institute for Adult Continuous Education. They were holding a special event to introduce their annual Learners' Week celebrations. I was notified that my name had been put forward to be considered for one of the nineteen specials awards they were making. A previous Creative Writing tutor had nominated me for an award because of an event that had taken place in the past year. I had encouraged a young girl to continue her education despite having been expelled from her school. Several of these children, banned from attending school, were receiving a few classes in English and maths in the same hall where we met for our current creative writing course. I used to chat with them if I arrived early. One day this girl asked me what we did in our class. On hearing we were potential writers, she asked if anyone wrote poetry. I told her that I did and then she showed me a poem she had written. Despite incorrect grammar and spelling, the message was very powerful. She went on to tell me of her deprived upbringing, which included sexual abuse by her mother's many boyfriends. I asked her if she would read the poem to our class. When I gave her an anthology of poetry from my collection she said that it was the first book she had ever owned.

We all encouraged her to continue writing poetry and to work at improving her English. She heeded the advice and at the end of the school year, had then managed to find permanent employment as a cleaner at the Crown Court with a regular wage. She had furthermore enrolled in an evening class to improve her language skills.

I had forgotten the occasion completely and as there were over two hundred names put forward for nineteen awards, I did not think I was likely to be chosen. Imagine my surprise to receive a letter saying I was to receive the Open University Learner of the Year award. I was invited to the ceremony to be held at Brangwyn Hall in Swansea two days before the graduation date. At the same time, I was asked to submit the names of nine people who would join me on the occasion for a celebration banquet and entertainment. Later I received a phone call from the BBC notifying me they were sending a producer to my house for an interview, which together with one from the tutor who nominated me, would be shown during the presentation. What a week I had to look forward to!

The videoed interview with Carwen Jones of the BBC came and went. I sent the names of special friends I wanted to invite to the presentation and decided that I would like to include the eye surgeon who had done so much to keep me sane during the last twelve months, and his wife. I also invited my brother's best friend, Peter Stevens, as I felt it would make up for my brother not being there. It was my greatest sorrow that Dennis, who had encouraged me to work for my degree, never lived long enough to know I had succeeded.

The week before these celebrations saw me give a talk to a class of ten-year-olds at a primary school in Penarth. It coincided with VE Day, 8th May. It was a wonderful occasion. The school, during assembly, re-enacted life in wartime Britain, with evacuee children arriving in Wales, waiting to be taken into the homes of the villagers. Then followed a further scene showing the housewives clutching their ration books and buying their week's rations at the butcher's shop. This was a great way to teach history. Later I followed this with a talk at a Cardiff girls' public school who were studying the world war two for their GCE examinations. Interestingly I did not receive as many questions from this audience as I did from the younger children. However, I do remember two questions particularly since it made me realise how little modern youth understood what living during a war was like. Having mentioned that we worked underground in the Filter Room, one girl asked 'But you didn't work at night, did you?' She imagined, I supposed, that Hitler's bomber crews worked a five-day week from 9am to 5pm! After I mentioned that five weeks after marrying Peter, I was sent abroad for a year, another question was 'You came home at weekends, right?' I realised how little modern children understood how life was during the wartime years.

Finally, the most exciting week of the year arrived. Together with three friends, I was driven to Swansea for the NIACE dinner. We were greeted outside the hall by a band of circus performers. There were jugglers, acrobats and fire-eaters. What else was in store? After aperitifs in the anteroom, we went into the main hall. Brangwyn Hall is an incredible building. It was constructed in 1934 and is a palace of Art Deco splendour. The decoration in the great hall was gilded and ornate; the whole room was splendid. For this occasion there were twenty-three large circular tables laid for dinner, one allocated to each prizewinner and their guests and four more for the organisers and VIPs. We enjoyed a beautifully prepared meal with copious wine on offer. My table was situated very near the front stage. We could see the sound engineers preparing for the entertainment and speeches. As we enjoyed coffee, we were entertained by a Welsh tenor, apparently well known but not to me. Then there descended from the vast ceiling two decorated ropes and an acrobat dressed in gold tights who performed some amazing manoeuvres between the two ropes, ascending and descending with speed and agility. Finally, the prizegiving began. Before each person was called to the platform, their photo was displayed and the video played of the interviews with both the nominator and the nominee. It was strange to watch a large version of myself speaking to the audience. Then my name was called and I was interviewed by one of the two BBC presenters present. Escorted to centre stage, I received my certificate and a large envelope presented by the director of students of the Open University. Finally, after all nineteen of us had gone through this procedure and we had finished our last drops of wine, we made our way home. It was an evening to remember. The funny thing was that I forget to open the large envelope until a month later. Inside I found a voucher for £100 for use with any further course I wished to take. What a pleasant surprise!

I was hardly over the excitement of the Swansea presentation when two days later it was time to prepare for the graduation ceremony.

I brought three friends with me. Whilst I had to go through the registration procedure and be measured for the appropriate robe, my friends went off and had a delicious lunch. Meanwhile, I was arrayed in a black robe with a sky blue and gold hood, appropriate for a bachelor grade. I was most disappointed; nobody wore a mortarboard. I do not know whether it is only the Open University that has dispensed with this item, but I felt a little cheated. Then I queued for the official photographs, which of course we all had to pay for. Finally, we were shown to our places in the hall. As I now walk with a stick, I was allocated a front row seat, making things easier for me. The rest of the audience then assembled. The students occupied almost half of the ground floor of the large St David's Hall. They were grouped according to their title, depending upon whether they were receiving a doctorate, a master or a bachelor of arts or science

NIACE Open University Student of the Year – awards ceremony

degree, an honorary degree or a special diploma. The guests not accommodated on the ground floor, were seated in the ranging tiers of seats reaching high into the hall. It seemed every seat was occupied. I saw my friends had managed to get good seats near the front.

The platform was soon filled with academics sporting gowns of every colour of the rainbow. They sat behind the throne, placed centre stage for the visiting director of students, who would make the presentations. Alongside was a further academic who would announce the names. The ceremony took over two hours as there were so many students graduating at various levels. The proceedings began with the formal speeches. Then the special moment came. We stood anxiously waiting for our names to be called. The honorary doctorates were the first to ascend the platform, then those receiving their earned doctorates, followed by the masters and then it was the turn of the bachelors. Since my name begins with the letter Y, I knew I had a long wait. However, the moment finally arrived and to my great surprise after I was handed my certificate, the be-gowned academic presenting it said 'I saw you two days ago, didn't I?' The same man had made the presentation to me for the NIACE award. Then he proceeded to have a chat with me for a minute or two. For that, I got an especially long clap from the audience as I left the platform. I guess I was the oldest there but finally I had done it. I had achieved my ambition after over seventy years. All that was left was to find the friends who had accompanied me, have a few more photos taken and then to retreat to the reception area for a well-earned glass of champagne and a few nibbles. By that time, I was really hungry.

Back home, the next months spent in campaigning for Lucentis for everyone took me back to the reality of being eighty-seven years old and not knowing what the future held for me. I was delighted when a series of requests came in for my talk on radar in the defence of Britain during world war two. Every occasion was different. I would gauge it to the audience of the day. The first one in mid-July was on behalf of the Penarth Heritage Trust and took place in the Turner Art Gallery. The audience of fifty was very mixed, young and old. However, I always judged its success by whether the audience asked interesting questions. There were many ex-service personnel present so the response was good. It seems that the vital work done by the RAF Filter Room to process radar information is completely unknown to the majority of the public and yet without it, Fighter Command would never have had the success against the German bombers and possibly Hitler would have attempted an invasion of Britain in 1941 instead of opening the second front with Russia. The British public in those days had little idea of how few fighter aircraft we had nor how few pilots were trained to fly them. I hope in some small way by giving these talks that the women plotters and Filterers will at last receive the credit that is their due.

Later in the year, I was booked for a further three talks within a week, a Men's Forum in Barry, a Women's' Institute in Penarth and then a talk to the history group of the University of the Third Age in Cowbridge. For this latter occasion, I had to learn how to use Powerpoint. This is a very powerful programme used to create and manipulate slideshows. I was fortunate that a friend was able to create this by extracting slides from the film found at the Imperial War Museum, highlighting the various aspects of my talk. The main problem was to remember to move on from one slide to the next especially when I was involved in complicated explanations of the work of the Filter Room. This meant a great deal more effort on my part but all was well. The audience for this occasion was particularly probing with their questions but I felt I had at least helped to give the work done by the members of the WAAF during those long years, greater recognition. The year's talks were to finish with the audience I enjoyed most of all. The Barry squadron of the Air Cadets are not very numerous but exceedingly keen. It was a delight to see these teenagers accepting discipline, looking smart and showing enthusiasm for serving their country. They were my favourite audience to date.

It was soon Christmas, not my favourite time of year as it had meant hours of hard work and little time for leisure during my past years in the hotel profession. This year was made memorable. After the Beijing Olympics, I had sent an email to all the Chinese academics who had stayed with me, congratulating them on the opening entertainment. I had two delightful replies, one from the young couple from Heilongjiang University and one from Zjiming Wang from Shandong. They each sent electronic all-singing Christmas cards to me. The one I received from Shandong was so entertaining. It lasted ten minutes, with constantly changing pictures of typical British Christmas scenes such as an iced cake, a holly wreath and a Christmas tree; all of them with ten little dancing Father Christmases and a girl's voice singing 'I wish you a Merry Christmas and a Happy New Year' in Chinese. It cheered me up immensely.

Now we are entering another new year. I wonder what it will hold for me. Are there other surprises good and bad in store? I am in my eighty-eighth year and realise however keen the ideas and the spirit may be, the physical frailties become more difficult to overcome as the days go by. I wonder how many more visits I will make to my family in the States and whether I will visit again those much-loved towns I know so well in Brittany, Andalusía or Mallorca. I wonder whether I will go blind. I have called this story 'Not an Ordinary Life' – most certainly it was not one I ever planned or expected. Yet despite the many sad occasions in my life, I realise I have lived through momentous times. I hope there are still some more interesting times to come. Above all, I value the friends I have made on the way. I have always said 'You may take away my possessions but not my people.'

POSTSCRIPT

As I look back over nearly nine decades of my life, I realise how greatly the lives of my generation differed from those of recent years. Young people today have more freedom to plan their way in life, decide on their training, chose their careers. I realise that many do not bother to do these things but it is there for the taking.

For my contemporaries, any plans or ambitions were swamped by history. I feel we were robbed of choice. To face a war when your country could be invaded altered your perspective. We had to grasp at any opportunity that arose and make the best of it, never knowing what future you had. I look back on lost dreams, unrealised hopes and impossible ambitions. Yet the difficulties of those years and the many hazards we faced moulded our characters. We faced up to events and overcame them or we lost our way.

Present-day Eileen – June 2009

I can see now the wrong decisions I made, the errors of judgement I committed and the chances I missed. I see too the challenges I faced and the fears I mastered. I often wonder how different my life would have

282

been had I been born twenty years earlier or twenty years later. I will never know. Yet the testing ground of world war two had advantages. We were moved out of the narrow world in which we were raised,

A winter view from Eileen's home in Wales

its customs and daily habits, into a kaleidoscope of a dangerous but exciting life. We were challenged. We met people of all nations and beliefs, from every social strata and I believe we were all the better for it.

Having seen my brother's wife, Jill, create her quilts of many pieces, many colours and many textures and seen how they are blended into a whole, I realise that life resembles a memory quilt in which every event has its place. I can see the carefree pieces of childhood, the dark ones of danger. I can see the misshapen ones when I was unkind and thoughtless and the abstract ones of disbelief. There are

283

pieces of disappointment and of strengths, of hidden deeds, good and bad and of great effort. This quilt of life is sewn together with the threads of strength and hope and it is bound by friendship and love. Finally, it is backed by the support of family and friends. It is the one I made myself.

One of Jill's abstract quilts

APPENDIX

It seemed a strange coincidence that I in a small way and my brother in a much greater way were both involved in space vehicles. I received the initial Big Ben code signal for the first origenitor of all jet propelled missiles, the V2 rocket or Vergeltungswaffe, which was launched by Germany against London (Chiswick), on 8th September 1944. Subsequently, in the 1960s, Dennis became manager of Space Instruments working on the unmanned probes which first landed on the Moon. These were launched by Jet Propulsion Laboratory, Pasadena, California, to test the atmosphere and landing conditions prior to manned landings of the Apollo spacecraft. I include here an article he published, describing the events of that first unmanned lunar landing, as a tribute to the work he, together with other scientists from Jet Propulsion Laboratory, have contributed towards the continuing knowledge we have of space.

MY JOURNEY

by Dennis H Le Croissette

It was a cool mid-January night and I was sleeping peacefully when the telephone rang. 'We have a problem!' – an excited voice said. 'On the spacecraft?' I asked. 'No, on one of your instruments.'

It was a rare week when I didn't get called in specially at least once to the space centre. So I dressed and drove out to the Jet Propulsion Laboratory to meet some on-duty engineers. We were all members of NASA's Project Surveyor, a lunar exploration programme in the late 1960s that predated the Apollo human landings on the Moon.

We were the pioneers. This was the first spacecraft designed to

285

'soft-land' gently on the lunar surface without damaging fragile scientific instruments. (Previous lunar landing probes, such as the Rangers, 'hard-landed', that is, crashed.) Our job was to obtain enough information to assure the future astronauts could safely land and walk on the Moon.

The briefing was simple. The Surveyor 7 spacecraft, last in the series, had already landed successfully inside crater Tycho, and one of our scientific instruments, a probe designed to measure surface characteristics, had been released from its housing. But it failed to deploy to the surface. We had to find some way to release the instrument so that it could carry out its vital task of surface analysis.

We checked the television monitors. From the vantage point of the camera, mounted a metre above the lunar surface, we could see the instrument caught in the structure. The TV pictures were like snapshots refreshed every few seconds. The Moon's surface could be seen clearly in the background.

'Let's check the mock-up,' someone said. We moved to another room. There stood a full-sized mock-up of the spacecraft, identical to the one on the Moon. Our team went to work. We discussed what had gone wrong. How could we correct it? What alternatives did we have? We brainstormed some methods for saving the instrument. Good ideas, crazy ideas, all ideas were discussed. Nothing was thrown out before being considered. By two hours later, we had devised a plausible way to release the instrument. An existing articulated arm on the spacecraft would be used to push the unit against the structure and break it free.

Would it work? Dare we try it? Would it affect the rest of the multi-million dollar spacecraft? I contemplated whether, after four years of responsibility for developing these instruments, my work was about to end in failure. Finally, the decision was made to go ahead.

Now we had to plan the data sequences to transmit to Surveyor 7. Hours sped by as all the calculations were checked and re-checked. But during this period the Moon had set at our Pasadena, California location, so Surveyor 7 could no longer receive signals sent by our local tracking antenna. We had to wait for the Moon to rise again. We continued with our meetings and rechecked our calculations. The process seemed endless.

Many hours later, we were still at our monitors staring at the TV camera's view of the stuck instrument. We gave the JPL team the go-ahead to try to release the instrument using the articulated arm.

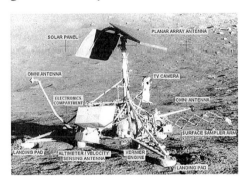

Sketch of instruments on Surveyor 7 uumanned spacecraft

The moves were made one agonizing, painstaking, meticulous step at a time. Send the command. Check the position. Send another command. Recheck the position. Repeat, repeat, repeat until we were ready for the final thrust.

A fresh set of operators came on duty but still our team remained. We had too much at stake to let others take over. The newcomers listened silently as we briefed them on the events of the day before. We were very tired now and worked under great strain. Tension was beginning to show in our faces as we reached the critical part of the operation. News of our difficulties had spread, but we were isolated at our screens with just short trips to a nearby machine that dispensed coffee and sandwiches.

As we watched the continuing efforts, I reflected on our task in this room on Planet Earth. We were controlling a device that was sitting on the Moon. That was the lunar surface showing our monitors. Humanity's dream of the ages had come true in front of my eyes.

The minutes ticked by. Slowly our confidence increased. The instrument was yielding. The structure was holding. We began to believe that the mission would be saved. The Chief of Operations was the first to put into words what several of us had been thinking. 'It's slowly moving down,' he said. No one replied. We were concentrating on the small-screen image of the spacecraft and trying to track the position of the instrument. JPL's operations centre was dimly lit to make the pictures easily visible. The eerie half-light gave an uncanny look to our scientific endeavours.

'I think it's breaking free,' I heard myself murmur. 'It looks good.'

We send the last and most important command in our sequence, the command designed to release the unit, and we waited for the resulting TV image to appear on our screen. Absolute quiet prevailed, except for the low hum of the air-conditioner. We all knew the next picture was crucial. Had the final push released the instrument?

It took us a moment to comprehend the refreshed image on the screen. Then spontaneously, a number of people stood up at their monitors and cheered. We had done it! The freed instrument could now analyse the lunar soil as it had been programmed to do. After the laughter and the handshaking were over, I realised that the stress of the last many hours had taken its toll. I closed my eyes for a moment as the excited chatter of the operators continued around me. This closed environment was all I had seen since I entered the building. I needed fresh air. But was it day or night? The cool night air refreshed me as I sat down on a bench just outside the building.

The burbling of an ornamental fountain was the only sound to be heard. As I sat on that bench, reliving the frenzied hours I had just spent, the strain lessened and my adrenaline ebbed. My life was returning to normal.

I leaned back and looked up at the sky. It was a clear night. And there – beloved by poets, romanticized by songwriters, prized by lovers – there, amid its panoply of stars, there was the Moon !

Dennis H Le Croissette, *a London-born physicist, served as Project Surveyor's scientific instrument development manager at JPL in the late 1960s. He later became a freelance science and humour writer based in Carlsbad, California.*